THE UNITED STATES IN THE GREAT WAR

BY

WILLIS J. ABBOT

AUTHOR OF

"THE NATIONS AT WAR"
"PANAMA AND THE CANAL"
"THE STORY OF OUR NAVY"
"THE STORY OF OUR ARMY"
"AIRCRAFT AND SUBMARINES"

WITH MANY ILLUSTRATIONS FROM DRAWINGS, IN
COLOR AND BLACK AND WHITE, AND PHOTOGRAPHS
TAKEN BY EXPERTS, MANY OF THEM UNDER FIRE

LESLIE-JUDGE CO.
PUBLISHERS   NEW YORK
1919

CONTENTS

CONTENTS

INTRODUCTION

THIS account of the participation of the United States in the Great World War is given to the public at the moment when representatives of all the nations are gathered in the historic halls of Versailles to formulate a treaty of peace which shall, so far as human foresight will permit, prevent in future any recurrence of the calamity which overwhelmed Christendom in the last four years.

The monumental palace built by kings for their own glory, and to house their obsequious courts, is to serve as the manger wherein to lay the babe of a worldwide democracy.

The great hall, which less than half a century ago resounded with the acclaims of those who, on the ruins of France, established the German Empire and committed its fortunes to the Imperial house of Hohenzollern, will now witness the disintegration of that empire, while the head of the fallen house lies in exile in a foreign country—a suppliant for the protection of a nation which only a few months ago he planned to rob.

In 1871 the halls of Versailles witnessed the apotheosis of the sword. To-day they behold the endeavors of those who have won by the sword to establish for the future a wiser, more humane, more Christian method of settling disputes among nations.

The United States was late in its entrance upon the war, but first of all the nations outside of France, to send its delegates to the peace conference. In these correlated facts there is a significance readily discernible by those who will stop to give them due consideration.

Ours has never been a military nation. We have had our wars—five of them in our 130 years of national existence. But they have been, unsought wars, forced upon us by conditions which we patiently strove to correct before taking up the sword. The measure of our aversion to war may fitly be judged by the complete unpreparedness for war which has attended our every entrance upon hostilities—and this last one more than any.

The United States gave formal notice of its entrance upon the prodigious struggle just ended after it had raged for two years and six months. Yet with the conflagration thus furiously roaring in our full view, and its sparks falling fast upon our territory to our own hurt, we made no preparation to join those who were doing their best to put it out. When belatedly convinced that, unless subdued, the flames of war would carry us down with the rest in one universal disaster, we had to begin preparations to take part in the fight from the very bottom. If the period of our participation in actual conflict was but brief, and indeed it scarcely exceeded six months, it was the fierce rush to fit ourselves to fight which showed most the temper of which the nation was made, and most impressed the enemy with the irresistible character of this last new and terrible force that he had aroused.

In the body of this book I have discussed briefly the futile question as to what nation won the war, and have shown that to each of the several belligerents on the side of the Entente is due so much of the credit that exclusive glory can be the meed of none.

As these words are being written the question before the world has less to do with the history of the fighting that is past, than with the question of the form of peace which is very present. If the United States was late upon the battlefield her envoys were early at the peace conference. By the personal presence there of the President of the United States ours was made a delegation that need yield nothing in point of

INTRODUCTION

dignity to that of any other nation. The position they held of complete detachment from any selfish national interest or ambition justified the anticipation that they would stand foremost as the representatives of peace with justice, a peace which should be permanent and mark the end of war. To this the President of the United States, alike as chief executive of the nation and in his capacity as a member of the Peace Conference, is committed. Back of him, so far as may be judged from the expressions of the newspapers of the country, the people stand as a unit in the conviction that such a peace can only be successfully established and permanently maintained by means of a League of Nations. The suggestion of such a league I think may fairly be said to have originated in the United States. If its actual creation shall be due to our influence in the Versailles Conference whatever there may be of regret for the tardiness of our appearance in the war may well be assuaged by the reflection that this great boon to humanity was due to American endeavors.

It is as yet too early to determine the extent to which the war waged for the protection of democracy may extend the system of democracy throughout the world. At this moment Russia is in complete anarchy, and Germany apparently on the verge of civil war. The duties of the Peace Conference are made inexpressibly more difficult by the fact that a great part of the territory, and of the people with whom it has to deal, is now without responsible government, a prey to disorder and to revolution. No great war ever ended without a prolonged period of precisely such unrest and turmoil. But we may well believe that out of this present chaos will be evolved a wider measure of democracy, a more just reorganization of society in the countries affected, and a peace that shall be enduring because it will be guaranteed by a League of Nations systematically organized, and directed by a code which shall have been formulated by the best representatives of democratic principles to-day.

The author desires to express his obligation to the corps of brilliant and devoted journalists who served as war correspondents during the progress of the struggle now ended. While the fighters made history, these writers recorded it. In many instances their letters from the front, written under the most trying circumstances, in water-logged trenches, dark and dismal dugouts, on the seat of a speeding lorry, or in some shell-torn hut with the guns roaring about them, had all the vivacity and spirit of well wrought literary productions. The work of such men as Philip Gibbs, Percival Gibbons, Frederick Palmer and Edwin L. James gave to readers of English throughout the world so vivid, picturesque and graphic an idea of the world conflict day by day that there is left to the historian little except the task of harmonizing conflicting reports and describing the broader strategy of the war of which the correspondent cannot be informed. At the beginning of the war it was the policy of the military authorities of all nations to bar the correspondents from the front and to circumscribe rigidly their freedom of expression. As the war progressed this policy was gradually abandoned. It is perhaps the best testimonial to the position which the capable and earnest correspondent bears in relation to the operations of the army to which he is accredited that these restrictions should have been relaxed, and the end of the war should have found the correspondents given every facility for observing and recording its progress.

WILLIS J. ABBOT.

Jan. 10, 1919.

THE UNITED STATES IN THE GREAT WAR

CHAPTER I

SITUATION IN EUROPE WHEN THE UNITED STATES ENTERED THE WAR—LIST OF THE WARRING NATIONS—OUR PEOPLE'S AVERSION TO WAR—SYMPATHY FOR FRANCE—EFFECT OF GERMAN ATROCITIES—THE GERMAN SUBMARINE CAMPAIGN—THE SINKING OF THE "LUSITANIA"—THE DIPLOMATIC DISCUSSION —THE PRESIDENTIAL ELECTION—GERMANY'S ARROGANT DEFIANCE—THE DECLARATION OF WAR

THE United States entered upon the Great War in Europe when, on the 6th of April, 1917, President Woodrow Wilson signed the war resolutions which had been adopted by the House of Representatives that morning, and by the Senate two days earlier.

All Europe, and part of Asia and Africa as well, was at that moment in the grip of war. The German armies seemed to be securely established in France and Belgium. Russia was in the throes of revolution, and had ceased to be a factor in the war activities of the Allies. What might come of the over-throw of her government, and the attempt to erect upon its ruins a new edifice of democracy it was too early to tell. It was not, however, too early to recognize the fact that as an aid to the Allies Russia could no longer be counted upon. At various points along her battle line in the east her soldiers were fraternizing with the Germans and Austrians in their front. The revolutionary powers, sedulously encouraged by Germany, were breaking down military discipline in the army so that soldiers no longer obeyed or even saluted their officers. The great divisions at the front were melting away, as the

soldiers were told by foreign intriguers that those who hastened home would be given tracts of land in the distribution of the property of the privileged classes which the revolutionary government had begun. Even at the moment it was clear that Russia could no longer be relied upon to keep the Central Powers busy along the eastern battle-front, and, as the months rolled by, the extent of the Russian defection, and the degree to which the intrigue of Germany with the revolutionary leaders had fomented it, convinced military men that the Allies must fight out their fight without hope of further assistance from that enormous state now fallen for the time into the grip of anarchy.

As a result of the Russian withdrawal the armies of both Germany and Austria along the eastern front were freed from any apprehension of the armies of the Czar, and were able to concentrate their assaults upon those more western forces still actively in the field. The effect of this was shown most disastrously in the check which the Austrians were able to put to the triumphant progress of the Italian forces which had fought their way gallantly into Austrian territory, through the difficult passes of the

© Harris & Ewing
Count Johann H. von Bernstorff, the former German Ambassador

though later revelations show that had the invaders made but one more effort they must have succeeded. Farther to the south, in Mesopotamia, the forces of General Maude had just taken Bagdad thus wiping out to some extent the memory of the loss of the British force under General Townshend at Kut-el-Amara. But for the moment the British operations in this part of Asia Minor seemed none too promising, for the revolution in Russia had put an abrupt end to the progress of the Russian armies about Lake Van, which prior to that outbreak had been pressing gallantly forward and giving every indication of ability to beat back the Turks and effect a juncture with the British forces.

Returning to the western front we find that the German grip upon France and Belgium appeared unshaken, though for the moment the German armies under Hindenburg were engaged in a retreat, undertaken for strategic purposes. Yet this retreat was not wholly voluntary, for almost at the moment when the American congress was debating war the British had struck the foe savagely near Arras and had driven him back with heavy

Dolomite and Julian Alps, had taken Goritzia and menaced the interior of Austria, and even Germany, through the Austrian back door. Freed from further apprehension of Russia Germany was able to send troops to Austria's aid, and held the Italians in check, until by the devious devices of intrigue and trickery their defensive power was undermined and a serious defeat threw their armies back into their own territory for a prolonged defensive.

In the region of the Balkans the moment of the entrance of the United States showed nothing encouraging to the Allied cause. Greece had not yet finally thrown off the domination of her pro-German King Constantine and his army, lurking in the rear, had made impotent the joint French and British army at Saloniki, so that the Germans and Austrians had been able to sweep down upon Serbia and overwhelm that people in an invasion which for ferocity and barbarity has perhaps never been paralleled in the history of war. Turkey, meantime, had every reason to be exultant. She had beaten back the British from the Dardanelles,

© Harris & Ewing
Captain Von Papen, Germany's Military Attaché in this country who characterized us in a letter as "Idiotic Yankees"

losses. Verdun was successfully continuing the gallant defense by which for more than two years it had upheld the French watch-word, "They shall not pass," while Paris in a new security, destined to be rudely shocked nearly a year later, had settled down to the conviction that the advance of the foe had been permanently checked far from her city gates.*

Such, then, roughly outlined, was the situation of the principal belligerents in the main theatre of war when the United States, after prolonged hesitation, determined to enter the conflict on the side of the Entente Allies.

There were at the moment, after the United States declared war upon the Central Powers, engaged in the war upon Germany and her Allies thirteen nations, namely: Great Britain, France, Russia, Belgium, Serbia, Japan, Italy, Montenegro, San Marino, Portugal, Rumania, and the United States. Their population exceeded 977,260,000 people.

Against these were marshalled the Central Powers, namely: Austria, Germany, Turkey, and Bulgaria. The forces opposed to the Entente Allies numbered at the moment of the entrance of the United States 156,572,000. But the disparity in numbers was more apparent than real. It has already been explained that the Russian revolution eliminated that nation from the list of effective belligerents. Serbia and Rumania had been put out of action by overwhelming defeat. Japan had never taken the slightest part in the fighting in western Europe where the war was to be decided, and even her naval services in the Pacific were of little value in view of the dominant strength of the British navy. Portugal contributed little to the course of the fighting and naturally such pigmy nations as Montenegro and San Marino were without military significance. And the predominance of British population is due to the incorporation in it of the teeming millions of India, and of British colonies in Asia and Africa whose part in the war bore no just proportion to the numbers of their inhabitants. It is fair to say that prior to the entrance of the United States the Entente Powers were outnumbered in actual fighting population, as they were almost in-

*A full description and history of the progress of the war which had reached this stage at the time of the entrance upon it of the United States will be found in the author's earlier volume "The Nations at War."

© Harris & Ewing

Captain Karl Boy-Ed, the former German Naval Attaché

variably outnumbered on every field of battle. The latter condition, however, was due more to the fact that the Germans had the advantage of a central position, and short interior lines, than to the disparity in total man-power between the two groups of belligerents.

After the entrance of the United States upon the war many other nations followed her into the conflict. Among them were Cuba, Panama, Greece, Siam, China, Brazil, and Peru. None of these contributed especially to the strength of the Allies unless it were Greece. Brazil, through the activity of her navy, was of some assistance in patrolling the seas.

Immediately upon the first outbreak in Europe President Wilson issued his proclamation of neutrality, and called upon the people of the United States to observe neutrality "in thought and deed." That was a task difficult of fulfilment. Indeed as the months wore on it became impossible. While it was quite true that among our people was a great body of German-Americans, as those either of German birth or immediate German lineage were called, the dominant intellectual forces in the nation were almost from the

"Barred Zones" and "Safety Lanes" Outlined in Germany's Note.

very outset favorably inclined to the Allies. They openly declared their sympathy, and, to a very great degree, advocated the entrance upon the war on the Allied side.

Beyond doubt it was the large admixture of English lineage and blood among our people which caused this attitude on the part of a section of the populace, numerically small but exerting an influence beyond its numbers. In the roster of those who urged incessantly the taking up of arms by the United States English names not only predominate—they almost monopolize the list. But in addition to the distinctly pro-British sentiment thus manifested there was a very

wide-spread feeling of earnest sympathy for France. Republics may, as the maxim has it, be ungrateful, but the sentiment of affection and gratitude to France springing from the aid she extended to us in our Revolutionary War is wide-spread among the American people, despite the large admixture among them in these latter days of foreign elements ignorant of our earlier history. Two incidents of the war fitly indicated the extent of this policy among our people.

One of the many gallant and cultured American boys who, even before their own nation entered the war, joined the French army as aviators and laid down their lives

The German submarine, *U-53*, which had the impudence to make a social call at Newport before going out to sink some British steamers off our coast. It is very likely, as has since been suggested, that this visit was also a threat calculated to frighten us out of going to war with Germany

German destroyers and submarine chasers lying in a foreign harbor

in that service, was Kiffen Rockwell. "I pay my part for Lafayette and Rochambeau" he answered proudly when someone asked him on the flying field in France what he was doing in a French uniform when his country clung to cold neutrality:

And later when the flood of American soldiers began pouring into France General John J. Pershing, Commander of the American Expeditionary Force, was taken to visit the tomb of Lafayette. Advancing he laid a wreath upon the sarcophagus with the brief and simple words which the whole world found eloquent,

"*Lafayette, we are here!*"

The heart of France, sorely burdened, though not crushed, under the heavy hand of the foe, revived at these words of promise, and Christendom rejoiced that opportunity had been given to a soldier of the United States to speak them.

This feeling of loyalty to the England whence our forefathers had come, and to the France which had helped us to win our independence, were dominant forces in bringing the United States into the war. That France had helped us against England did not in the least embarrass those who felt that now was the time when we should fight shoulder to shoulder against a common foe. For that common foe was Germany, and history showed that it was a German king on England's throne, an alien monarch scarce able to speak the English tongue, who forced our forefathers into revolt and strove to crush English liberty in the English colonies. The English people, and their most representative figures in parliament, were with the American colonists in their struggle for liberty—and the wisest and most philosophic of Englishmen to-day admit that the fight which won American liberty saved English liberty as well.

The effect of such considerations upon American public sentiment favoring war upon Germany was enormously enhanced by the news of the frightful atrocities committed by the Germans in their march through Belgium. These atrocities, unparalleled in the records of modern warfare—unless it be by the barbarities perpetrated by the Germans themselves in the march to Pekin, at the time of the Boxer rebellion in China—shocked the civilized world. The callous government of the Kaiser, seemingly incapable of comprehending the fact that the bayoneting of babes, the ravishing and mutilation of women, and the wholesale slaughter of inoffensive civilians could arouse an antagonism throughout the world that might be fatal to Germany, at first did not take the trouble to deny commission of the crimes. Later it strove to excuse them as the necessary accompaniments of a state of war.*

To the indignation which the atrocities committed by the German army had aroused in the American mind was added the wrath awakened by the course of the German submarine campaign. In the end this assault upon our rights on the high seas was made by the President the reason for declaring war upon Germany. Technically, it was perhaps the determining cause, but no observer of the slow awakening of the war spirit in the United States can doubt that resentment for the unspeakable barbarities of Germany in the war, and determination that German

military autocracy should not overwhelm the democracies of England and France had quite as much to do with it as had the German assault upon our commerce.

Indeed it was rather the manner of the German submarine campaign than the fact that it was prosecuted that stung the American people into war. It is perfectly conceivable that the Germans might have so used their U-boats as to have accomplished nearly as much as they did toward destroying British commerce, shutting off supplies of munitions, and bringing England to the verge

A typical American-built submarine chaser. These small craft were turned out by the thousands and were ever ready to make it hot for any enemy submarine which visited our waters. Several such visitors never returned to their bases.

*For a more comprehensive account of German atrocities see "The Nations at War," p. 19.

of starvation, without spurring America to the fighting point.

But the same criminal fatuity which prevented their resting content with having stolen Belgium without inflicting unspeakable tortures upon its people, made it impossible for the Germans to prosecute their submarine warfare in accordance with the humane dictates of the law of nations.

was destined to become one of our chief causes of complaint against the Kaiser's government. Had Germany, on her part, carefully observed the dictates of the law of the nations on the sea, while calmly and steadily pointing out the infractions of it by Great Britain, 1917 might have told a different story.

Instead of this, maddened by the spectacle

Life savers at Whitby hauling in the lifeboat which made several vain attempts to reach the hospital ship *Rohilla*, sunk off the east coast of England

There was beyond doubt a certain sympathy for Germany at sea among the American people. To their sporting spirit the hopeless inferiority of the German navy to that of Great Britain gave to the effort to accomplish something by means of the pigmy undersea boats an element of peculiar gallantry. Moreover, the desire of the British to suppress trade with Germany at every point led that nation, with its great naval supremacy, to establish rules of blockade that were not in precise compliance with the hitherto accepted laws of nations, and which at times caused loss to American citizens using the high seas in thorough accord with international law.

Such resentment against Great Britain as was aroused by these methods in the United States was artfully stimulated and extended by that German propaganda which

of enormous neutral fleets bringing to her enemies cannon, shells, high-explosives, arms, uniforms, and all imaginable munitions of war, she cast off all restraint and sent out her submarines to prey on the ships not of her foes alone, but of the neutral nations, among which the United States was the greatest.

And more than this. While Great Britain had invaded the property rights of our people, causing them some loss and great inconvenience, the submarine campaigns of Germany were directed against life as well as property, and before the United States sprang to war more than 220 of her people had been sacrificed to the mad savagery of the submarines.

The proclamation by the German Government of its creation of a "war zone," comprehending all the waters immediately surrounding the British Isles and her announced intention of destroying all enemy vessels found within that zone, "without its always being possible to warn the crew or passengers of their danger," first forced upon our Government recognition of the gravity of the German menace to the rights of neutrals on the high seas.

The United States instantly protested.

submarine, the Germans urged, were forced to come to the surface, and dispatch a boat to examine the papers of a suspected craft before destroying her, it was always possible that naval aid summoned by wireless by the victim would destroy the submarine itself. As for putting the passengers and crew in safety that, according to the humane view of the Boches, was amply accomplished by

Photo by Paul Thompson

German submarines lying at their docks at Wilhelmshaven

It denounced the whole theory of a "war zone." It restated the principle of international law that a suspected vessel shall not be destroyed until she has been visited and her belligerent character, or the contraband quality of her cargo established by due examination. Even then she may not be sunk until her passengers and crew have been placed in safety.

The response of the German Government, adhered to until the collapse of that government as the result of its utter defeat in the war, was that all established principles of international law should yield to the peculiar qualities and needs of the submarine boat. These boats, it pointed out, were small, weak both structurally and defensively, able to perform their functions only when unseen, or at least when exposed to view for only the briefest possible time. If a

crowding them into open boats, hundreds of miles from shore in the bleakest and stormiest gales of midwinter.

While diplomatic discussion of these sharply divergent views was in progress, Germany gave effect to her programme by sinking vessels, both belligerent and neutral, on which American citizens lost their lives. But the crowning and most atrocious act of aggression was the destruction by submarine torpedo, and without warning of the British passenger liner *Lusitania*, with the loss of 1,198 lives of whom 114 were Americans.

The storm of wrath aroused in the United States by this crime was so great that only the seemingly indomitable determination of the Administration to keep the peace averted the immediate entrance of the nation upon the war. The people had not yet settled down to the recognition of the fact that war changes all conditions. Those who had business in Europe, and many of those who sought pleasure there, had no idea of relinquishing their right to travel thither, on unarmed vessels, in safety over the sea which belonged quite as much to the individual American as to the Kaiser himself.

Perhaps the German Government was itself appalled by the storm its crime aroused. Although it was announced that the submarine commander who had sunk the *Lusitania* had been decorated, his identity was sedulously concealed and was not known to the world when the war ended. Bronze medals— which were struck off in Germany to commemorate the exploit and prepared as was afterward learned several days before the actual sinking—were hurriedly suppressed. Though the school children of several German cities were given a holiday when the news of the great victory over unarmed men, women, and children was received, this fact was afterward stoutly and falsely denied by German authorities. The German ambassador at Washington, Count Von Bernstorff, tried to palliate the offense by pointing out that before the sailing of the ship he had caused advertisements to be published warning Americans who had taken passage that they would sail at their own peril.

But this rather heightened than allayed the popular wrath. The people declared that a murder was made none the less criminal by the announcement in advance that it was to be committed in cold blood. Moreover, public opinion bitterly criticised the President for not having made the appearance of these advertisements the occasion for sending a battleship to convoy the *Lusitania*, and warning Germany that an attack upon her would be an act of war against the United States.

While a large part of the people was demanding war the President turned to diplomacy for redress. It may be noted here that never did his diplomatic endeavors succeed, nor ever was there coaxed out of Germany so much as an official repudiation of the act of the man who sank the ship. After the lapse of years, and the abundant revenge which our forces have taken for this atrocity, it seems curious to reflect that in his note of protest President Wilson ascribed the crime to a misapprehension of orders on the part of the captain of the submarine. But the concluding paragraph of the note put strength and encouragement into the hearts of those Americans who, even at that early day, recognized the duty resting upon our nation to cleanse the blot of Hohenzollernism from the face of Europe. The President's note concluded:

The Imperial German Government will not expect the Government of the United States to omit any word or act necessary to the performance of its sacred duty of maintaining the rights of the United States and its citizens and of safe-guarding their free exercise and enjoyment.

That was written May 13, 1915. Though the Imperial German Government increased, rather than lessened, the frequency of its attacks upon the rights of American citizens, it lacked but one month of being two years before the United States acted upon "its sacred duty" of maintaining those rights.

Germany was less lethargic. Her work of piratical assaults upon neutrals on the high seas proceeded apace, as though she

The cargo submarine *Deutschland*, the first undersea boat to cross the ocean, sailing up the Weser River on her return to Bremen, her home port

The American steamer *Gulflight* settling by the head after she had been torpedoed

felt assured that no response more vigorous than a diplomatic note would proceed from the United States. On the 9th of August the British liner, *Arabic*, was torpedoed without warning. No lives were lost, but 26 Americans were exposed to the hardships of a night in open boats. A note of protest brought from the Huns the grudging assurance that "liners will not be sunk by submarines without warning, and without assuring the safety of non-combatants, provided that the liners do not try to escape or to offer resistance." This was unsatisfactory, as it offered no protection to American sailors on freight vessels, and assumed that placing passengers in open boats on a tempestuous sea was assuring their safety. Even at that, it expressed too great a measure of humanity for the Germans to maintain, and in less than two weeks the liner *Hesperian* was torpedoed without warning.

The people of this nation were getting very weary of the German policy of promising reform while continuing its offensive course. And about this time there began to appear a series of revelations concerning plots against our good order and interests by German emissaries—not unconnected with the diplomatic service—that added to the popular discontent. It was discovered that incendiary fires in ammunition plants and strikes in works of the same character were being fomented by German agents. Our State Department was being deceived with forged passports—a work in which attachés of the German Embassy, Captain Boy-Ed and Captain Von Papen, took an active part. The existence of a subsidized German propaganda was demonstrated. Papers emanating from Dr. Dumba, the Austrian Ambassador, fell into the hands of the State Department, showing that functionary to be busily engaged in encouraging strikes in such great steel works as those at Bethlehem. As a result he was summarily sent home. An intercepted letter from Captain Von Papen disclosed that warrior of intrigue as advising "these idiotic Yankees to hold their tongues." It was daily made more clear that the embassy which Germany maintained here in a nominal spirit of friendliness was in fact a nest of conspiracy against our industries and our internal peace, and that the spirit which animated its officials, from Ambassador Von Bernstorff down, was one of cynical contempt for the United States and resentment for the part she was playing in the war. After relations were broken off it was dis-

The officers of the Dutch steamer *New Amsterdam* bringing, under threat of destruction, their ship's papers to the commander of this German submarine

covered that German diplomacy was actually trying to embroil us in war with Mexico and Japan.

Much of the German intrigue was directed against the enormous business in munitions of war for the Allies which had sprung up in the United States. Although German public men privately admitted the entire legality of this trade they bitterly denounced it in public as a gross violation of neutrality. It is a fact, unpleasant to consider in the light of later events, that at this period the manufacturers of the United States would quite as readily have made munitions for Germany as for England and France. The only difficulty was that Germany had no means of getting the finished product to her armies. So being unable to profit herself by the trade she denounced it bitterly as unneutral and barbarous. American business men were depicted as turning the wounds and blood of German soldiers into tainted money, and every effort was made to stir up German-Americans to open and to stealthy attacks on the business. Congress was be-

seeched to lay an embargo on the export of arms, and when that expedient failed, the coarser devices of blowing up the plants and fomenting strikes were applied.

In its resentment over German atrocities committed upon the people in conquered nations of Europe, and in wrath because of German aggressions upon our own rights and liberties, the American people were far in advance of the American Government. Yet even among them the war spirit lagged. It is one of the most curious records of politics that the presidential campaign of 1916 was won by the democrats with the slogan "He kept us out of war."

The reasonable implication was that "he," President Wilson, would continue to keep us out of war. Yet it must have been apparent to the members of the administration, fighting the political battle for their own retention in office, that the continued abstention of the United States from sharing in the conflict would be impossible. That fact was apparent to careful unofficial observers. How much more so must it have been evident to those in the government possessing precise knowledge of all the diplomatic correspondence between the countries, and all the reports of the officials stationed in belligerent lands?

Everywhere throughout the United States pacifist societies sprung up, usually suspiciously well supplied with funds from unascertainable sources, and not infrequently provided with executive officers with suggestively German names. The German language press, which was moribund at the beginning of the war, took on a new prosperity, and in the majority of instances was strenuously pro-German in all issues which involved a clash between the United States and the government of the Kaiser. The undoubted evidences of overwhelming pacifist sentiment in the United States, and the apparent indications—illusory as it later proved—of widespread disloyalty among German-Americans seemingly encouraged the German Government to renewed aggressions. Long afterward, when relations between the two governments had almost reached the snapping point, the Kaiser's Minister of Foreign Affairs truculently reminded Ambassador Gerard that there were 500,000 German Reservists in the United States.

"And we have 500,001 lamp-posts for their accommodation, Your Excellency," was the ambassador's apt and instant retort.

A German U-boat being sent where she will do no more harm. By the time this occurred submarining was becoming unpopular in the German navy

An American vessel at the moment she was hit by a torpedo fired by an enemy submarine. She did not sink, however, and she subsequently had her revenge

Meanwhile, Germany proceeded steadily with her submarine campaign of "ruthlessness." The sinking of the *Lusitania* had never been disavowed. No adequate promise to adhere to the principles upheld by all civilized nations had yet been made by Germany, and even the grudging agreement not to sink without warning regular liners was frequently violated—notably by the sinking of the Dutch liners *Tubantia* and *Palembang*. In March, 1916, the Channel steamer *Sussex* was torpedoed and sunk with great loss of life, many American citizens being among the victims. Germany was still evasive, sometimes arrogant. But the *Sussex* incident served to bring matters sharply to an issue, for on April 19th, in a message to Congress, President Wilson declared that

Unless the Imperial German Government should now immediately declare and effect an abandonment of its present methods of warfare against passenger and freight vessels, the Government can have no choice but to sever diplomatic relations with the Government of the German Empire altogether.

This was very much in the nature of an ultimatum. True, to sever diplomatic relations is not tantamount to a declaration of war, but in troublesome times it is almost invariably followed by such a declaration.

The German Government evidently recognized the gravity of the situation for it responded with the declaration that the German navy would at once

receive the following orders for submarine warfare in accordance with the general principle of visit, search and destruction of merchant vessels recognized by international law: Such vessels, both within and without the area declared as a naval war-zone, shall not be sunk without warning, and without saving human life, unless the ship attempt to escape and offer resistance.

But in connection with this belated agreement to recognize the rules of civilized nations the Germans advanced the proposition that in return for it the President should endeavor to lead the British to mitigate in some way the strictness of her blockade. The point was clearly foreign to the matter at issue. Because Germany was at last willing to obey international law was no reason why the United States should attempt to coerce Great Britain on any point. This the President pointed out in his response to Germany, but it was made evident nearly a year later, when Germany utterly and flagrantly repudiated her promise, why the conditional clause had been so shrewdly attached to it.

Looking back on the months immediately preceding the declaration of war, with the mind full of the recent evidence of what American participation in the struggle has meant to Germany, one cannot but feel that the character of the democratic presidential campaign, and its result, must have completely deceived the German Government.

For it witnessed the triumphant election of a candidate whose own utterances had always been pacifist in tone, who had refused to take seriously the appeals of a great part of the nation for at least adequate preparation for possible war, and who had been urged for reëlection by his closest supporters on the pacifist theory expressed by the ceaseless repetition of the phrase: "He kept us out of war."

Could any foreign government, viewing these conditions, and ignorant of the Republican factional fight which did in fact accomplish Mr. Wilson's election, construe the result other than as a positive declaration of the American people against entrance upon the war?

Germany unquestionably so construed it. The year 1917 opened with a vigorous renewal of the submarine warfare upon vessels of every class and nationality. In a month 96 vessels, many of them neutral, had been sunk in the war zone. Not only passenger ships but even hospital ships, marked clearly with the red cross, fell victims to German piracy. The *Britannic* and the *Braemar Castle*, hospital ships both, were sunk in the Ægean Sea, and the attitude of the Huns toward helpless non-combatants generally was indicated by the statement made by Mr. Bonar Law, in the House of Commons in February, 1918, that up to that date 14,120 non-combatant men, women, and children,

The warning published as an advertisement in the press of America by the German Embassy just before the *Lusitania* sailed

of British race alone, had been done to death by the German submarines.

So persistent was the violation of German promises to the United States, so flagrant the defiance of those principles of international law upon which the President had insisted that men began to think that Germany actually wished to draw us into the conflict. Her public men expressed entire contempt for our military and naval strength, and even some of our own people, regarding the 3,000 miles of ocean that separated us from Europe, thought the conflict would be not unlike the duel which Abraham Lincoln suggested should be fought with axes at a distance of sixty paces.

Whatever the German purpose, the practical result of their policy was to force us into the conflict. For while many of our people desired war as a protest against German aggression, the Administration at Washington had made the submarine campaign the specific ground of its complaint. This campaign was prosecuted with increased vigor. Admiral Von Tirpitz succeeded in convincing the German Government that, if freed from all consideration for neutral rights or opinions, he could, with the ruthless employment of his submarine boats, starve England into subjection in three months.

In compliance with this policy the German Government directed Ambassador Von Bernstorff to notify Washington that after February 1st—the very next day—neutral ships, equally with those of belligerents, would be sunk in the war zone without warning and without mercy.

This was a flat repudiation of all promises made to the United States. The notice was accompanied by the insulting proposition

The medal which was designed in Germany and distributed to commemorate the sinking of the *Lusitania*. With it was distributed information giving the size and tonnage of the great liner all set forth in the most approved style of German brag. It is said, and generally believed, that these medals were struck off before the crime was committed.

S. S. *Lusitania*, the largest and most celebrated victim of Germany's ruthless submarine campaign. She was sunk May 7, 1915, with 1,951 persons on board of whom 1,198 perished

President Wilson reading to Congress his famous war message on April 2, 1917. When he left the Capitol after reading this message he had built himself a monument which will stand while this nation lives. The entire country, as ex-Secretary
of State Root expressed it, stood unitedly behind President Wilson in the gravest emergency that the nation had ever been
compelled to meet. When President Wilson asked for war his words were not directed against a people but against an artificial evil. When he had finished speaking, the final day for imperialism and its abuses had begun. Everywhere throughout
the world, save in those unfortunate lands where the iron hand of despotism was clinched for one last blow, this lofty message
was received with limitless rejoicing. From that time forth President Wilson became and remained the foremost spokesman of
the Allied cause.

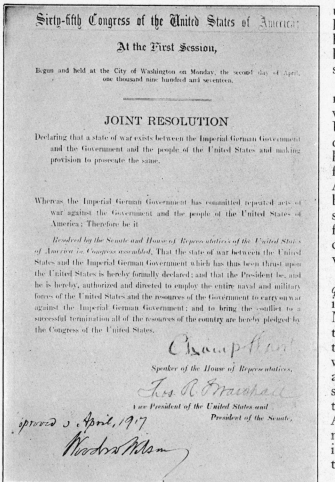

Fac-simile of our Declaration of War

utmost courtesy he was sent to his home, while the United States Ambassador to Berlin was being bullied by the German Government, and insulted by the German people.

In eighteen days after the beginning of ruthless submarine warfare 177 vessels were sunk, one being an American ship. Up to April 3d, just preceding our declaration of war, 19 American ships had been sunk, and 8 others unsuccessfully attacked. The temper of the American people was not improved by the fact that three of the vessels sunk were Belgian relief ships carrying from the United States food freely contributed for the aid of the Belgian victims of German barbarity.

March 14th, the American ship *Algonquin* was sunk and her people exposed in open boats for twenty-nine hours. March 19th brought news of the destruction of the *City of Memphis, Illinois,* and the *Vigilancia.* Fifteen American sailors were drowned. The President had already called Congress in Special Session, but these occurrences caused him to set the date two weeks earlier—to April 2d. Before the Congress could meet, news came of another sinking in the North Sea and the loss of the crew.

The nation by this time was fairly roused to the occasion. Patriotic meetings were held in all the cities, and men without regard to party pledged their support to the Administration in the impending crisis. But the pacifists were correspondingly active. At Madison Square Garden, New York, a gathering of citizens that packed the huge hall and called upon the President in no uncertain tones to declare war upon Germany was followed within the week by a meeting of pacifists, of no smaller proportions, which stoutly opposed war and vehemently called upon the President to submit the issue to a referendum of all the voters of the United States before making the final declaration.

In the vigor and noise of their agitation, the pacifists seemed superficially to be the dominant faction. Indeed, comparatively few wanted war—the nation was about to accept it as a most abhorrent necessity violently thrust upon the United States by German aggressions. If the referendum had been

that the United States might send one ship a week to England, Germany picking the port and prescribing the way in which the ship should be painted and what sort of a nondescript flag it should fly. London *Punch* picturesquely and accurately depicted American sentiment concerning this arrogant proposition.

The Kaiser was shown saying haughtily to Uncle Sam: "You may sail once a week to Falmouth." To which the latter, hands in pockets and hat and cigar at a defiant angle retorts: "And you may go, all the time, to hell."

The situation had become intolerable. Within 24 hours Von Bernstorff had received his passports and was dismissed.

"The President could have done no less," he remarked philosophically. He knew, as the people of the United States did not, what he had been plotting in secret. With the

ordered and the question asked had been "Do we want war?" it would probably have been answered by an overwhelming vote of "No!" But the question was, in fact, "Must we fight to protect our national honor, our national integrity, our national safety?" and to this the one answer, though given in sorrow, was "Yes!"

The Congress met at noon on April 2d. After organization and a few polite tributes to the first woman ever seated in the House of Representatives as a member, the House adjourned until night. When it reassembled it presented a dignified and historic spectacle. Directly before the Speaker's stand sat the members of the Supreme Court. The diplomatic gallery to one side was crowded with diplomats in uniform or evening dress— the representatives of Germany and Austria being conspicuous by their absence. The galleries were crowded with privileged spectators each one of whom displayed an American flag or the white badge of pacifism. At half-past eight the doors opened and the Senate marched in, headed by the vice-President. Again the American flag was much in evidence, though one or two irre-

concilable pacifists among the senators failed to display it.

When the President entered and mounting the rostrum with quick, nervous steps was presented to the joint session, the tumult was unbounded. All were instantly on their feet—pacifists with the rest—cheering and waving their national emblems. Grave justices of the Supreme Court shouted like boys at a baseball game, as the President stood impassively waiting for quiet that he might begin his address.

The President's address was both grave and eloquent. The hesitation and incertitude which had characterized some of his earlier utterances were gone, but the deep regret he felt at the engulfing of the nation in war was clearly apparent. He strove to discriminate between the German Government and its people, saying that for the latter "We have no feeling but one of sympathy and friendship." But he denounced the German autocracy and concluded his appeal for war in these solemn phrases:

The world must be made safe for democracy. Its peace must be planted upon the tested foundations

Photograph by Kodel & Herbert, N. Y.

West Street, New York, congested with freight which cannot be shipped to foreign ports owing to Germany's ruthless submarine campaign

of political liberty. We have no selfish ends to serve. We desire no conquest, no dominion. We seek no indemnities for ourselves, no material compensation for the sacrifices we shall freely make. We are but one of the champions of the rights of mankind. We shall be satisfied when those rights have been made as secure as the faith and the freedom of nations can make them. . . .

To such a task we can dedicate our lives and our fortunes, everything that we are and everything that we have, with the pride of those who know that the day has come when America is privileged to spend her blood and her might for the principles that gave her birth and happiness and the peace which she has treasured.

God helping her, she can do no other.

indeed break out with a severe rash of patriotic bunting, but from this Western towns were largely exempt. There were no street mass meetings. The seeker for excitement and dramatic detail was in the position of Captain Robley D. Evans, when he looked up in the midst of the Battle of Santiago to find his ship destitute of a battle flag. "What the devil's the use of a battle without a battle flag?" cried "Fighting Bob" disgustedly and soon had two flying. The United States had not yet come to its excitement. It only slowly roused to the point of noisy enthusiasm. But determination and the will to win were growing every day.

This liner was steaming across a placid sea when she was sighted by a German U-boat which instantly opened fire. As the torpedo hit its mark the engine room was wrecked by a terrific explosion. The crew was rescued by a British patrol boat.

Amid renewed cheering the President left the Hall and was swiftly driven back to the White House. To all intents and purposes the nation was from that moment at war. At war for the first time since 1812 with a formidable foreign foe. Yet to observers, not alone in Washington but in other great cities of the land, the amazing feature of the crisis was the total lack of excitement, indeed of enthusiasm. There were no cheering mobs flaunting flags and parading the streets. There were no mob assaults upon the most outspoken of Germans. New York and eastern cities did

Congress was not slow in granting all the President had asked. The Joint Resolutions declaring a state of war to exist were passed by the Senate April 4th and by the House April 5th. There was debate, of course, and an acrimonious one. Six senators voted against war. In the House the vote for it was unanimous save for the single ballot of a socialist representative who felt forced to vote according to the international tenets of his party. The same day the President issued his proclamation to all the world and the United States was at war.

CHAPTER II

OUR NATIONAL UNPREPAREDNESS—THE STRUGGLE OVER CONSCRIPTION—
FORCES OPPOSED TO THE DRAFT—SCENE AT THE FIRST DRAWING OF NUMBERS
—MOBILIZATION OF THE NATIONAL ARMY—LACK OF SUPPLIES—WORK OF THE
WAR WELFARE SOCIETIES—LIFE IN THE CANTONMENTS—THE SOLDIERS'
FOOD—SPORTS AND GAMES—MILITARY TRAINING—LIFE IN THE FOREIGN
CAMPS

THE nation was thus at war. In the face of an emergency that few had expected would so soon confront the American people, the question was asked and not for the first time, "What is our preparation for war; how are we equipped to give battle to the nations of central Europe that for fifty years have been preparing for precisely this emergency, and for four years have been turning their already well-drilled soldiers into battle-tried veterans?"

The United States indeed was sadly deficient in all that goes toward national defense. There had been in progress for some years an active agitation, conducted by far-seeing citizens, for the expansion of the military and naval forces of the United States. The propaganda received but little encouragement from men in active political life. Even the President frowned on it and dismissed it contemptuously within but a few months of the time when we were called upon to give battle to the greatest of all military powers. But the pertinacity of the friends of preparedness compelled a certain amount of provision for the needs of national defense, and June 3, 1916, an act of Congress fixed the total strength of the regular army at 293,000 men, the national guard at 409,000, while by a later act the personnel of the navy was fixed at 87,000 men. The men needed

were to be obtained by volunteer enlistment only.

This was a notable step forward for this nation in the matter of provision for national defense, but how trifling it was in the face of a world in arms may be judged by the fact that at that very moment the losses in the French, German, or British armies were exceeding each week the total number of men we provided for our defense. Even as it was the small number asked was not obtained through the methods of volunteering. When war was declared in April of 1917 the regular army lacked more than 100,000 of the number authorized. The navy had done somewhat better proportionately, but it, too, was short of its requisite quota when the nation made that entrance upon the war which all its leading men should have foreseen was inevitable.

The slowness of volunteer enlistments was by no means due to any hesitation on the part of the American people to enlist for the defense of the nation when they were needed. But they had been assured, were almost daily being assured, by the leading men in the national government that there was not the slightest chance of our being involved in the European tempest. At the moment a spluttering struggle with one or the other of the claimants to power in Mexico was keeping our army on the southwestern border, engaged in peculiarly harassing police duty. Men who would have leaped at the chance to fight for their country and for humanity in France refused to take up arms in a petty quarrel for no conceivable ends in Mexico. The fact that it was not unwillingness to serve, but hesitation because of the character of the service asked was clearly shown by the tremendous jump in enlistments when war upon Germany was

Chicago's elevated fleet landing recruits for the Navy

© International Film Service, Inc.

the enlistments in the regular army totalled 204,754, or more than three times as many as during the preceding twelve-month.

Over the enactment of a law for the conscription of the youth of the land into the armies there raged for some time a fierce debate in Congress, the press, and amongst the people. It had been more than half a century since the United States had asked anything other than voluntary military service of her sons. The Civil War had been fought for years before actually declared. Between April 1, a few the method of the draft was applied and days before the declaration of war, and September 5, when the draft became operative, had volunteered held themselves of finer

The U. S. cruiser *Recruit* at anchor in Union Square, New York, winning volunteers for Uncle Sam's fleet through the seas of oratory which surge over her decks

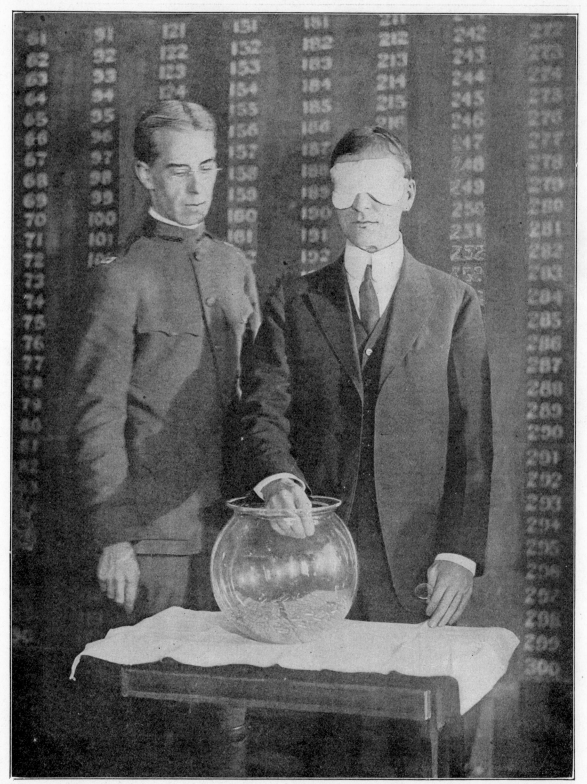

Secretary of War, Newton D. Baker, drawing the first number from the bowl in the draft which began June 27, 1918

© G. V. Buck, Washington, D. C.

President Wilson leading the great preparedness parade in Washington on June 14, 1916. The parade is passing the Treasury Building. The President is exercising the prerogative of his exalted office by dressing comfortably and sensibly

quality and higher patriotism than the conscripts.

To those who urged at the very outset that the volunteer system would not bring forward in season the enormous numbers of men that would be needed in the colossal conflict upon which we were entering, the opponents of the draft declared that there was no way to judge of the extent of the volunteering when it became known that the volunteers would see service in foreign parts. They insisted, and with reason, that the sluggishness of enlistments when men had nothing

Philadelphia's 25,000 drafted men receiving their farewell tribute

better than police duty on the Mexican border to look forward to was no criterion by which to judge the numbers who would come forward for fighting in France.

To a very great extent the struggle between the opposing schools of thought settled down to a debate over a matter of sentiment. The direct question whether enough men would volunteer to fight the battles of their country in so huge a struggle was one that could not have been decided in advance of a test, and to make the test and fail would have been disastrous. Most observers agree that the event showed that it would have been suicidal to have relied altogether on voluntary enlistments, although the promise of its advocates that it would bring out the very flower of the land and create an army

Wives and sweethearts saying last farewells to the men of the "Fighting Sixty-Ninth"

Drafted men of the National Army marching up Fifth Avenue, later known as the Avenue of the Allies, in New York. These were the kind of scenes which characterized the draft in New York in the World War in contrast to the disgraceful draft riots of the Civil War

Fifth Avenue, New York, decorated with the flags of the Allies during the Fourth Liberty Loan campaign and known as the Avenue of the Allies made up wholly of self-sacrificing patriots was most enticing.

Indeed it began very early during the discussion to be apparent to observers with good opportunities for studying what was going on that the continuance of volunteer enlistments would in fact be most disastrous to the country, and that the more successful it proved in raising large numbers of men the more hurt it would do in the end to the nation. For, precisely as its advocates had urged, the volunteer system brought at once to the army in a patriotic burst of enthusiasm the very flower of American youth. Offices, stores, and workshops were stripped of their best men. The ranks were being filled up with men who were naturally fit to be officers. Foreseeing a long war with the inevitable exhaustion of this class of soldiers, public men began to ask themselves whence would come the officers to lead the later armies that must be formed.

It seemed, too, obviously unjust that to the less patriotic should come the business opportunities that would be opened at home with a great part of the manhood of the nation gone off to the war. There was danger that political power might pass into the hands of the class that was too selfish, or too cowardly to fight. This would have been equally a menace to the country and an injustice to the men at the front. All told, the arguments for universal military service, the selection of the active participants to be by draft, seemed unanswerable. Nevertheless, when the Administration on April 6th introduced a bill of that character it encountered immediate and vigorous opposition. Southern members of Congress professed to fear that it might lead to a race war by accustoming negroes to the use of arms. Others thought conscription an affront to the patriotism of the people. The Speaker of the House of Representatives distinguished himself by remarking that out his way "people saw mighty little difference between a conscript and a convict." The democrat who happened to be the chairman of the

The drafted men of Milwaukee, Wisconsin, being given a rousing send off by their fellow townsmen. If the Kaiser counted upon disloyalty among the thousands of Milwaukee citizens of German extraction scenes such as this must have disillusioned him

House Committee on Military Affairs so strenuously opposed conscription that he refused to advocate the bill, fathered by a democratic president, and it was necessary to call upon the ranking republican member to press it. In Representative Julius Kahn the measure found a friend, and a wise champion whose earnest and non-partisan efforts in behalf of our proper military organization will not soon be forgotten by the people.

With the nation at war, and our allies crying loudly for aid in the field the controversy raged for weeks. House and Senate, each adhering to its own point of view, passed divergent bills and a long-drawn-out conference between committees of the two houses followed. It was not until May 16th that the army bill passed the House. The day after it ran the gauntlet of the Senate. In the House certain timid souls were willing to dodge responsibility by having it passed without a roll-call. In the Senate eight votes were cast against it. Immediately upon signing the bill the President issued a proclamation calling for a first draft of 500,000 men and fixing June 5, 1917, as registration day.

There was a certain amount of apprehension lest there should be widespread and even violent opposition to the draft. The United States had long prided itself upon having kept its people free from the heavy demand for military service which the European nations made upon their citizens, and many saw in this emergency legislation the beginning of a permanent system of militarism here. Such people were outspoken in their

© Committee on Public Information

A doughboy consuming the famous Salvation Army doughnuts

opposition to the draft. To them were added those who were conscientiously opposed to war and who, despite the endeavors made by Congress to respect their convictions, had not been assured exemption from service. Lastly, there was a very considerable body of American citizens who were either openly or covertly in sympathy with Germany and who could hardly be expected to give hearty

A great gathering of new recruits listening to patriotic addresses of distinguished civilian and military authorities at Camp Lewis, Washington

At the outset it appeared that all these forces of discontent with the draft might combine and offer an opposition that might be serious. But nothing of the sort occurred. It will ever be to the credit of the patriotism and the good sense of the people of the United States that however general may have been the feeling of bitter disappointment that at last we had been forced to the adoption of the military measures which, as practiced by foreign nations we had always condemned, there arose in this moment, so critical to our

A company of the now famous Rainbow Division having their equipment inspected at Camp Mills on Long Island just before "going over"

support to a war upon what was in many instances the country of their birth.

A company street at Camp Devens, Mass., showing members of Company E ready for an inspection. Every article of equipment must be in its exact place

nation, no opposition to the Government's war measures that was sufficiently extended to warrant general attention. Throughout the nation the registration passed off without incident and at the end of the day the names of nearly 11,000,000 Americans, of the ages between twenty-one and thirty-one, had been inscribed upon the rolls of possible defenders of their country upon the field of battle.

Photograph by Central News Photo Service
Some New Jersey drafted men digging trenches at Camp Dix, N. J.

July 20th saw the first drawing of numbers for the selection from the registration lists of those who should first enter the service. The occasion was an historic one and a contemporary description of the scene will be interesting. The drawing was held in one of the rooms of the Senate Office Building and was conducted by Secretary of War Baker. An eye witness writes of the scene:

A handkerchief was tied about the eyes of Secretary Baker, the camera squad focused their instruments, the calcium light of the movie operators played upon

Cornell cadets having a tent-pitching drill on the beautiful campus of Cornell University at Ithaca. N. Y

A rollicking modern version of Valley Forge

the big blackboards in the rear, and the lottery began.

Secretary Baker plunged his hand into the large glass jar containing the 10,500 numbers inclosed in capsules and drew one, announcing to the spectators, "I have drawn the first number." A clerk assigned by the War Department opened the capsule and announced "258." An officer seated at the long table upon which were spread the tally sheets repeated the number, and another clerk walked to a large blackboard at the rear and wrote upon it the figures. Senator Chamberlain of Oregon, likewise blindfolded, drew the second number. He was plainly nervous. His hand was guided to the top of the jar, which was fourteen inches in diameter. "The second number is 2,522," said the announcer, and again there came the click of the cameras, the rustle of copy paper, and the murmur of excited men and women who thronged the committee room.

Members of Congress and high officials of the army attended the start of the drawing. Eight numbers were drawn by officials before the ceremony became routine, with students from various universities acting as the blindfolded withdrawers of the fateful capsules.

A round of applause greeted the appearance of General Crowder, who had worked tirelessly for days perfecting the details of the nation-wide lottery. Adjt. Gen. McCain, too, was applauded by the throng which crowded the committee rooms. Members of the Senate and House Committees on Military Affairs and other members of Congress occupied seats of honor at the drawing.

The unprecedented ceremony seemed particularly to impress Representative Julius Kahn, who had led the fight in the House on the Army Draft bill. "It is an inspiring sight," he commented as he left the room soon after the proceedings settled down to a routine basis. Mr. Kahn was born in Germany and came to the United States when a child.

As the eighth number was drawn by an official, Secretary Baker said: "We will wait a moment while the photographers remove their apparatus. Meanwhile, I want to ask that perfect quiet prevail. This is a most important occasion and absolute quiet is necessary."

John Phillips, a student of Princeton University, was the first "regular teller" who took his place at the glass jar and began to draw out the capsules—black-looking affairs, because the paper upon which the numbers were written was coated black on the outer surface. It was impossible for any one to examine the exterior of a capsule and ascertain the number within. The blindfolding lent an additional touch of the dramatic to the event, but it was unnecessary. Every few minutes Major Gen. C. A. Devol, delegated by Secretary Baker to guard the glass container, walked over to stir the capsules with a long wooden spoon. On the handle of the spoon was a piece of bunting, red, white, and blue. General Devol stirred deeply, bringing the capsules at the bottom to the top and a few moments later sending the capsules at the top to the bottom. While this stirring process was on there was a momentary pause in the recording of the numbers. The only interruptions were the frequent changes of tired announcers and tabulators and the removal of the blackboards. When a group of five hundred had been written the first section of the board was taken out to be photographed to establish an absolute record, while a second section was substituted. The lottery ended at 2:15 o'clock on the morning of July 21st, and later the same day the figures were officially checked and rechecked in the office of General Crowder. There were a number of tally sheets kept simultaneously, in addition to the recording of the drawn numbers on two blackboards, and every number was gone over and checked by a force of experts under the supervision of army officers. The result of the drawing was set into type at the Government Printing Office. "Master sheets" containing the numbers in the order

A favorite amusement of the candidate officers at the Negro officers, training camp at Fort Des Moines, Iowa

in which they were drawn were then sent by General Crowder to each Governor and distributed to each local registration board.

In August of 1917 the War Department ordered the mobilization, in four instalments, of this first draft of 687,000 men. Five

per cent. were to proceed directly to the camps; the remainder were to be called later. The men were classified in various ways according to their social and industrial condition. The effort was made to defer the actual calling of married men with dependent families, and of men whose trades

A tug of war at Camp Mills, L. I. In spite of the hard, intensive training the boys found time for games

California national guardsmen, inducted into the National Army, are having their first mess at Camp Kearny, San Diego, California

The scientifically balanced ration which keeps up the health rate

At the absorbing task of eating the "chow"

©International Film Service, Inc.

Amateur soldier cooks amid their pots and pans learning their job

Lined up for mess at the N. Y. State Cadet Training Camp at Peekskill, N. Y.

© International Film Service, Inc.

Newly drafted men lined up for mess in a National Army camp

A traveling kitchen at rest while the kitchen squad is at work preparing mess

© Underwood & Underwood.

Making wholesome bread by the wholesale for thousands of hungry boys

Uncle Sam's army loaves being handled like cord wood

© Underwood & Underwood

Rookies going over the top for the first time. Some regulars are holding the enemy trenches and acting the part of the hated Boche

of Frenchmen go to the front without a military band as they marched through the boulevards, and scarcely with the tap of a drum to mark the step. So we shall find that in the United States, when the time came to send our boys abroad, they were marched forth secretly at night, being taken to their ships under cover of darkness and dropping down the harbors without any ceremony attendant upon their departure. This was of course due to the necessity of keeping the movements of our troops secret lest lurking submarines might waylay and sink the heavy-laden transports on their way across.

or callings were such as to make them necessary in keeping up the industrial activity of the nation.

In September this first instalment began to appear at the camps and cantonments scattered over the country. In many of the greater cities, notably New York and Washington, the departure of the first detachments of conscripts were signalized by great public manifestations. But this war curiously enough was destitute very largely of the pageants and spectacles which have ordinarily accompanied the departure of a nation's troops. The writer was in Paris at the outbreak of war, and saw tens of thousands

The cantonments to which the drafted men were sent immediately upon being mustered into the army were great villages of frame houses; in fact, actual towns. Each one was designed to house an infantry division of approximately 40,000. In this division would be comprehended two brigades of infantry and one of field artillery; one regiment of engineers, one field signal battalion, three machine gun battalions, and the necessary motor and horse trains for the transport of supplies, ammunition, and sanitary appurtenances. The men reached these camps in four instalments,

Charging from behind a bomb shelter—the second man from the right is about to throw a hand bomb. The motion of throwing causes it to explode in six seconds

the mobilization being completed by October.

The method of distributing the troops once they had arrived at the cantonments in which they were to receive military instruction before departing for France was somewhat complicated. It was the effort of the military authorities to keep men coming from the same neighborhood together. But this purpose was qualified somewhat by the necessity of keeping those who followed the same technical trade in a coherent body as much as possible. The National Army of the United States, being drawn from all sections and strata of our people, comprehended among its soldiers men trained in every industry and in every art. They could take a locomotive to pieces and rebuild it; they could lay the track of a railroad or they could construct an automobile truck. Though the endeavor had been to leave in civil life workmen necessary to the industrial life of the nation, the army was itself a great hive of trained workmen who could go into almost any land, however much devastated, rebuild it, and maintain themselves there without outside assistance.

To supply these men with the necessaries of life was in itself a collosal task. Readers will recall how wide-spread and vociferous was the complaint of lack of uniforms and

equipment at the beginning of the creation of the army. The country did not thoroughly understand that this nation was not like Germany in having devoted its best energies for fifty years to the creation and storing of military supplies against a war which its rulers knew must come. In the nations of continental Europe, even in France the moment war was declared the uniforms, guns, and equipment for the entire army were ready at fixed places and every man of military age in the nation knew at what spot he could report. To the American mind that system has always been repugnant. In time of peace we have persistently thought of peace and refused to prepare for war. Accordingly, when confronted with the problem of equipping more than a million men for service which it was desired should begin within six months we found many perplexities in the situation and the men themselves suffered not a little from the lack of suitable clothing in winter camps. Fortunately enough, there was in this war, unlike the situation during our Spanish war, no complaint whatsoever regarding the quality or the quantity of food furnished the armies. We had no "embalmed beef" scandal. Unquestionably the success of this branch of the commissary department was due to the fact that the great food producers of the

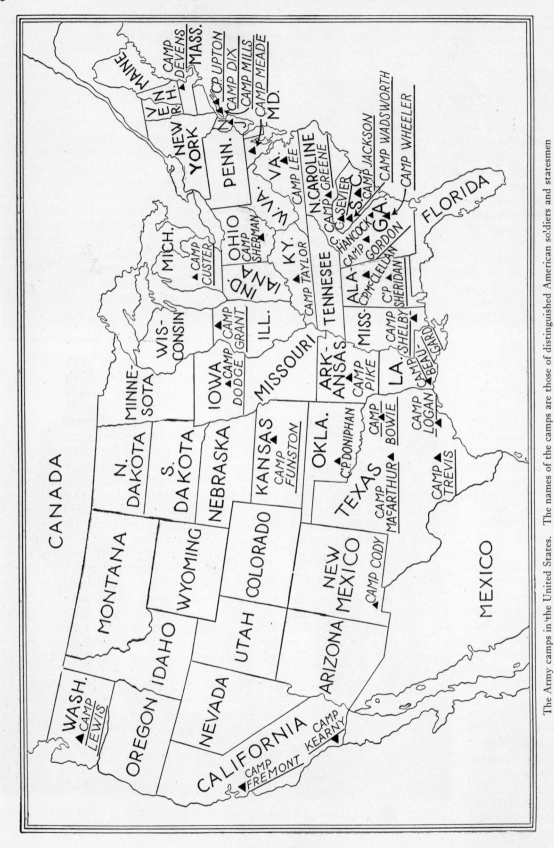

The Army camps in the United States. The names of the camps are those of distinguished American soldiers and statesmen

United States had for three years, prior to our entrance into the war, been feeding the armies of the Allies. Their methods were properly systematized, and to feed our armies simply necessitated an extension and amplification of them.

We had hardly entered into the war when patriotic and humane people throughout the country recognized the necessity of furnishing to our soldiers something more than mere food and raiment and as a result such organizations as the Young Men's Christian Association, the Red Cross, The Knights of Columbus and others took up the task of ameliorating the condition of the soldiers and sailors. Here again our men profited by the fact that the war was old to the world if new to the United States, for all of these organizations had been doing much to help cheer and comfort the soldiers of our Allies abroad. What was done by them, not in our camps alone and not in the United States alone, merits a history of its own and in due time no doubt that volume will be supplied. Their huts established in every camp, their uniformed secretaries working amid the men and trying in every possible way to bring cheer into hard lives; the entertainments they organized with theatrical talent from Broadway, often volunteered with the characteristic liberality of the dramatic profession—all these things make up a record well worth

telling in full, and the liberality of the American people in meeting the cost of this helpful service passed all earlier achievements. The "drives" for charity were as widely extended and as earnestly pressed as those involved in placing a national loan, and the amounts expended cannot have fallen far short of a billion dollars during the period of the war.

Some description of incidents of life at the various camps will be of interest to those who did not serve in the army, and may perhaps arouse recollections, at once pleasant and painful, among those who did. What happened in one camp was as a rule that which happened in all, for everything was done by routine and on a schedule which was followed universally. The American genius for standardization was applied to the organization of camps as to the building of motors. Let us quote at this point the day's schedule at a typical camp:

General Pershing and General Sibert talking with President Poincaré and General Pétain. General Pétain, the saviour of Verdun, has since been made a Marshal of France

An American artillery regiment on its way to the fighting zone in France. The marksmanship of our gunners amazed the Germans

5.45	Reveille
6 – 6.15	Calisthenics
6.30– 7	Breakfast
7 – 7.30	Police of Quarters
7.30– 8.45	School of the Soldier
8.45– 9.45	School of the Squad
9.45–10.15	Inspection of Quarters
10.15–10.45	Semaphore Signalling Drill
10.45–11.45	Reading and Explanation of Articles of War
12 – 1	Dinner
1 – 1.30	Issue and Exchange of Equipment
1.30– 2.15	School of the Soldier
2.30– 3.15	School of the Squad
3.15– 4	Instruction and Guard Duty
4.15– 5	Calisthenics
5 – 5.45	Rest Period
5.45	Retreat
6	Supper
10.30	Tattoo
10.45	Taps

The men were hardly landed in their camps before they began work on the rudiments of drill. The hand salute which is given so airily by men passing on the street is not so readily learned. Several hours are spent in drilling in this simple performance. After that, divided up into squads of eight men, they were taught to march in step. This seems like a simple task but recruits have left on record the fact that they did not find it so easy. One writes:

Back and forth, back and forth, we marched on the black strip of drill ground between barracks. I had never walked so much in my life, and sweat rolled from every pore. My back ached dully; my feet burned. But the Second Lieutenant (a youth with a pale, thin fringe above his lip) continued to command sharply "One, Two, Three, Four; One, Two, Three, Four!"

Suddenly he wheeled about and came up to me briskly.

"Get in step!" he shouted, glaring at me. "You are not dead yet."

The muscles of my jaws twitched, and I breathed an oath of vengeance. But I fell in step and I kept up with the count.

In the construction of the camps the chief features were the barracks. These were rough frame buildings, of two stories, with a low-pitched roof covered with fire-proof roofing. The building contained bunks for 150 to 200 men, or about one company. The main floor housed the mess room and kitchen, and in some instances a company hall used for purposes of recreation. Remarkable speed was shown in the erection of these edifices, the record time being said to have been made by a contractor at Camp Pike, near Little Rock, Ark. It is claimed that on a bare piece of ground at nine one morning he set a gang of carpenters to work and at 11.55 had a company barracks all complete, cleaned up, and the workmen away busy on another job.

But to return to the vital question food:

At mealtimes, to the call of the bugle the men were marched to each mess hall, and there in single file carrying in their hands the metal plate and mug from which each must eat, whatever his home training in the matter of porcelain, they marched past the service table where the dishes of each were piled high with food, and his cup filled with steaming coffee. Quantity seemed to be the first consideration, though from none of the camps did there ever arise any complaint of the quality of the food served. But certainly the assortment and amount piled on each plate were not designed for weaklings, and in the case of most of the men, who took it greedily, would have revolted the more delicate appetites they cherished in civilian life.

Sample menus may not be uninteresting. Here are typical meals:

BREAKFAST
Steak, potatoes, rice, and coffee.

DINNER
Meat stew, mashed potatoes, boiled onions, peas, bread and butter, pudding or pie, and tea, coffee or lemonade for a beverage.

SUPPER
Fried bacon, canned salmon, potato salad, a vegetable, bread and butter, and peaches or some other canned fruit.

This is a typical menu for an ordinary day, and though in the National Army there were gathered youths who in civil life had led pampered lives there was no complaint about this provender. Hunger, stimulated by plenty of work in the open air and regular hours, furnished the best sauce.

And there was indeed plenty of both work and play in the open air. As the schedule shows, drilling occupied most of the time, but even with drills, trench digging, long hikes and bayonet practice, the whole routine of the soldier's physical exercise was not completed. After hours of this sort of work the boys would turn to athletics for recreation, and baseball, football, and all varieties of athletic sports engaged most of their leisure time. The athletic field of one cantonment was equipped with not less than sixteen separate baseball diamonds and many a half holiday saw sixteen separate games going on, each with its enthusiastic crowd of "fans" rooting for their favorite team. Another camp had twenty-six football gridirons and it was not extraordinary for all twenty-six to be occupied at the same time. Then the twenty-six crowds of spectators was something to more than match the biggest November game in the Yale bowl or the Harvard stadium. Boxing, too, was a favorite sport and the wide-spread draft had caught in its net several hundred practiced pugilists who were assigned to instructor's duty. At times as many as a thousand men would be engaged in taking a fistic lesson, directed by an instructor perched on a lofty platform with assistants circulating among the crowd and helping the boys in the rudimentary art of handling their fists. All physical work of this character, and even boyish games like leap frog and prisoners' base, were encouraged by the instructors at the camps. The good effect they had on the

A column of American artillery passing through a village of Picardy on their way to the first-line trenches

physical training of the men to fit them for war suggests the reflection that it might not be unwise to encourage men to play a little more in fitting themselves for peace.

There were in all sixteen cantonments for the National Army and sixteen for the National Guard. Besides these there were officers' training camps and special camps for the marine corps, the aviation force, and for the reception of men whose training was completed and who were being concentrated immediately prior to being put on transports and sent to the foreign battlefields. A full list of the National Army and National Guard cantonments with their locations and the geographical distribution of the troops which were assigned to each will be of general interest:

NATIONAL ARMY CANTONMENTS

The names borne by the various camps are those of distinguished soldiers of the United States

SITE	ORGANIZ-ATION	TROOPS FROM—	CAMP
Ayer, Mass.	76th Division.	Maine, New Hampshire. Vermont, Massachusetts, Rhode Island, and Connecticut.	Devens
Yaphank, Long Island, N. Y.	77th Division.	Metropolitan portion of New York.	Upton
Wrightstown, N. J.	78th Division.	Remainder of New York and Northern Pennsylvania.	Dix
Annapolis Junction, Md.	79th Division.	Southern Pennsylvania,	Meade
Petersburg, Va.	80th Division.	New Jersey, Virginia, Maryland, Delaware, and District of Columbia.	Lee
Columbia, S. C.	81st Division.	Tennessee, North Carolina, South Carolina, and Florida.	Jackson
Atlanta, Ga.	82d Division.	Georgia and Alabama.	Gordon
Chillicothe, Ohio.	83d Division.	Ohio and West Virginia.	Sherman
Louisville, Ky.	84th Division.	Indiana and Kentucky.	Taylor
Battle Creek, Mich.	85th Division.	Michigan and Wisconsin.	Custer
Rockford, Ill.	86th Division.	Illinois.	Grant
Little Rock, Ark.	87th Division.	Arkansas, Louisiana, and Mississippi.	Pike
Des Moines, Iowa.	88th Division.	Minnesota, Iowa, Nebraska, North Dakota, and South Dakota.	Dodge
Fort Riley, Kan.	89th Division.	Kansas, Missouri, and Colorado.	Funston
Fort Sam Houston, Tex.	90th Division.	Texas, Arizona, New Mexico, and Oklahoma.	Travis

SITE	ORGANIZ-ATION	TROOPS FROM—	CAMP
American Lake, Wash.	91st Division.	Washington, Oregon, California, Nevada, Utah, Idaho, Montana, and Wyoming.	Lewis
Charlotte, N. C.	26th (old 5) Division.	Maine, New Hampshire, Vermont, Massachusetts, Rhode Island, and Connecticut.	Greene
Spartanburg, S. C.	27th (old 6) Division.	New York.	Wadsworth
Augusta, Ga.	28th (old 7) Division.	Pennsylvania.	Hancock
Anniston, Ala.	29th (old 8) Division.	New Jersey, Virginia, Maryland, Delaware, and District of Columbia.	McClellan
Greenville, S. C.	30th (old 9) Division.	Tennessee, North Carolina, and South Carolina.	Sevier
Macon, Ga.	31st (old 10) Division.	Georgia, Alabama, and Florida.	Wheeler
Waco, Tex.	32d (old 11) Division.	Michigan and Wisconsin.	MacArthur
Houston, Tex.	32d (old 12) Division.	Illinois.	Logan
Deming, N. Mex.	34th (old 13) Division.	Minnesota, Iowa, Nebraska, North Dakota, and South Dakota.	Cody
Fort Sill, Okla.	35th (old 14) Division.	Missouri and Kansas.	Doniphan
Fort Worth, Tex.	36th (old 15) Division.	Texas and Oklahoma.	Bowie
Montgomery, Ala.	37th (old 16) Division.	Ohio and West Virginia.	Sheridan.
Hattiesburg, Miss.	38th (old 17) Division.	Indiana and Kentucky	Shelby
Alexandria, La.	39th (old 18) Division	Louisiana, Mississippi, and Arkansas.	Beauregard
Linda Vista, Cal.	40th (old 19) Division.	California, Nevada, Utah, Colorado, Arizona, and New Mexico.	Kearny
Palo Alto, Cal.	41st (old 20) Division.	Washington, Oregon, Montana, Idaho, and Wyoming.	Fremont
Garden City, L. I., N. Y.	42d Division.	Most of the Middle and far Western States.	Mills

After the men had finished their course of training in the respective cantonments they were taken to various ports on the Atlantic seaboard and shipped to Europe. In both England and France there were other instruction camps in which the men were taught more precisely the rudiments of war under the tuition of foreign officers fresh from the front and with years of experience in actual battle. Of the methods of transportation across the three thousand miles of water which separated us from the seat of war I shall have more to say in the succeeding chapter. The instruction in the European camps was from the very first briefer than had been planned. For our men had hardly begun to arrive in continental Europe before it became apparent that the need for their presence on the battle line was already pressing. As a result just as rapidly as they could be given even a rudimentary idea of their duties, they were pushed forward and their education was completed

American soldiers on a practice hike, marching through a typical French village

in the harsh and bloody post-graduate school of the trenches.

In both England and France our troops were greeted as though they were the saviors of the nation. Particularly was this true in the latter country for there the situation had been the more desperate and the ravages of the Hun more frightful. One little French seaport, St. Nazaire, which had for centuries dragged out a humdrum existence as a port of the third or fourth class, entered by no great ocean liners and far from the track of tourist travel, was suddenly galvanized into amazing life and development. Great docks and breakwaters were constructed for the reception of the ships bringing the Yankee forces. Railroads were laid out and constructed for direct connection with Paris and the battlefront. Camps capable of holding 100,000 men were established. The villagers tried to learn English and the sleepy little sailors' town was quick to see the possibility of profit in the inundation of strangers and suddenly transformed itself into a sort of Coney Island with amusement and refreshment places on every hand.

How the Americans adapted themselves to the situation and to their new manner of life was told most graphically by a friendly foreign observer in September of 1917 who wrote thus in an English magazine:

The American troops in their billets, their camps, their training grounds, their rifle and gun practice grounds near the front, are already absolutely at home. The French villagers have adopted now a Franco-American language—sister tongue, though different, to the now classic Anglo-French spoken for three years from Calais downward. The American troops have made themselves at home, have settled all their arrangements with businesslike finality, and are out to do their job thoroughly. Their bases near the front seemed to me already definitely organized. They are settled in villages, where they disturb the villagers by aggressive sanitation. They have abolished all dung-hills, to the old farmers' amazement and alarm. They have purified the water, cleaned up the streets, cottages, and farmyards. The villagers, at first terrified by these wild measures, are now reconciled, and every little village grocery sells American matches, American tobacco, American groceries, sterilized milk, "canned goods," American mustard, and everything American except American whisky. For at the messes, where I was received with open arms as an ally of to-day and forever—no American officer makes any doubt about that—cold American purified water and French coffee with American sterilized milk are the only drinks. Villages of France have become American, and American café au lait colored cars and motor bikes with side-cars tear all over the country driven by university boys turned chauffeurs.

Our new allies are learning from us both—from us old allies, English and French. I first saw a French division in horizon blue teach the new American Army, in khaki and wearing British trench helmets what a modern battle is like. It was a moving sight. It was poignant, really, when one heard that the French division had just come back from Verdun and was enacting over again in play what it had just done in terrible and glorious earnest. The American Staff stood on a knoll watching, with the French Staff explaining. On the edge of the hill to the left of the staff the new American Army watched. Further to the left the French troops came on. Every "poilu" among them had just come from the real thing. He grinned as he played at war this time, and one felt how he must enjoy playing at it.

The lines advanced in open formation, then stopped for the barrage fire to be pushed forward. Flares were sent up to signal to the artillery. There was another step forward under barrage fire, another (sham) barrage fire, more flares and rockets, the horizon-blue line crept cautiously around to take the first trenches, the machine-gun parties came up. One more barrage fire and more signals, then the boche trenches below us were taken.

It was all exactly as it would have been in real war. The American troops understood and appreciated keenly. Who would not? These play-actors in the hollow at our feet had just come from the real tragedy, and had fought and won, but had paid the price of victory.

The American soldier (officers told me) understands the manœuvre well. The officers find that their men are quick at grasping individual field work, i. e., make admirable noncommissioned officers with initiative, enterprise, and intelligence. French officers, many of whom speak English perfectly, while several American officers I met speak very good French, give enthusiastic and intelligent assistance. French and Americans are not much alike in method or by temperament. I heard a French officer describing a battle with perfect technical accuracy, but also with dramatic expressiveness and with the literary sense. An American officer immediately translated the French into American, and it was American—short, sharp, almost crackling with crisp Americanisms. It was the same battle described, but the difference in the descriptions was delightful to note. Differences are nothing. The French are keen to teach, the Americans, if possible, keener still to learn.

British instructors and American pupils understand each other equally well. I never was more amused, pleased, cheered, and bucked up than by watching British Sergeant instructors training American officer cadets. Imagine a typical British Sergeant, with three years of war behind him and with seven or more years of British military training before that, spending every ounce of his energy, every particle of his keenness, and every word of his vocabulary teaching young Americans what they will have to do in a few months' time, and the young Americans using every muscle of their bodies, all their alertness, and all their keenness, too, to make themselves ready for the fight that all are yearning to be in.

Parties of American officer cadets dug line upon line of sham trenches, killed dummy boches on the way, dashed through four lines of trenches, dug themselves in at the last, and began instant rapid fire at more boche targets. "Advance!" said the Sergeant. A second later "Go!" and the young chaps leaped out. "Kill 'em sweet and clean! Clean killing is what we want!" shouted the Sergeant. The young Americans were at the dummies and each dug his dummy with a wild "Yah!" or college yell or scream. "Go on!" roared the Sergeant; "there are more boches beyond. Clean killing is what we want." And the Americans charged at several more lines of dummies before they leaped into the front trench and began firing.

Before the war ended more than 1,500,000 young Americans shared in this life of the foreign training camps. Let us consider the way in which the Government performed the herculean task of taking them across the 3,000 mile barrier of the tossing Atlantic.

© Committee on Public Information

American troops in Château-Thierry which has since become one of the world-famous sites of the war

CHAPTER III

GIVEN an army of not less than 3,500,000 men, which it was the intent of the United States to raise and equip, and recognizing the fact that the fighting of this army would have to be done beyond seas, how was it to be carried to the field of battle?

That was the problem that confronted the authorities of the United States while the men were doing their bit with hard drill and preparatory work in the cantonments. For long years of neglect had reduced our merchant marine to proportions that were utterly ridiculous in the face of the existing emergency. Of our own resources we could not have taken 50,000 men a month across the Atlantic—and the least number that would comply with the need would be 250,000. England naturally was willing to help with her prodigious fleet, but her own troops from the colonies had to be ferried across and meantime the Germans were sinking ships at the rate of not less than half a million tons a month. Of course the remedy was to build new ships, but that took time and the enemy was beginning to exult over what he believed would be the permanent incapacity of our nation to get its soldiers to the front in season to be a factor in the war. He estimated the amount of tonnage afloat that would be needed for the transportation of each soldier to France and his maintenance there at six tons, and asked with some degree

of reason where in the world the United States could secure this twelve or fourteen millions of tons before Germany had brought the war to a victorious end.

What was done by this nation in this crisis was one of the finest examples of organized and efficient effort the world has ever seen. Ships were needed. "Very well, we will build them," was the response of the nation. The Emergency Fleet Corporation was created by Congress with a capital of $50,000,000 and the work begun. Ship yards were established all over the United States. Contracts were let to private bidders. Public yards were speeded up. There was a long controversy over the question of whether only steel ships should be built, or some part of the construction should be of wood. A compromise was effected, but in the end the greater part of the tonnage was of steel. Ships were built on the Great Lakes, of proportions that would permit their passage through the docks of the Welland Canal, or were of such size that it was necessary to cut them in two and tow the sections through the canal and to a point below the rapids of the St. Lawrence, there to be put together again and steam bravely out to sea. After half a century in which the need for internal development had diverted the attention of the people of the United States from the ocean-carrying trade, in which they had once ranked first, the stern demands of war once again lured them upon the ocean and they determined to reassert their old supremacy there.

We had ready to hand a very considerable nucleus of a fleet of transports in the ships belonging to German companies which had been interned in our ports at the outbreak of the war. There were eighty-seven of these, representing a total of more than 500,000 tons. Greatest of all was the liner *Vaterland*, which, when taken over by the United States,

45

The *Vaterland*, rechristened the *Leviathan*, carried almost 10,000 soldiers each voyage to fight Germany

was rechristened the *Leviathan*. This, the largest merchant vessel in the world, of 54,000 tons was, like many other of the German ships, treacherously crippled by her crew by the destruction of vital parts of the machinery. But although in the case of this great ship alone the repairs cost no less than $1,000,000 they were swiftly made by American mechanics—though the Germans had boasted that she could be repaired nowhere but in her home port—and she was set afloat to carry more than 10,000 American soldiers abroad on each trip to give battle to her former owners. Her contribution in all was 94,195 fighting men landed in France. By charter, purchase, and construction the American Government ultimately acquired so great a fleet that when the armistice was signed we had transported more than 2,500,000 men across the ocean.

It was no slight task to begin with to get the men from the cantonments which were scattered the length and breadth of the land to the waiting ships. Boston, New York, Philadelphia, and Newport News were the chief ports whence troops were shipped, although other seaports were occasionally used.

© Committee on Public Information

Interior of boiler of S. S. *Pommern*, now U. S. S. *Rappahannock*, showing how the German crew melted the boiler by dry firing

Near the principal sailing ports were great concentration camps, such as Camp Merritt, in New Jersey, near the port of Hoboken. To these camps the men about to sail were brought from all over the country. There was very little ceremony about it all. For pomp and martial display this was the least picturesque of all wars. Mustered in their home camps at early dawn, marched without music to waiting troop trains, transported in crowded day coaches across half the continent in many instances, without crowds to speed them on their way the boys despatched about the business of fighting the Hun must have felt a lamentable lack of romance about the circumstances attendant upon their departure.

While every possible effort was made to conserve the health and comfort of the troops

© Committee on Public Information

The wrecked engine room of the German ship which became the U. S. S. *George Washington*

A latecomer being sworn in at the pier just before the transport sailed

en route the troop trains at best were but a dismal form of traveling. Each had its kitchen car in which the company cooks practised their art, and food was plentiful at regular hours. At fixed periods along the line, if the journey was a long one, the train was stopped and the men mustered outside for exercise. In the main, however, the journeys were uneventful and uninteresting, and the thousands of our people who may have wondered at the loud shouts with which a loaded troop train greeted every station at which there was sign of life may have conjectured that the only variety that attended the soldiers' journey was an occasional chance to yell.

Meantime at Hoboken, or some other port, the ships destined to carry the troops speeding thither from across country were being prepared. The transports were manned in the main by members of the Naval Reserves, patriotic boys, often college students who volunteered for that service early in the war. The thousands of young men in this service were the very pick of our youth, and it is hoped that the experience of seafaring life they enjoyed during the war may encourage many of them to take up as a life profession the American merchant marine which it is believed will be established on a prodigious scale as a result of the fleets built for war purposes.

Wives and sweethearts, friends and relatives at the pier saying those final words, so commonplace and yet so moving, to their boys setting forth for the great adventure on one of the first transports to leave our shores

© International Film Service

This illustrates the spirit in which our boys set out to "lick the Huns." They came back with the same spirit even though wounded

Some of the first of our soldiers marching up the gangway on to the ocean ferry which was to land almost two and a half million of them on foreign soil before the victory was won

Photograph from London *Daily Mirror*

A German submarine commander showed the customary German respect for the property and lives of unoffending neutrals by setting afire in mid ocean this neutral ship

A typical scene on a transport in mid ocean. Very few American transports were lost in spite of Germany's silly threats and cruel and treacherous efforts to make these threats good

Photograph from London *Daily Mirror*

British destroyers are hurrying to the rescue of the surviving victims of this submarine atrocity where the Germans did not succeed in living up to their ideal of "sinking without a trace"

The transports were steamships of every sort. Only a very few had been built especially for this purpose because the United States had had little need for moving troops about the world except to her colonies in the Philippines. Most of the transports, therefore, were liners that had been adapted to this use. Some were among the most gorgeous of the ocean palaces which were stripped of their tapestries, paintings, and decorative features, fitted with bunks and set to the stern duties of war. Many had been owned by our foes. Besides the German ships already mentioned 14 Austrian ships aggregating about 70,000 tons were taken by the federal government. The skill with which the German sailors had secretly wrecked the machinery of their ships, acting upon instructions from their government, made their immediate use impossible. As a result of the first survey made after the seizure the American engineers declared that it would take at least 18 months to complete the necessary repairs. Germans exultingly insisted they could not be repaired at all outside of Germany. They

failed to take into account American ingenuity and efficiency. In fact, all the ships were made ready for service within nine months. But at first the machinery and vitals of these vessels presented a sorry spectacle. Valves had been thrown overboard, pipes cut and the sections removed, bolts, nuts, and other articles had been dropped into the machinery where they would do the most hurt, and bearings had been filled with emery to cut them as soon the engines might be started. In certain ships explosives had been secreted in the engines with the idea that on starting them up they would blow everything, including the new engineers, to pieces. It was all a piece of Hun frightfulness and destruction very carefully worked out. The way in which the engineers of the United States navy grappled with this mechanical chaos and reduced it to order, in many cases so improving the engines of the ships that they made several knots an hour in our service more than they had before, was a triumph of professional skill. Of course when put into our service the names of the German vessels were changed with

Photograph by Western Newspaper Union

This German submarine was caught napping and found herself at the mercy of the American destroyer *Fanning*. The officers and crew are on deck eager to save their lives by surrendering to a chivalrous foe. The Germans instinctively realized that their enemies were not as base and cruel as they were

S. S. *Antilles* of the U. S. Army transport service arriving at a French port laden with American troops. She was later sunk on a return voyage by a German submarine

the exception of three that, by a delicate attention, the Huns, before they went war-mad, had named *George Washington*, *President Lincoln*, and *President Grant*. The *Prinz Eitel Freidrich*, a raider which had escaped from its British pursuers only by running into Hampton Roads, was renamed *Baron DeKalb* and took the very first detachment of American troops to France. The *Kronprinzessin Cecelie*, which at the opening of the war was on her way to Europe with a large shipment of gold for Germany and which turned and fled into Bar Harbor, was renamed the *Mount Vernon* and was badly damaged, though not sunk, as the result of a torpedo wound inflicted by her former owners.

As each transport filled up with its quota of precious human cargo, it was moved from its pier to a previously assigned anchorage in the bay, safe behind the submarine net stretched across the harbor's entrance. A ring of ever-watchful cruisers and destroyers surrounded the gradually increasing number of transports. In a way, perhaps, these few days of anchorage were the most difficult of the whole trip. With land in sight on all sides, with the high towers and

at night the bright lights of Manhattan, suggesting all the joys of the country's metropolis, with nothing of any real importance to do, and with what seemed unending delays to the start for France, it was at times hard for this crowd, eager to get nearer to the enemy, to reconcile itself to the utter impossibility of either getting shore leave or of being off on the road to war and glory.

However, the day of days at last arrived. The embarkation was completed. The squadron, divided into several groups, each with its own escort of destroyers and cruisers, passed through the Narrows and before many hours had gone was on the high ocean. The various groups separated, each travelling a different route, and though they might come in sight of each other on the way over more than once they were not to meet again until they all had safely reached that port "somewhere in France."

Life aboard the transports soon settled down to more or less of a routine. For the first few days many of the men, most of whom had never been on salt water before, had neither strength nor desire enough to do anything. They were experiencing their first taste of the great joykiller of the briny deep.

seasickness. But being in tip-top condition and leading the most regular of lives they quickly recovered and again began to take interest in life and in "chow," especially in "chow." It was a good thing that a paternal government had provided tons and tons of food. For, once over the seasickness, every soldier boy seemed to make it his chief object in life to make up as quickly and completely as possible for whatever meals he had missed.

Besides eating there were plenty of other things to do. All the "passengers" suddenly became one great strident body devoted for many hours every day to the difficult task of acquiring a speaking knowledge of French. Not all France ever held as many varied "patois" of its musical tongue as could be heard any day on any of the transports. Then there were boxing bouts every night during which the participants got their fair share of exercising their muscles, while the spectators would make valiant efforts to regain for their tongues that stability which they must have lost during their French linguistic studies.

Of course there was more serious work to be done, too, now. Setting-up drill morning, afternoon, and evening kept the soldiers from going stale, while the naval crews never once let up preparing for possible submarines by frequent gun practice. All hands, officers and men, both military and naval, took part in frequent fire and life boat drills. A certain number of men, too, were assigned each day to stand their share of watching for submarines. Many a keen and eager military eye would report a periscope which upon closer inspection by someone more accustomed to the sea and its flotsam would prove

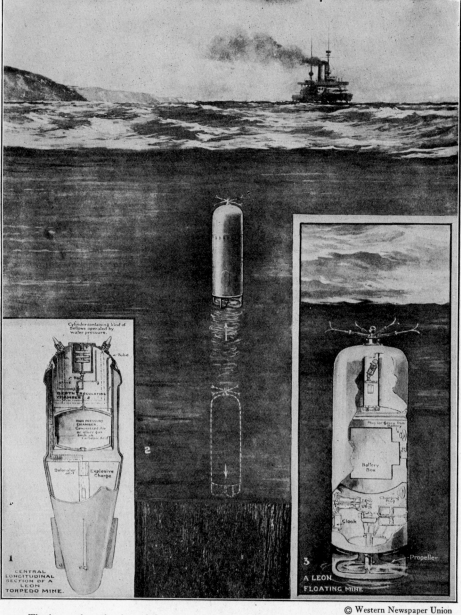

The internal mechanism of that dreaded modern instrument of destruction, a floating mine

to be nothing more danger-ous than a log or a barrel. The manœuvres of the group units and of the naval escort fur-nished another source of con-siderable in-terest.

The twelfth day usually the convoy entered the danger zone. Interest wherever it had began to lag immediately became renew-ed. One of the escorting ships wigwagged that in a few hours the trans-port was to make rendez-vous with some additional de-stroyers that had come from one of our naval

U. S. transport *Neptune* and other American troop ships arriving at St. Nazaire, France

bases in France to meet us. And almost at the exact time appointed there hove into sight three United States destroyers. Added to the escort which had come all the way across, they made such a formidable pro-tection, that even a small squadron of sub-marines would not have had much of a chance.

Soon after their arrival came that day's boat drill. The life boats now were swung to the level of the promenade deck rail and were lashed there. Portable steps were placed before each boat all along the deck. The destroyers were continually cutting in and out amongst the transports. Lookout was kept even more carefully and by larger numbers of men. Reports of suspicious looking objects increased in proportion. But nothing happened.

The convoy was now within a day and a half's journey from port. Long before that time was up the French pilot had come aboard and brought the ship into port.

There, stretched out in the quaintness and beauty of western France, lay the country whose men, women, and children had for four weary years fought the battle of liberty. And how those of them who were compara-tively fortunate, inhabiting that small corner of valiant France far from the "battle front," greeted this latest force from their mighty sister republic across the wide ocean! Cheer upon cheer rang out as each transport came in sight. The Stars and Stripes were to be seen everywhere, on houses and in the hands of the people who somehow never missed the arrival of a single transport, no matter how little official news there was to be had about its arrival.

As the boats proceeded to their anchorage the bands struck up the "Star-Spangled Banner." The boys in olive-drab stood at attention and so did all the French, man, woman, and child. Renewed cheering broke out as soon as the music had stopped. A few moments later that other tune of liberty

General Pershing on his arrival at Boulogne reviewing the French marines in company with two French generals

dear to every loyal French heart and to every freedom-loving heart the wide world over, the "Marseillaise" sent forth its thrilling notes, accompanied by the stirring voices of the natives.

Not all the transports had as uneventful a passage as the group whose journey from the United States to France has been described. The first loss suffered by the transport service was the sinking of the former liner *Antilles*. Though under convoy she was attacked by a German submarine on October 1, 1917, while returning to the United States from France. Sixty-seven men, most of them wounded soldiers, went down with her.

The second, and unfortunately much more serious loss, was the sinking of the former Anchor liner *Tuscania*. This boat, then under charter to the Cunard line, formed part of the British fleet employed in assisting in the transportation of the United States forces. Within sight of the Irish coast, and, though guarded by convoy, she was attacked by a submarine in the early evening of February 5, 1918. The torpedo struck the liner amidship. Though British destroyers came to her rescue immediately and only a short time later British trawlers arrived, the

death toll was large, amounting to 204. The boat almost immediately after having been struck keeled over at a dangerous angle which prevented the launching of most of the life boats on the port side. Of the few that were launched some capsized. In spite of the quite apparent danger the American troops aboard conducted themselves with great calmness and discipline. In all, 2,179 officers and soldiers, consisting of National Guardsmen from Michigan and Wisconsin, with part of the first Forestry Engineers and three Aero Squadrons chiefly from New York, were aboard the ill-fated ship.

The *Oronsa*, with only 250 men aboard, was sunk on April 29, 1918. Three of the crew were lost. Two transports were sent to the bottom in May, 1918. On the 24th the British S. S. *Moravia* was sunk in the English Channel and 55 out of the 500 men aboard laid down their lives. On the 31st the former Hamburg-American liner, *President Lincoln*, of 18,168 tons, one of the largest of the German ships taken over by the United States Government, was attacked some 600 miles out of a French port on her return to the United States. Though she was sunk, assistance arrived so quickly that only 27 lives were lost.

Another large former Hamburg-American liner, the *Covington* (formerly *Cincinnati*), of 16,399 tons met the same fate on July 1, 1918, off the French coast. Fortunately she carried neither troops nor passengers. But 6 members of her crew made the supreme sacrifice for their country's liberty.

September 6, 1918, the British S. S. *Persic*, with 2,800 U. S. troops aboard, was attacked 200 miles off the English coast. Badly damaged she managed to keep afloat and was finally beached without any loss of life. The attack was one of the most venturesome in the history of submarine warfare. Not only was the *Persic* one of a large group of transports, but she was also heavily guarded by destroyers and warships. One of the former, it was reported unofficially, sent the submarine to the bottom of the sea.

The last and the most costly loss on the open sea was suffered when the transport *Otranto*, one of a group of transports under strong convoy, collided during the night of October 6, 1918, with the British P. & O liner *Kashmir* in the North Channel between Ireland and Scotland, off the bleak Island of Islay. A very high sea was running and a dense fog added its share to the difficulties created by the collision. Though destroyers did their best to assist the unfortunate vessel and its unhappy load of soldiers and sailors, the weather doomed many a brave man to death who, under more favorable conditions, might have been saved. The *Otranto* was dashed to pieces on the sharp rocks of Islay and so were many of the life boats. Of

699 men aboard 372 were drowned or missing. Many of these succumbed to the exposure they had suffered before they were rescued. Though the place and conditions in which the collision happened were horrible enough to break the courage of the stoutest heart, once more American valor and discipline asserted themselves. From all sides it has been testified that both those who lived and those who died acted with the utmost courage and self-control.

One other boat, the former Hamburg-American liner *America*, was lost to the transport service, at least temporarily. On October 15, 1918, while lying at her dock in Hoboken, N. J., almost ready to sail and already having some 300 soldiers aboard, she suddenly began to sink and before long was resting on the bottom with only her superstructure visible above the water. Three of her crew were lost, but the rest as well as all the soldiers were saved. The "accident" was due to the treachery of German sympathizers.

The transportation of United States forces to Europe was a task remarkable not only for the surprisingly small percentage of losses suffered at sea, but also for its magnitude. The first ship carrying military personnel sailed on May 8, 1917, having on

French Official-Pictorial Press

Official visit of Mr. Sharp, American Ambassador to France, to American aviation headquarters at the front

A typical scene in a French port where American transports are docking.   Sleepy and picturesque little ports like St. Nazaire
became among the busiest in the world

board Base Hospital 4 and members of the
Reserve Nurses Corps. The Commander-
in-Chief of the U. S. Expeditionary Force,
General Pershing, and his staff, sailed on
May 28, 1917, landed in London June 8th
and arrived in Paris June 13, 1917.

From then on an ever-increasing flow of
troops, regulars, National Guards, and National Army men, with their various different
special service detachments, soon began to
indicate that the United States would before
long surpass the most optimistic expectations
in respect to the number of troops which
could be sent every month. Official embarkation figures announced by the Department of War are:

1917	May	1,718
	June	12,261
	July	12,988
	August	18,323
	Sept.	32,523
	Oct.	38,259
	Nov.	23,016
	Dec.	48,840
1918	Jan.	46,776
	Feb.	48,027
	March	83,811
	April	117,212
	May	244,345
	June	276,372

July	306,185
August	290,818
September	261,415
Oct. 1-21.	131,398
Total	1,994,287
Marines	14,644
	2,008,931

The greater part of our forces which went
direct to France were landed at either Brest
or St. Nazaire. The latter which was exclusively an American port of landing had
been prior to the war a little, sleepy French
hamlet at the mouth of the Loire, with a
good harbor, but off the lines of trade so
that it had never more than a fishing fleet
and a few tramp steamers to accommodate.
The Americans descended upon it and made
it one of the great harbors of the world.
Enormous concrete breakwaters and docks
were built. Warehouses to accommodate
food and raiment for a city of half a million
people were there. Railroads were built
into the interior, and railroad sidings covered
broad acres of what had been rural country.
Millions upon millions of dollars were spent
in construction work, while the money spent
by our soldiers who began coming in by

The arsenal at Brest where the Fourth Division of the U. S. Fleet twice visited during the war

the scores of thousands soon began to make the thrifty French peasants feel as though they had encountered the days of an El Dorado.

They were quick enough to grasp the opportunity. The little shops in the narrow streets were suddenly multiplied an hundred fold and began the sale of goods of a sort never dreamed of in that village. They do say that some of the souvenirs and articles with that unmistakable Parisian air which our soldier and sailor boys eagerly snapped up were manufactured in our own New Jersey and sent over to gratify our demand. But that may be mere slander. At any rate, the United States made of St. Nazaire a busy mart of trade, a great shipping and railroad centre, and multiplied its population about 1,000 per cent. in a few months. One wonders what will be its destiny now that the war is over.

We established also training camps in England where a portion of our men received their final instruction before going to the front. An American writer has set down a pleasing account of one of these which may be worth quoting:

As the visitor strolls through the sinuous streets of an ancient city of England he at once notices that a change has come over this quiet place, for it is full of bustle and animation, and the English that is spoken is not uttered with the local intonation. Strange to say the voices are those of Southerners and the ear soon becomes accustomed to the drawl of the Marylander, of the Alabaman, of the Tennesseean and of the Virginian. Here and there one can detect the burr of the Iowan and the Ohioan.

If you address them they answer briefly and to the point. A few regulars there are—very few, they belong to that corps d'elite, the United States Marines. . . . The camp is merely a passing one, men come there after landing on British soil, and undergo a sort of quarantine for about a week, when they depart to be trained on French territory.

"We don't mind staying here for the winter, but next Spring must see us off. We don't want to miss the big drive, and a big drive it is going to be next Spring. Cuba, the Philippines won't be in it with that drive," says a fine Marylander, a sergeant in the aforesaid marines. The American officers are emphatic and sincere in their praise of their British confréres who have helped, and are still helping them with zeal and chivalry. Our officers are known as liaison officers, to the British Tommies they are "Elizas"—their best attempt to pronounce that French word. It is one more word to be added to what may be called the "Napoo" language or rather dialect.

A stroll through the lanes of the cantonments compels the visitor to admire the way in which the British authorities have paved the way for our latest allies. A "pharmacy" where every day the boys can get a pill if they want one—"for in wartime a man can have a pill for a sore throat, a broken leg, or any other thing he thinks he has got," remarks the guide. An isolation

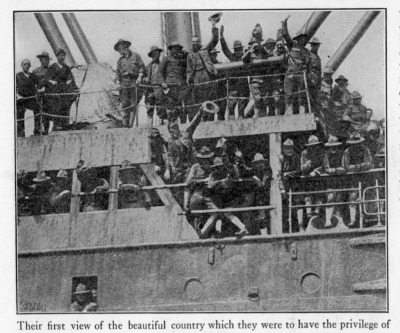

Their first view of the beautiful country which they were to have the privilege of helping to save

ward, two or three hospitals, "dry" canteens, messrooms, bathrooms, banks, and express company, clubs, chapels, everything has been provided. The principal medical officer in charge relates an interesting bit of statistics: "I saw long ago that we were going to come in fast and I went to work at once—2,000 of us, that was the number then; 20,000 now." In a way the camp looks somewhat akin to a mining camp in Colorado with its huts as "banks." The only bank not to be found is one wherein poker chips or dice are rattled.

The first American troops were landed in France in June, 1917. They came to a land in which little had been prepared for them. Though they came as strangers they were met with an enthusiastic

Five thousand of the vanguard of America's army crossing Westminster Bridge after a memorable march through the cheering throngs of London

Austrian and German prisoners digging sewers in an American camp under the direction of our soldiers

American mechanical and organizing enterprise soon made itself felt in France. This is an American built powder mill with docks in the foreground. It was the largest in France

The American Expeditionary Force was aided in every possible way by the soldiers of France. Here some poilus are helping American Marines put up winter quarters

Secretary of War, Newton D. Baker, and General Pershing inspecting American warehouses in France

welcome by the French people who hailed them as saviors and as the implacable enemies of the Boche. Within three months a new complexion had come upon the little towns which were made subject to American occupation. To begin with the villagers were amazed, and to some extent aggrieved, by finding their homes made the subject of aggressive sanitation regulations. The French village, for all its picturesqueness, does not conform to those rules of sanitation which have become compulsory in the American Army, and of which Surgeon General Gorgas has been the great author and executor. It was not long after the arrival of the "Sammies," as the French for a time called our men, despite their protests, before the dunghills which from time immemorial had been a decorative feature of the front yards of French cottages had disappeared. The water supply was purified, the streets and farmyards cleaned up. After the villagers had become reconciled to these revolutionary reforms, they took up most cheerfully the business of extracting from the pocket of the American soldier the American dollar. If northern France had suffered cruelly from the invasion of the Boche and the devastation he had accomplished, southwestern France during the American occupation profited as never before in its existence. Everything that could appeal to an American soldier or sailor was for sale with the single exception of American drinks. That particular source of cheer was effectively denied our men at the front.

Just outside of each village or cantonment was the field on which the newcomers were drilled in the art of war. Here they had in the early days what at first was denied to those in training camps at home, instruction at the hands of men who had actually done what they were teaching the greenhorns to do.

It was late in October, 1917, that the American forces first came into conflict with the enemy. This does not mean that at that early date our troops were ready to take and hold a sector of the battle line, or to join in an assault of the enemy's positions. But at that period began the practice of sending detachments of the American army into the trenches and merging them with French or

© Committee on Public Information

These American soldiers in the training area in France are being instructed in trench building by a veteran Scotch sergeant

© Committee on Public Information

Because of their universal training in baseball, our national game, our "boys" easily learned and speedily excelled in the art of throwing hand grenades

A British Army Captain instructing members of an American machine gun company in the use of the Vickers Light   Machine Gun in a training camp in France

British commands in order that they might see something of actual warfare.   Naturally the points chosen were not those at which the firing was fiercest.   And in this particular instance our soldiers were sent into the trenches in the neighborhood of the Vosges mountains not far from the line of Lorraine.

They entered the trenches under cover of the night, and being the first Americans to reach the actual front were greeted by the French with a welcome that was no less hearty because owing to the proximity of the enemy it had necessarily to be silent.   They were gripped by the hands, hugged, and even kissed on both cheeks after the French fashion, but somewhat to American disgust.

October 27th the first shot was fired by an American artillerist at the enemy.   There is a long story of unpreparedness behind the fact that this missile, discharged with a certain degree of ceremony, though fired by an American artillery-man, had to be discharged from a French 75, we having no guns of our own on the field. History relates that the gunner was red-headed, the shot was loudly cheered, and the

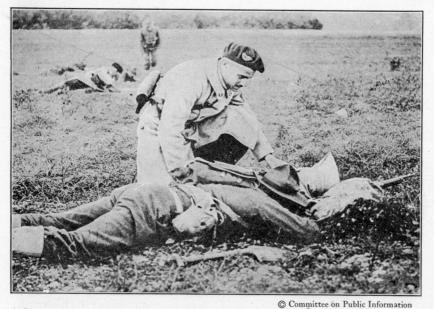

A French soldier instructor showing an American how to protect himself with a single bag of sand

shell case was sent as a trophy to President Wilson. History does not relate what damage the missile did in the enemy's lines.

A night or two later the Americans on that sector had their first experience of the perilous invasion of No Man's Land. A dozen or more accompanied by French veterans who knew the ropes, equipped with hand grenades, rifles, revolvers, and trench knives, with their steel helmets firmly strapped on clambered over the top and set forth on their midnight excursion. After finding the gap in their own barbed wire, they wriggled along in the dark on their stomachs, stopping their progress as now and then a flare from the enemy's lines lighted up the blackness, and patrolled thus the disputed territory between the two lines of trenches. There were no casualties in this first expedition. But a few days later, on the 5th of November, the Americans were destined to lose their first comrades as prisoners to the enemy, while three were shot dead, being the first to fall under the Stars and Stripes on a European battlefield.

American soldiers resting beside the road on their way to the assault upon the Hindenburg Line

The occasion was a raid made by a German force against a sector of the line held mainly by Americans. The latter occupied a salient which must have been carefully spied out by the enemy for they put down a barrage immediately behind it, preventing any retreat by the occupying force, while with a

In this beautiful spot in France well back of the devastated area these American soldiers are being instructed in the art of throwing hand grenades—in which they soon excelled

heavy artillery fire they cut away the wire in front. Then in overwhelming numbers they attacked. Many made their way into the American trenches and for a time there was hand-to-hand fighting in these deep and narrow gullies. Fragmentary reports by eye witnesses show how little the new soldier understands the art of such fighting. One of the wounded Americans said, "I was standing in a communicating trench waiting for orders. I heard a noise back of me and looked around in time to see a German fire in my direction. I felt a bullet hit my arm." It was not long, however, before Americans learned not to wait for orders when they heard the enemy descending upon their trenches.

In this raid three Americans were killed, the first actually to fall in battle in this war. They were:

GRESHAM, JAMES B. (Corporal) of Evansville, Ind.
ENRIGHT, THOMAS F. (private) of Pittsburg, Penn.
HAY, MERLE D. (private) of Glidden, Iowa.

Near a little village in Lorraine, and in its torn and rent churchyard, are three graves each surrounded by a neat white fence with a wooden cross at the head. Here lie the first three Americans to fall in the war for democracy. With a guard of French infantrymen clad in their horizon blue, on one side, and a detachment of American soldiers on the other, with both the Tri-color and the Stars and Stripes floating over the scene as a bugler played taps and minute guns were fired, the bodies of these first of our heroes were laid away. A French major-general spoke fitting words over the graves and ended his tribute with this appeal and prophecy:

"We will therefore ask that the mortal remains of these young men be left here, left with us forever. We inscribe on the tombs 'Here lie the first soldiers of the Republic of the United States to fall on the soil of France for liberty and justice.' The passerby will stop and uncover his head. Travellers and men of heart will go out of their way to come here and pay their respective tributes.

"Private Enright, Corporal Gresham, Private Hay! In the name of France I thank you. God receive your souls. Farewell."

The first American infantry units to reach Picardy halted by the roadside on their march to the front

CHAPTER IV

THE FIRST AMERICANS TO GO—WORK OF OUR AMBULANCE CORPS—THE
COMMISSION FOR THE RELIEF OF BELGIUM—OUR MEN IN THE FRENCH FOREIGN
LEGION—THE LAFAYETTE ESCADRILLE—OUR FIGHTERS IN THE AIR—THE
MARTYRS

NO HIS-
TORY of
the United
States in the
Great War could be
complete which failed
to recount some of
the deeds of those
ardent young Ameri-
cans who, while the
President himself
questioned and de-
layed, offered their
lives to the cause of
democracy and of
humanity. There is
no nobler roster of
war's heroes than
that upon which are
inscribed the names
of the young men who sacrificed their lives
in France, whether as ambulance workers,
aviators, or fighters on the battlefield, before
their hesitant country had recognized its
duty and come to their aid and to that of
imperilled civilization.

Earliest in the field were the volunteers
for ambulance work, and of these easily
first was Richard Norton, organizer of the
American Volunteer Motor Ambulance Corps.
Two months after the declaration of war
in 1914 he had ten ambulances in the field,
all manned of course by volunteers like
himself. By the time the United States
entered the conflict he had charge of more
than one hundred cars. Doing somewhat
similar work was the Field Service of the
American Ambulance of which A. Piatt
Andrew, a Princeton man, was organizer and
director. Before the United States came in
this organization had more than two hundred
cars in service.

Men died in the ambulance service even
as they did serving the great guns, or leading

the charge. To attempt the roster of all the
devoted young Americans who thus gave up
their lives for others would be indeed impossible, but the stories of a few may stimu-
late emulation in future wars—if future wars
there have to be.

Of Richard Hall, a young graduate of the
University of Michigan at Ann Arbor, a
friend tells in the memorial volume "Friends
of France":

All this time as in all the past months Richard Neville
Hall calmly drove his car up the winding, shell-swept
artery of the mountain of war—past crazed mules,
broken-down artillery carts, swearing drivers, stricken
horses, wounded stragglers still able to hobble—past
long convoys of Boche prisoners, silent, descending in
twos, guarded by a handful of men—past all the personnel of war, great and small (for there is but one road,
one road on which to travel, one road for the enemy to
shell)—past *abris*, bomb-proofs, subterranean huts to
arrive at the *postes de secours*, where silent men moved
mysteriously in the mist under the great trees where
the cars were loaded with an ever-ready supply of
still more quiet figures (though some made sounds),
mere bundles in blankets.

Hall saw to it that those quiet bundles were carefully
and rapidly installed—right side up, for instance—for
it is dark and the *brancardiers* are dull folk, deadened
by the dead they carry; then rolled down into the
valley below where little towns bear stolidly their
daily burden of shells thrown from somewhere in
Bocheland over the mountain to somewhere in France
—the bleeding bodies in the car a mere corpuscle in the
full crimson stream, the ever-rolling tide from the
trenches to the hospital, of the blood of life, and the
blood of death.

At midnight Christmas Eve he left the valley to get
his load of wounded for the last time. Alone, ahead of
him two hours of lonely driving up the mountain.
Perhaps he was thinking of other Christmas Eves, perhaps of his distant home, and of those who were thinking
of him. . . .

Matter, the next American to pass, found him by the
roadside half way up the mountain. His face was
calm and his hands still in position to grasp the wheel.
. . . A shell had struck the car and killed him in-

Some of the many Americans in France who volunteered for service with the Foreign Legion of the French Army long before the United States entered the war. It is said that there were fully fifty thousand Americans fighting with the Allies before our declaration of war

© Underwood & Underwood

The private residence of Mr. Paris Singer in Devonshire, England, which he gave to the authorities to be used as the American Women's Hospital

stantly, painlessly. A chance shell in a thousand had struck him at his post, in the morning of his youth.

The whole world will long remember the heroic defense of Verdun by the French who swore a mighty oath "They shall not pass" and kept it in the face of the whole army of the Crown Prince. There were Americans there, too, and although not among the fighting corps their gallantry compares well with that of any poilu. Consider this story of the rescue of William Barber, an American ambulance driver, by a colleague identified long after as Walter H. Wheeler of Yonkers, N. Y.

Fifth night.—Got to post O.K. Heavy traffic; firing; road stinking of dead flesh. On way back heard forlorn cry of Barber. Stopped and found him in arms of Frenchman by side of road. Nerves gone, so he couldn't talk straight. Car had been hit; he was wounded; pumping hell out of road ahead where his car was. He had crawled back; was afraid to let him wait. Dragged him into front alongside of me and made a dash; never drove so fast in all my life. Passed his car; whole back shot off and wheels gone. Got to last bridge and found artillery coming across in opposite direction. Crawled across one side on remains of a railroad track. Grabbed leading horses of a battery by bridle and jammed them over on one side of road; commanding riders to wait; must have thought I was an officer; because they did; hurried back and drove across. Got to headquarters O.K. and got Barber into

dressing room. Worst wound was on his back but a glancing one. He will pull through.

And then there were the young Americans who, under the leadership of Herbert Hoover, fed for years the starving victims of German rapacity in Belgium. This is no place to describe the work of the Commission for Relief in Belgium. Whole volumes will yet be written on that topic and the tale still be left half untold. But a picturesque description of the nature of the work, from the pen of Professor Vernon Kellogg, one of Hoover's right-hand men, will not be out of place:

Rice from Rangoon, corn from Argentina, beans from Manchuria, wheat and meat and fats from America; and all, with other things of the regular programme, such as sugar, condensed milk, coffee and cocoa, salt, salad oil, dried fish, etc., in great quantities to be brought across wide oceans, through the dangerous mine-strewn Channel, and landed safely and regularly in Rotterdam, to be there speedily transferred from ocean vessels into canal boats, and urged on into Belgium and northern France, and from these taken again by railroad cars and horse-drawn carts to the communal warehouses and soup kitchens; and always and ever, through all the months, to get there *in time*—these were the buying and transporting problems of the Commission. One hundred thousand tons a month of food-stuffs from the world over, in great shiploads to Rotterdam; one hundred thousand tons a month

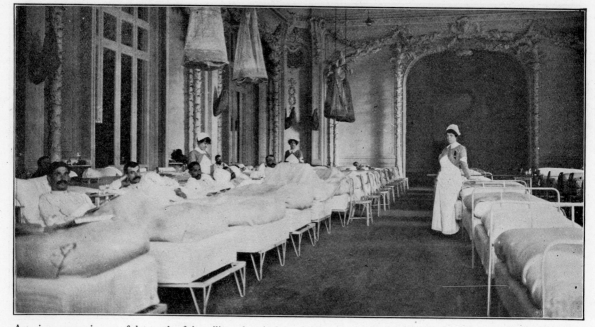

American nurses in one of the wards of the military hospital, established by the French in the magnificent winter palace at Pau

thence in ever more and more divided quantities to the province and district storehouses, to the regional storehouses and mills, to the communal centres and finally to the mouths of the people. And all to be done economically, speedily, and regularly; to be done, that is, with "engineering efficiency."

It would be interesting to go more into detail concerning the work of the hundreds of young Americans who volunteered for service with Hoover. In most cases they were college men—many of them Rhodes students at Oxford. The work was arduous, compelling great personal devotion and a high degree of tact and self-restraint. It is not at all surprising to learn that after what they saw in Belgium and France during their period of enforced neutrality most of these gallant lads gladly took up arms with the American army when the chance to fight was given them.

It is appropriate here to tell the stories of some of the gallant young Americans who, long before their country recognized its moral obligation to come to the aid of the nations that were fighting for civilization against the Hun, had offered themselves for the cause of democracy. We have spoken already of Kiffen Rockwell and of Victor Chapman, both of whom gave up their lives in the course of duty.

Another was William Thaw, class of 1915 at Yale, who enlisted in the famous *Légion Étrangère* of France—the foreign legion that Ouida made

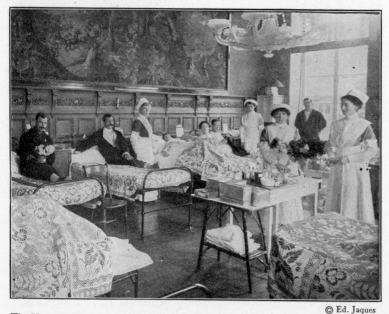

© Ed. Jaques

The Hadfield Ward of the Singer palace after its transformation into a hospital, with American nurses in charge

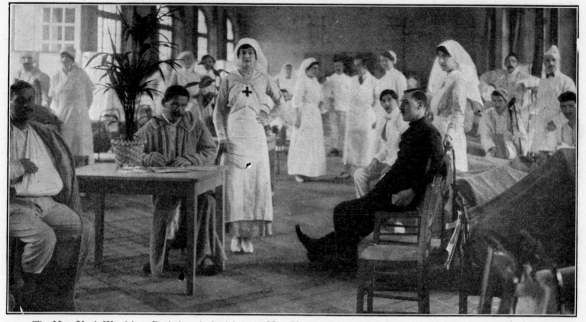

The New York Ward in a Paris hospital with some New York girls as nurses and some New York boys as patients

famous in "Under Two Flags." He served in the *Légion* only about six months when he was transferred to the French aviation service. There he remained until the end, the only original member of the Escadrille in service at the time of peace. His description of life in the *Légion* is illuminating as to the sort and conditions of society there encountered. A brief excerpt will be interesting:

Talk about your college education, it isn't in it with what a fellow can learn being thrown in with a bunch of men like this. There are about 1,200 here (we sleep on straw on the floor of the *Ecole Professionel pour Jeunes Filles*) and in our section (we sleep and drill by sections) there is *some* mixture including a Columbia Professor, called Shorty, an old tutor who has numerous Ph. D.'s, M.A.s, etc., a preacher from Georgia, a pro. gambler from Missouri, a former light weight second rater, two dusky gentlemen, one from Louisiana and the other from Ceylon, a couple of hard guys from the Gopher gang of lower N.Y., a Swede, a Norwegian, a number of Poles, Brazilians, Belgians, etc. So you see it's some bunch. I sleep between the prize-fighter and a chap who used to work for the Curtiss Co. As for the daily routine it reminds me of the Hill School and then some; only instead of getting demerits for being naughty you get short rations and prison.

© George Grantham Bain

Dr. Alexis Carrell of the Rockefeller Institute, who discovered, among other things, a drainage method which permits healing chemicals to be introduced into deep wounds. The method saved many lives during the war. Marvelous instances of his work in facial surgery were shown in motion pictures sent from France for use in our medical colleges

Mr. Piatt Andrew (centre) in charge of the American Ambulance Service in France, and some of the members of his staff

Chapman too, gave a picture of life in the Legion. His story of one Christmas day is worth reading:

Xmas in the trenches was interesting but not too exciting. Beginning the evening before "conversations" in the form of calls. "Boches," "*Ca va,*" etc. In response "*Bon camarade,*" "cigarettes," "*nous boirons champagne a Paris,*" etc. Christmas morning a Russian up the line who spoke good German wished them the greetings of the season, to which the Boches responded that instead of nice wishes they would be very grateful to the French if the latter buried their compatriot who had lain before their trenches for the last two months. The Russian walked out to see if it were so, returned to the line, got a French officer and a truce was established. The burial ceremony performed, a German Colonel distributed cigars and cigarettes, and another German officer took a picture of the group. We of course were one half mile down the line so did not see the ceremony, though our Lieutenant attended. No shooting was interchanged all day and last night absolute stillness, though we were warned to be on the alert. This morning Nedim, a picturesque, childish Turk, began again standing on the trenches and yelling at the opposite side. Besconsoledose, a cautious Portuguese, warned him not to expose himself so, and since he spoke German made a few remarks, showing his head. He turned to get down and—fell; a bullet having entered the back of his skull; groans, a puddle of blood.

Another American in the Legion, though of French parentage, was E. Morlae, who wrote of its American members in the *Atlantic Monthly* thus:

Even the Americans were not all of one stripe. J. J. Carey had been a newspaper artist, and Bob Scanlon,

An American hospital ambulance being loaded with wounded soldiers

American Ambulance Field Service, Section No. 10, the cars and equipment for which were given by the New York Stock Exchange. This picture was taken just before the Section's departure for the Near East

a burly negro, an artist with his fists in the squared ring. Alan Seeger had something of the poet in him. Dennis Dowd was lawyer; Edwin Boligny a lovable adventurer. There was D. W. King, the sprig of a well-known family. William Thaw of Pittsburg, started with us, though he joined the flying corps later on. Then there were James Bach, of New York, B. S. Hall who hailed from Kentucky, Professor Ohlinger, of Columbia, Phelizot who had shot enough big game in Africa to feed a regiment. There were Delpenche and Capdevielle, and little Trinkard from New York. Bob Subiron came, I imagine, from the states in general for he had been a professional automobile racer. The Rockville brothers, journalists, signed on from Georgia; and last though not least was Friedrich Wilhelm Zinn, from Battle Creek, Mich.

It will ever be to the glory of our American colleges that in the early days of the war so many of their young undergraduates went to the war under foreign flags, despairing of the entry of their own country upon a conflict which so enlisted the sympathies of generous youth. One of these in the Legion, though not listed by Morlae, was Henry W. Farnsworth, of Dedham, Mass., who,

though no longer an undergraduate, was just out of Harvard when he enlisted. He was killed in the battle of Fortin de Navarin, in September, 1915. No better description

William P. Fay of New York (left) as an ambulance driver visiting a first-line trench

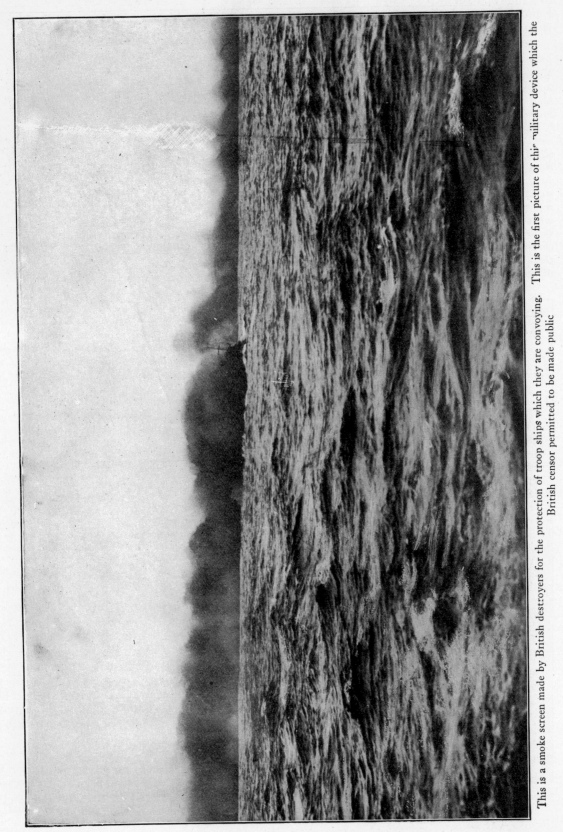

This is a smoke screen made by British destroyers for the protection of troop ships which they are convoying. This is the first picture of this military device which the British censor permitted to be made public

of a night patrol in No Man's Land has ever been written than this of his:

The patrol is selected in the afternoon. At sunset we meet to make the plans and tell every man his duty; then at dark, our pockets are filled with cartridges, a drawn bayonet in the belt, and our magazines loaded to the brim. We go along the *boyau* to the *petite poste* from which it is decided to leave. All along the line the sentinels wish us good luck and a safe return. In the *petite poste* we clamp on the bayonets, blow noses, clear throats, and prepare for three hours of utter silence. At a word from the chief we form in line in the prescribed order. The sentries

Christmas presents being hoisted aboard the U. S. S. *Jason* for the boys "over there"

wish us luck for the last time, and the chief jumps up on the edge of the trenches, and begins to work his way quickly through the barbed wire. Once outside he disappears in the beet weeds and one after another we follow.

Then begins the crawl to the appointed spot. We go slowly with frequent halts. Every sound must be analyzed. On the occasion of the would-be ambush I admit I went to sleep after awhile in the warm, fresh clover where we lay. It was the adjutant himself who woke me up with a slight hiss, but as he chose me again the next night he does not seem to have thought it a serious matter.

Then, too, once home, we do not mount guard all the rest of the night, and are allowed to sleep in the morning; also there are small but pleasing discussions of the affair, and above all the hope of some night leaping out of the darkness hand to hand with the Germans.

"Alan Seeger," wrote Legionnaire Morlae, "had something of the poet about him." The world outside the trenches came to learn how true was the poetic sentiment that animated this young graduate of Harvard who gave his life for France. His lines: "I have a rendezvous with Death," became perhaps the best known of all the real poetry that the war inspired. His prose too, was of the best. The accompanying quotation gives a clear idea of the dismal life of the trenches:

This style of warfare is extremely modern and for the artilleryman is doubtless very interesting, but for the poor common soldier it is anything but romantic. His rôle is simply to dig himself a hole in the ground and to

U. S. S. *Jason* which carried to France the eighty carloads of Christmas presents

keep hidden in it as tightly as possible. Continually under the fire of opposing batteries, he is yet never allowed to get a glimpse of the enemy. Exposed to all the dangers of war, but with none of its enthusiasms or splendid *élan* he is condemned to sit like an animal in its burrow and hear the shells whistle over his head and take their little toll from his comrades.

The winter morning dawns with gray skies and the hoar frost on the fields. His feet are numb, his canteen frozen, but he is not allowed to make a fire. The winter night falls with its prospect of sentry duty, and the continual apprehension of the hurried call to arms; he is not permitted to light a candle, but must fold himself in his blanket and lie down cramped in the dirty straw as best he may. How different from the popular notion of the evening camp-fire, the songs and good cheer!

And of those other gallant and sacrificial young Americans for whom this soldier and poet of the Legion fitly sung the last sad lay:

There was Edmond Genet, great great grandson of the Citizen Genet whom the Revolutionary government of France sent to this country in 1792 as its minister. In the third generation the French blood still told and young Genet, nineteen years old and already having seen service in the United States navy, enlisted first in the Légion Étrangère and afterwards in the American Escadrille where he met his death. He had foreseen his fate. "I expect to have to give up my life on the battlefield," he wrote, "I care nothing about that. Death

Refugees being moved from Flushing, Holland, to Middlesbrough, England, in order to relieve the congestion at Flushing

Seeger was indeed a true poet—the poet of the trenches. He wrote for himself, as for Chapman, for Farnsworth, for McConnell, for Prince, for Genet, for Poe of the Black Watch and for Starr of the Coldstream Guards the best of all epitaphs in his "Ode in Memory of the American Volunteers Fallen for France":

And on those furthest rims of hallowed ground
Where the forlorn, the gallant charge expires,
When the slain bugler long has ceased to sound,
And on the tangled wires
The last wild rally staggers, crumbles, stops,
Withered beneath the shrapnel's iron showers—
Now heaven be thanked we gave a few brave drops,
Now heaven be thanked, a few brave drops were ours.

to me is but the beginning of another life—sweeter and better. I do not fear it." In a letter written just after the reëlection of President Wilson, an event which because of the nature of the campaign that had been waged was thought by those abroad to presage the continuance of American neutrality, Genet expressed the bitterness felt at our national attitude by the brave youths who had rushed forth at the first call of France for aid:

It couldn't be possible for Americans in America to feel the same bitter way as Americans over here among the very scenes of this war's horrors. It's incomprehensible over there where peace reigns supreme.

American beans arriving to save the lives of the starving peoples of the regions devastated by the Germans

Come over here and you'll be engulfed like the rest of us in the realization of the whole civilized world arming itself against this intrusion of utter brutality and militaristic arrogance. Peace—God forbid such happiness until the invaders have been victoriously driven back, behind their own borders, knowing the lesson of their folly in treading ruthlessly upon unoffending neutral territory and all the rest of their deeds of piracy, and all the blood of France and Belgium has dried up.

Neither the Légion Étrangère nor the French Army engaged the allegiance of all the young Americans whose spirit impelled them to take part in the fight upon Prussianism long before their nation was willing to take that step. French aviation attracted many, and out of the Escadrille Lafayette, which first engaged the endeavors of young American aviators, grew the Escadrille Americaine. The British Army, too, found favor with many of our youth. Most of these were mute if not inglorious—gallant young fellows who made their way over the Canadian border and enlisted in the Canada troops that did such magnificent service on every battlefield from the North Sea to the Dardanelles. History will in time perhaps do justice to these gallant volunteers who, on being asked by recruiting sergeants from what province of Canada they came, smilingly replied "Texas" or "Missouri" or "Kentucky." Of some of those who were able to go direct to the front and enlist in English regiments some historical record already exists.

Among these latter was John P. Poe, class of '95 at Princeton, known first to

Belgians interned in Holland arriving at Flushing

© London *Daily Mirror*

Nine of the ninety little Belgian refugees from Louvain who were guests of Mr. Walter Chamberlain on his estate, Harborne Hall, in England

the college football world as "Johnny" Poe, and afterward extending that fame and carrying his endearing diminutive to Cuba, the Philippines, and about every Latin-American republic which offered him a chance to serve either for or against a revolution. The European explosion of 1914 gave Poe his great chance, and before the end of that year he was enrolled in the Coldstream Guards—an historic regiment of Highlanders with a record of a century and more of fighting inscribed upon its rolls. "I am trying to feel more at home in a kilt," wrote Poe to a friend at this stage in his career, "and while they are cool the legs get dirty for quite a way above the knees." Poe was a fighter rather than a writer, and of his all too brief service in the Black Watch, or the "Ladies from Hell" as the Germans called the kilted troops, little record is left. He was killed in a charge near Bethune in the latter part of September and lies buried on the battlefield.

In the same command with Poe and like

him fated to meet death fighting under a foreign flag was Dillwyn Parrish Starr, of Philadelphia, a Harvard man and like Poe a football player of note. His foreign service began in the American Red Cross ambulance service, but like hosts of the young men who began with that purely humane part in the war he found his blood raised to fighting heat by what he saw and he soon entered the British armored car service. He served in Flanders and later in Gallipoli and has left a graphic account of the battle of Achi Baba in which he participated:

Well, the attack has been made and was a complete failure here. Almost four thousand men went out and very few came back. Some monitors and ships bombarded Achi Baba for two hours. The Turks during this moved down into a gully and came back after it to their second line and massed four deep to meet our men. I was on higher ground with four guns and could clearly see our charges of the 6th and the morning of the 7th. The men went out in a hail of bullets and it was a wonderful sight to see them. Many of them fell close to our parapets, though a good number reached the Turkish trenches there to be killed. On the morning of the 7th, the Turks made a counter attack and drove our men out of the lightly held trenches they had taken. Our guns fortunately took a lot of them; my two guns fired a thousand rounds into their closely formed mass.

In a long record of gallantry and self-sacrifice all comparisons are futile and offensive, but I think that in days to come the people of America will learn to look upon the brilliant and daring youths who in the first days of the war formed the Lafayette Escadrille that young Americans might fight together for France in the air formed the very best of our contribution in payment of our debt for Lafayette and Rochambeau.

The story of the foundation of that historic flying battle corps is told by one of its two surviving members, Elliott C. Cowdin, who ascribes all credit for its creation to Norman Prince, a Harvard graduate of the class of 1908. Cowdin thus describes its beginnings:

Norman Prince had spent many years, and made many friends in France, and felt it his privilege and duty to serve her in the hour of her need. . . . Knowing there were many Americans in the Foreign Legion and the various ambulance units, and being one of the pioneer aviators of the United States, he conceived the idea of forming an aero squadron, composed exclusively of Americans, to join the French Army.

It was a difficult task. Most Americans resident in Paris refused to have anything to do with the project lest they violate the neutrality rulings of their own country. The French Government was indifferent. Its officials declared they had more would-be aviators among their own people than they could provide planes for. But with pertinacity Prince overcame all obstacles, and, as Cowdin writes:

Early in May (1916) we were all mobilized at the Alsatian front as the "Lafayette Squadron" with French officers, Captain Thenault and Lieutenant de Laage in command. The original members, besides those officers, were: Norman Prince, William Thaw, Victor Chapman, and Kiffen Rockwell of the Foreign Legion; James McConnell, who had already done good work in the American Ambulance before joining the French Aviation; Bert Hall and myself. Five of the original nine have been killed at the front.

The American loss was in fact five out of the original *seven* for the two commanding officers were French. First to go was Chapman of whom mention has been made more than once in this narrative. James McConnell who witnessed one of his later battles tells the story of it thus:

I remember one curious incident that occurred while I was in the Verdun sector. Victor Chapman, who was doing combat work with the American Escadrille,

The Germans driving 314 men and women between the ages 15 and 60 out of the village of Guiscard, France, to place them at forced labor in Germany. They include practically all the skilled workmen of the village

after a brush with four German aeroplanes was forced to descend to our field. Not only had he received a bad scalp wound from a bullet, but his machine had been riddled and nearly wrecked. One bullet had even severed a metal stability control. By all the rules of aviation he should have lost control of his aeroplane and met with a fatal accident. But Chapman was an expert pilot. He simply held on to the broken rod with one hand, while with the other he steered the machine. This needed all the strength at his command, but he had the power and the skill necessary to bring him safely to earth. A surgeon immediately dressed his wound, our mechanics repaired his machine. The repairs completed he was off and up again in pursuit of some more Boches. I must say that everyone considered him a remarkable pilot. He was absolutely fearless and always willing and able to fly more than was ever required of him. His machine was a sieve of patched-up holes.

Chapman's head was bound up with bandages covering the wounds received in that very conflict when a few days later he was killed. He was not on duty, but high in air was returning from a visit to a distant hospital whither he had been to carry some oranges to a wounded colleague. In the distance he saw three planes holding his friends Captain Thenault, Prince, and Lufbery sore beset by six Germans. Without hesitation he dived to the attack. His friends at the moment did not know he was there. All they knew was that two of their assailants hastily disappeared, and beating off the others they returned to their field. When Chapman, too, failed to return inquiry was made and another pilot who had seen the fray from a distance reported that while the three Nieuports were attacking six Germans he saw a fourth Nieuport come up with all possible speed, dive into the thick of the fight, and then suddenly fall to the ground as though out of control. In that machine flying fast to the aid of his friends was Victor Chapman. A chance shot brought him down. What better word could have been spoken of his supreme sacrifice than that uttered by the Prime Minister of France, M. Briand, who said he was "the living symbol of American idealism."

Norman Prince, who had created the squadron, died in an accident—not the death that he would have chosen for he was eminently a fighting aviator. In his last expedition he downed his fifth Boche, thus qualifying as an ace. It was on the return from this exploit that his machine, landing in the dark, struck a wire and he sustained fatal injuries. Before this he had figured in 122 engagements, was officially credited with having brought down five of the enemy, and had four others to his credit but not officially recorded. He had won the Croix de la Guerre, the Medaille Militaire, and the Croix de la Legion d'Honneur. But his greatest glory in history will be that he created the Lafayette Escadrille.

Lufbery, the famous American ace, from Wallingford, Conn., in his Nieuport, not long before he fought his last battle

Lawrence Scanlon, of Long Island, fell 500 feet and crashed through the roof of the bakery of the French aviation school at Avord and emerged from the débris entirely unhurt

James McConnell, of North Carolina, served first in the American Field Ambulance, and, being stirred like so many young Americans by the atrocities of which the enemy was guilty, went into active service against the foe in the Escadrille. He was to a great degree the historian of the flying corps, his book "Flying for France" being the best of all contemporary contributions to the literature of the air. As an example of his literary style this extract from a letter written while he was still in the ambulance service may well interest:

Ogilvie got his car and we got our stretchers out to take away the *blessés*. There were a few of us grouped about, some seven or eight—and near—with the wounded just put on stretchers, when—Bang! Bang! Bang!—three more shells.

We had already thrown ourselves on the ground, and then finding we were still alive, feverishly loaded the car. "Good God! I've stalled it!" said the driver—then the cranking—would it never start—try again—thank Heaven it was off. Hardly thirty seconds after, whish-sh-bang! bang! Two more came. We retired to a cellar for a few minutes as the three dead could stay there while it was so terribly dangerous. At last we emerged and were about to lift Mignot's body when both arms moved. Was he alive, after all? No, it was only the electric wires he was lying on that had stimulated his muscles. The car turned the corner with the three dead, and we ran back to the caserne. There we found the rest of our Section very shaken

indeed. A shell had burst just outside of the house where the nine were making merry and the violence of the impact had hurled all of them to the ground. Two feet nearer and the whole lot would have been killed.

At the time of McConnell's death Edmond Genet, to whom reference has been made, was flying with him. He tells the story of how the body of the lost air-fighter was found:

Jim M'Connell has just gallantly earned a lonely grave out beyond the present fighting-lines. I wrote to you last Tuesday—the day he and I were out together, when we had to return, wounded, without him, and with no definite news of him. Since then the Germans were forced back further and finally French troops came across a badly smashed Nieuport with the body of a sergeant pilot beside the ruins. All identification papers were gone, and the d——d Boches had even taken off the flying clothes, and even the boots, and left the body where it had fallen. The number of the machine was sent in and so we knew it was Mac's.

The following morning, after a flight over the lines, I spiralled down over the location given and found the wreck—almost unrecognizable as an aeroplane, crushed into the ground at the edge of a shell-torn and wrecked little village. I circled over it for a few minutes and then back to camp to report. Our captain flew over that way the same morning to see about the body. When he returned he told us about the clothes and shoes having been stolen, and said that Mac had been buried

James R. McConnell, the American ace who lost his life flying for the French and who was the author of a book entitled "Flying for France"

Lufbery had, like most of the flyers, a knack of writing well about the service that he loved. In *Everybody's Magazine* he gave a description of a raid in which he took part as pilot of a huge Voisin plane. The objective was the Metz-Sablon railway station:

A few minutes later I found myself over the spacious station of Metz. This was our objective. The machine in front of me executed a semi-circle in order to give the slower aeroplanes a chance to come up. Handicapped by my 140 h.p. I took no part in this manœuvre, but flew straight to the point where I was first to arrive.

Our coming must have been announced as several enemy machines came from every direction to meet us. One of them turned toward me. Quickly I turned my head to see if my observer was on guard. His machine gun was pointed at the enemy, his finger on the trigger. At a distance of one hundred and fifty metres, the enemy machine made a brisk movement to get beyond our range, turning to enable its gunner to fire at us. But this manœuvre was useless for the greater number of the bi-plane machines have two guns, one stationary, which fires from the front, the other mounted on a turret in the rear.

I kept my eye on my adversary. I could clearly see the black painted cross on his fusilage and helm. The fight began. We exchanged a shower of bullets. The

beside the road next to which he had fallen. There is no doubt but that he was killed during the combat in the air, and the machine crashed down full speed to the earth. Since that day I've chased two Boche machines but could get up to neither, but I'll get one yet and more than one, or be dropped myself to avenge poor Mac.

Poor Genet himself fell a little more than a month later, and was the first aviator to die after the United States entered the war.

King of the American aces was Raoul Lufbery, of Wallingford, Conn., an American by birth and a Frenchman on his mother's side. He had been something of a soldier of fortune for years and had enjoyed some flying experience before joining the Lafayette Escadrille. He developed extraordinary skill as a fighting pilot, and at the time of his death was credited with having brought down eighteen enemy planes. The Croix de Guerre, the Medaille Militaire, the Croix de la Legion d'Honneur, and the Military Cross for Distinguished Services, a British decoration, were all his. Though not, like so many of his associates, a college man,

Platt Andrew, Director of the American Ambulance Field Service in France

Boche *piqued*, apparently having had enough. I did not think it worth my while to follow him, as there was nothing now to obstruct our way, and I had an important mission to fulfil.

Through the wind shield I could distinguish railroad tracks, trains, stationary and on the move, stores of goods, hangars, etc.

My observer tapped me on the shoulder and signed for me to go ahead. Another tap informed me that all the bombs had been dropped. Our mission was accomplished. All that remained for us to do now was to get back to camp as soon as possible. The Boches were hurrying up in numbers. We had to keep a watch on all sides. We were surprised by a monoplane Fokker which hurled at us a shower of bullets and departed before we had time to respond. Two or three short, sharp familiar sounds told me my machine was hit. But my motor continued its regular throb, and my observer reported that the gasoline tank was untouched.

Norman Prince, who also gave his life flying for France

The wind blowing from the north facilitated our return. In a short time we were over our lines. Then I laughed without knowing why. I looked at my observer and he, too, laughed. We were both feeling good.

Lufbery attained the rank of Major in the American Squadron but was not destined to survive the war. In May, 1918, in a battle over the city of Toul with a huge German machine, his machine was seen to burst into flames and his body was thrown out. He was of course killed instantly. A comrade, Kenneth P. Copeland, in a letter home told of the funeral services and I quote his closing words:

He was given a full military burial; with the salutes of the firing squad and the two repetitions of taps, one answering the other from the west. General E. made a brief address, one of the finest talks I have ever heard any man give—while throughout all the ceremony French and American planes circled the field. In all my life I have never heard taps blown so beautifully as on that afternoon—even some of the officers there joined the women in quietly dabbing at their eyes with white handkerchiefs. France and the United States had truly assembled to pay a last tribute to one of their soldiers. My only prayer is that somehow, through some means, I can do something as much for my country before I too wander west—if in that direction I am to travel.

James Norman Hall, another great American aviator, who helped to make America's famous air record in France

The next day the writer of these touching lines himself fell in combat with the Boche.

William Hohenzollern, the deposed Kaiser of Germany, and the most notorious criminal in the world

CHAPTER V

WHILE the United States was thus gathering itself together in preparation for the plunge into the European maelstrom there was no cessation in the fighting abroad. Rather was it pressed with greater vigor and desperation, for the Germans, although they scoffed at the idea of the United States exerting a really commanding influence over the war, nevertheless exerted every endeavor to win a decisive victory before our troops could be brought into action. The nations of the Entente Alliance, on the other hand, seeing in the coming of the American troops the aid which would end in victory, set themselves to resist stubbornly all attacks, and to hold their own until that aid could be made effective.

The cheering with which the people of the United States greeted their entrance upon the war had scarcely died away when the British began at Arras a tremendous offensive upon a wide front between Lens and St. Quentin. The battle line included the famous Vimy Ridge, which dominates the plain of Douai and the coal fields of Lens— coveted objectives which the Allies were not destined to win for many long months. The battle then opened was one of the greatest of the war. The battle line was forty-five miles long. More than in any earlier action the airplanes, both those of the Allies and enemy planes, were in evidence, scouting, bombing, and fighting among themselves in the midst of cold, snowy, and sleety weather most unseasonable for April.

The first British attack, opened on April 9th, was made against positions which the enemy had held for two years, and which they had made, in their own estimation, impregnable. The belt of wire entanglements before their trenches was hundreds of yards deep, and indescribably tangled. It was against this form of obstacle that the newly invented "tanks" or land cruisers were most effective. These were automobiles, oftentimes the "flivvers" beloved of the American farmer, on which had been built a structure of steel, mounting usually three machine guns, or sometimes light rapid firers. The tanks were propelled on "caterpillar wheels," or endless belts of jointed, flat platforms which revolved slowly, and carried the whole structure forward, on a road thus laid for it as it advanced. The car with its superstructure is about 23 feet long, by 9 feet over all, weighs about 20,000 pounds without armor, is propelled by 120-horsepower and makes from $2\frac{1}{2}$ to 5 miles an hour according to the ground it must traverse. Because of the breadth of the steel plates upon which it moved the pressure on the ground is said to be less than that of the hoof of a horse or the foot of a man; accordingly soft ground or even mud interferes but little with its progress. The machine cannot tip over, it can descend one side of a trench and climb up the other at most incredible angles. It can break down trees, go through houses, and nothing short of a direct hit by a shell will put it out of action. Because of its power to plow through all obstacles the tank has

Liquid fire was one of the Germans' diabolical innovations during the war.   These French soldiers are giving the enemy a very bitter taste of their own medicine

These French artillerymen during the great German offensive in March, 1918, have just received from an aeroplane the signal of the enemy's approach and are rushing to man their gun

been especially serviceable in breaking down entanglements of barbed wire.

When they were first employed, these ungainly and powerful machines aroused the merriment of the men who marched by their side quite as much as the terror of those against whom their lumbering charges were directed.

Philip Gibbs tells two stories of the operations of tanks in the battle of the Somme:

A "tank" had been coming along slowly in a lumbering way, crawling over the interminable succession of shell craters, lurching over and down, and into and out of old German trenches, nosing heavily into soft earth, and grunting up again, and sitting poised on broken parapets as though quite winded by this exercise, and then waddling forward in the wake of the infantry.

Then it faced the ruins of the château, and stared at them very steadily for quite a long time, as though wondering whether it should eat them or crush them. Our men were hiding behind ridges of shell craters, keeping low from the swish of machine-gun bullets, and imploring the "tank" to "get on with it." Then it moved forward in a mon-

strous way, not swerving much to the left or right, but heaving itself on jerkily, like a dragon with indigestion, but very fierce. Fire leaped from its nostrils. The German machine guns splashed its sides with bullets, which ricochetted off. Not all those bullets kept it back. It got on top of the enemy's trench, trudged down the length of it, laying its sandbags flat and sweeping it with fire.

The German machine guns were silent, and when our men followed the "tank," shouting and cheering,

French 155's in action on the Oise River in France

British and French troops awaiting the enemy in hastily constructed intrenchments during the last German offensive of 1918.
This was just before the Americans came in numbers to the aid of their hard-pressed allies

they found a few German gunners standing with their hands up as a sign of surrender to the monster who had come upon them.

One of the most remarkable "tank" adventures was in the direction of Gueudecourt, where our troops were held up yesterday in the usual way—that is to say, by

French and American officers during the Battle of Picardy making arrangements
for American troops to take over a sector

the raking fire of machine guns. They made two attacks, but could not get beyond that screen of bullets.

Then a "tank" strolled along, rolled over the trench, with fire flashing from its flanks, and delivered it into the hands of the infantry with nearly 400 prisoners, who waved white flags above the parapet. That was not all. The "tank" exhilarated by this success, went lolloping along the way in search of new adventures. It went quite alone and only stopped for minor repairs when it was surrounded by a horde of German soldiers. These men closed upon it with great pluck, for it was firing in a most deadly way, and tried to kill it. They flung bombs at it, clambered on its back, and tried to smash it with the butt-ends of rifles, jabbed it with bayonets, fired revolvers and rifles at it, and made a wild pandemonium about it.

Then our infantry arrived, attracted by the tumult of the scene, and drove the enemy back. But the "tank" had done deadly work, and between 200 and 300 killed and wounded Germans lay about its ungainly carcase. For a little while it seemed that the "tank"

British troops in the act of assaulting at La Boiselle in France

also was out of action, but after a little attention, and a good deal of grinding and grunting, it heaved itself up and waddled away.

In seven days' fighting before Arras the British gained five miles, took 22,000 prisoners, and 200 guns. It was in the course of this fighting that troops from our neighbor to the north, Canada, greatly distinguished themselves. Vimy Ridge, a vital strategic point, taken before by the French, and later by the British, only to be lost again, was gallantly carried by the Canadian troops. In their ranks were many men of United States citizenship who had wearied of waiting for this country to enter the war and had crossed our northern border to enlist with the men of the Dominion. One of these, a young Texan, who was wounded in the battle of Vimy Ridge, learning that the United States had at last entered the conflict, went up to the assault with the Stars and Stripes on his bayonet, and fell thus. It was the first appearance of our flag on a European battlefield.

The British fighting in this section was the more determined because the soldiers had passed through the country devastated in Hinden-

burg's retreat which began on March 16th, and had been able to see for themselves what German ruthlessness meant. The region which the enemy ravaged was about 40 miles long, and 25 deep. It had contained before the war between 350 and 400 towns and villages, and some 200,000 people. The Germans burned, blew up, or otherwise obliterated the towns and villages, and of the 200,000 human beings took nearly half— including thousands of women and young girls—into slavery. Banks and private safes were robbed of their money. Private homes

A British raiding party getting clear of a sap and rushing toward the German trenches

French artillerymen installing one of the 155's on the Somme.   This is a rush job

were pillaged and burned from sheer lust of destruction. Even the little farmhouses and gardens of the peasants were ruthlessly destroyed. The savagery of the retreating Huns was shown by the fiendish zeal they manifested in destroying property that could have been of no use to a farmer. Portraits were hacked to pieces. Mirrors smashed with revolver shot. Filth defiled everything. Wells were poisoned. The trees of orchards were girdled or chopped down. Men versed

in the Scriptures recalled that in Dueteronomy XX it is written: "When thou shalt besiege a city a long time in making war against it then shalt thou not destroy the trees thereof by forcing an ax against them; for thou mayest eat of them, and thou shalt not cut them down (for the tree of the field is man's life) to employ them in the siege. Only the trees which thou knowest that they be not trees for meat, thou shalt destroy and cut them down." But the Germans, though talking much of "Gott," gave little heed to sacred things. Churches were stripped of every valuable thing before being burned or blown to pieces. In some of the demolished towns the retreating Germans left notes to this effect:

"*You see what we have done here. Well, this is what is going to happen all the way back to the French frontier.*"

And in other places they were malignantly ironical. "*Nicht argern; nur wundern*" was the German legend that met the British in several places that seemed no longer to bear any sign of having been spots of human habitation. "Do not be an-

A French anti-aircraft gun in action on the Oise in France

A sample of some of the difficulties the Allied and American troops had to overcome before they broke the Hindenburg line

noyed; only be astonished" was the meaning.

A British war correspondent summed up the hellish destruction in a paragraph when he wrote:

Even if we grant that the destruction of houses in the wake of retreat is the recognized cruelty of war there are other things I have seen which are not pardonable, even under that damnable code of morality. In Bapaume and Péronne, in Roye and Nesle and Lianecourt, and all these places over a wide area the German soldiers not only blew out the fronts of houses, but with picks and axes smashed mirrors and furniture and picture frames. As a friend of mine said, a cheapjack would not give fourpence for anything left in Péronne, and that is strictly true also of Bapaume. There is nothing but filth in those two towns. Family portraits have been kicked into the gutters. Black bonnets of old women who once lived in those houses lie about the rubbish heaps and by some strange, fitful freak these are almost the only signs left of the inhabitants who lived here before the Germans wrecked their houses.

While the British were pressing the fighting in the vicinity of Arras, the French were pushing forward their offensive on the Aisne. General Nivelle, the French Commander-in-Chief in April, 1917, pushed forward an attack on a 25-mile front between Soissons and Rheims. This was the southern pivot of the famous "Hindenburg line," the position of the impregnability of which the Germans long boasted, but which was broken more than once by the British and French before the final attacks under the dominant generalship of Foch in 1918 smashed the whole line out of any coherent shape. In

This is the kind of gun which made its appearance on the western front when the Allies caught up with the Germans in heavy artillery

French tanks awaiting repairs after having wrought great havoc among the enemy.   They were wounded in action

this second battle of the Aisne the Crown Prince had nominal command of the German armies, and received from his Imperial parent a telegram of congratulations upon his "death-defying perseverance and irresistible attack," and conveying to the soldiers assurance that "all who fight and bleed there shall know that the whole of Germany will remember their deeds, and is at one with them to carry through the fight for existence to a victorious end."

The victorious end did not come then, nor indeed did it ever come, though in the early spring of 1918 the Germans drove back across this same devastated territory for gains which brought them nearer to Paris than they had been since the opening weeks of the war, and set the whole Allied world aghast with dread until a handful of American marines at Belleau Wood checked the onrush and turned back the Huns in a retreat that ended in ultimate defeat.

But for the remainder of the year 1917, while America was striking her gait and the Atlantic ferry was slowly carrying our fighting men across to the fields of France, the British and the French pushed on the fighting in Flanders, along the Aisne and Ailette rivers, and at Verdun.   Hard fighting it was, brave and bloody, but although the record week by week showed notable successes on the part of the Allies it was all in the end ineffective, and without bearing upon the outcome of the war, except in so far as it wore down the German man-power to a point from which it was impossible for Germany to recover.

In Italy the moment of the entrance of the United States upon the war found the Italians seemingly in secure possession of the Austrian stronghold of Goritzia, holding the line of the Isonzo River, and threatening Trieste on the one hand and the back door of Austria on the other.   Yet this advance lagged during the summer months of 1917 to an extent which seemed scarcely explainable even by the difficult character of the plain of the Carso over which they had to fight their way.   That volcanic plateau was a desolate waste of rocks and caves, destitute of water, and fortified at every point by the Austrian enemy who had installed machine guns innumerable, and batteries of

The tanks used by the British in the East made a new type of ship of the desert

The Italians in their mountain lines fought under appalling difficulties. The wounded men had to be lowered down precipices, often more than a thousand feet high, to emergency hospitals or waiting ambulances below. The American Red Cross played a large part in Italy.

These tanks are awaiting orders. They are parked so as to reduce to a minimum the danger of observation

10-inchers by which the whole plain was swept. A long aqueduct, advancing with the troops, had to be built to supply the Italian forces with water.

Difficult though the *terrain* was it did not wholly explain the sluggishness of the Italian advance which early in June came to a complete standstill. The world did not know, though the headquarters of the Allies must have known, that the Italians were stopped, not by the valor of their enemies, but by the lethargy of their friends. Cadorna's army, which had advanced thus gloriously over almost unimaginable obstacles to the very doors of supreme victory, was suddenly experiencing a severe shortage in all the supplies necessary to a vigorous cam-

paign. Cannon and the needed ammunition, rails for the extension of railroads and rolling stock to equip them, food, clothing, small arms, and the countless munitions necessary to keep an army in the field were running low. Appeals were made to the Allies for aid, but the response came but slowly. Meantime, the Russian débâcle had occurred and the Austrians, freed from apprehension from that quarter, were able to give their entire attention to Italy. Germany was freed from the Russian menace likewise and was able to add her aid. Yet it is a striking tribute to the Italian valor that neither the gallantry of one side nor the discouragement of the other caused the disaster which, in the autumn, overwhelmed Cadorna's forces. The reverse was due to German intrigue, socialist propaganda, and the treachery of a comparatively few Italians.

The first news came to the world in the shape of reports that on October 24th the Austro-German armies had burst through the Italian front in the Julian Alps and had crossed the Isonzo and were pouring down into the Venetian plain. As the news was amplified it appeared that the Second Italian Army, under General Capello, had for some inexplicable reason yielded to the enemy practically without resistance and that the foe pouring through the gap thus caused had compelled the retirement of

This small dog is a tank mascot. He has often been under fire

the whole Italian Army from the Cranic Alps to the sea. The fruit of three years of the most gallant fighting known during the whole war was thrown away in a day or two. Goritzia was sacrificed, the line of the Isonzo abandoned, the menace to Trieste was withdrawn, and suddenly Italy from being magnificently on the offensive found itself driven back to its own territory with the cities of her northern plain and magnificent Venice herself in danger of capture by the Huns. In one week the enemy had taken 250,000

pacified front great bodies of troops and sent them into the Julian Alps to aid her ally. That alone would not have accomplished the sinister results that followed, for the Italian troops under any fair conditions were capable of coping with all comers. But at this moment they were sorely reduced in munitions of war and in no condition to resist an attack in force. To this fact was added the more sinister influences of disaffection and intrigue.

The spot chosen for the attack was on the

Germans attacking a British tank. This was typical of the desperate hand-to-hand fighting which was so common in the war in spite of long-range guns

prisoners and 2,300 guns and there seemed no likelihood of stopping his progress.

What was the reason for this colossal defeat suddenly inflicted upon an army which had been resting upon its arms seemingly secure in well-earned positions?

Once more credit must be given to Germany for having turned the reverses of her allies into victory. Her military leaders had no doubt contemplated with alarm the steady advance of the Italians and the continued reverses of the Austrians, but while Russia remained in the field were unable to intervene. But with the withdrawal of the Russians the Germans withdrew from that

lines at Tolmino, Monte San Gabriele, and Monte San Daniele. General Von Bülow was in command of the German forces, with Germans commanding Austrian divisions. Austrian names had disappeared entirely from the list of those in high command. Before opening fire with their artillery the Germans put into effect the more subtile method of intrigue for breaking down their enemy's defense. An Italian authority explains it thus:

"Opposite the Second Italian Army the Austrians had placed regiments composed largely of Socialists, and these utilized the war-weariness of opponents, similarly in-

These Italian troops having just reached the summit of a mountain are starting to attack the Austrians in an effort to dis-
lodge them

fected, to convince the latter that an end of the fighting would come if the soldiers on both sides should refuse to kill each other any longer. Fraternization followed, and an exchange of promises to do no more shooting. Then the demoralized—and demoralizing— Austrian division was withdrawn, and in its place were put German shock troops. These it was that, almost unopposed, smashed through the Italian line and began the flanking movement of which the results have been so disastrous to Italy."

It was not all German intrigue that caused this disaffection. There was only too much evidence that Italian Socialists, the followers of the discredited ex-Premier Giolitti, pacifists, and even some agencies of the Vatican had worked to attain this discreditable end. Immediately after the disaster General Cadorna bitterly denounced the "treachery"— using that word—of certain divisions, while the War Office in its bulletin made the distinct charge of cowardice. But the harsh words were quickly suppressed by the censors, and the defeat allowed to pass as though caused by the enemy's superior force. The fact remains, however, that certain regiments in abandoning certain strategic positions did so apparently not because overcome by superior force, but cheering, singing, and giving every indication that they were deluded into

Vinceremo (we shall win)! After capturing this mountain top the Italians put up
this sign with letters two yards high and illuminated at night

the belief that by their act the war would be ended.

The gap opened by treachery on the 24th of October, 1917, was big enough to disorganize the whole Italian line and within three days the whole Italian Army was in retreat. It must have been a bitter moment for the gallant Italian soldiers. From the mountain peaks which they had carried by such engineering skill, industry, persistence, and loss of life, through the narrow passes which they had penetrated against the fire of the enemy's batteries on every peak and crest, they had now to retire with the exultant Austrians snapping at their heels. It was a mournful retreat but an orderly one.

The Italians underwent herculean labors in getting great guns such as this on to the mountain tops

By November 1st the Italians had been driven from the line of the Tagliamento, which they had fortified heavily and hoped to hold. They were short of artillery and of ammunition. The enemy at this time reported the capture of 180,000 men and 15,000 guns. After another brief halt at the Livenza River, where, according to German reports, 17,000 more prisoners and 800 guns were lost, the Italians fell back to the line of the Piave.

When the Tagliamento had been passed by the Teutons the world suddenly awoke to what was happening. The Allied governments, that had looked complacently upon Italy fighting her own battles so long as she could fight them victoriously, perceived that her defeat now was a menace to their whole cause. Not only would the Germans sweep down over the northern plains, taking Vicenza, Verona, and even glorious Venice for added counters in the game of brag and barter that would attend the final peace conference, but they might move to the westward and strike at France by the back door of the Riviera. With one accord France, Great Britain, and the United States

rushed to the rescue. At last Italy's appeals were heeded.

A triune command representing the Allies was created, and on this General Cadorna was given place, General Foch and Sir Harry Wilson being the other two. As supreme commander of the Italian forces in the field General Armando Diaz succeeded Cadorna.

It appeared now for a time that the line of the Piave was to be to Italy what Verdun had been to France—a symbol of national

Austrians in the Italian Alps. They went back quicker than they came

Italian soldiers knee deep in snow rushing toward the enemy   They wear white uniforms to render them inconspicuous

determination to conquer. As in the case of Verdun the strategists said that the Piave was a line without true strategical importance or strength. Occupation of it left the left flank resting on the mountains, a very perilous and insufficient defense. Further south, pointed out the strategists, was the Adige River, a line along which would extend from Lake Garda to the sea, and be therefore impregnable on either flank. True, this would uncover Venice and probably lead to her capture, but Venice, while artistically and historically important. was without military significance.

At this all Italy sprang to arms. Sacrifice Venice, the Queen of the Adriatic! Permit the Austrians to come back, to swagger again in the Plaza of St. Mark's after having turned them out? Never! All Italy decreed the

Piave line, and adopted for its rallying cry *"Da qui non se passe !"*, the equivalent of the French motto at Verdun, "They shall not pass!" Up too surged the hot blood of the Garibaldians of 1866 with their battle cry *"Italia fara da se !"*

Venice was in a panic, and indeed the whole world—to which the Adriatic city throned in state upon her hundred isles seemed a shrine sacred to all humanity—held its breath as it viewed the closer approach of the Huns to that treasure house of art and beauty. Curiously enough, it was the historic Huns under the ruthless Attila who, raiding northern Italy, caused its people to take refuge in the lagoons and islands whence in due time Venice uprose. Now after the lapse of centuries new barbarians were at the door of the city that had grown great, rich, and beautiful. No people reverence and appreciate more their art treasures than the Venetians. Perhaps it may be admitted that they have a lively sense of the material advantages these treasures bring to them in normal times in the throngs of visitors from every land. From the earliest days of the war every imaginable precaution had been taken to preserve these treasures from possible injury. The horses of St. Mark's descended from their elevated

Transporting an Italian gun across a chasm at a dizzy height by aërial ropeway

Italian soldiers carrying building materials up a snow-clad mountain to build sheds above the clouds

station above the cathedral's portico and were taken to Rome, where they were comfortably stabled in the ruined baths of Diocletian. St. Mark's itself was banked about with sand bags within and without; though meticulous as were the precautions, they would have availed little against a single shell from a giant Austrian howitzer. To protect the neighboring Doges' Palace it was at first planned to build an entirely distinct structure of brick around and over it. But engineers reported that the piles on which the Palace, like all the rest of Venice, stands would not support the additional load, so that project was abandoned, and the more exposed portions of the edifice banked up with sand bags. The statue of Colleone, esteemed by artists the greatest in the world, was covered by sand bags until the near approach of the Germans suggested that not merely destruction but theft needed to be guarded against, and it was lowered from its pedestal and shipped to Rome.

So the Italians clung to the line of the Piave with a persistence that denoted real soldierly devotion. Though the enemy had broken over at Zenson, the gap he made there in the Italian lines was too narrow to be serviceable. On the lower river the Italian resistance could not be shaken. Floating defenses were employed with great skill. Not only were flat-bottomed English monitors of light draft and with the heaviest guns brought into service, but the Italians built floats on which they mounted powerful naval guns which drove the invaders away from the river banks. Early in November the Teutons began crossing the low delta of the Piave

An Italian sentry at his outlook post in the mountains

tacked fiercely all along the mountain front, captured, according to Berlin, 15,000 prisoners and seized some positions not without strategic value.

But as the roar of the great guns and the rattle of the lesser arms died away came noiselessly through the air the delicate and feathery missiles that were to end, for the time at least, Austro-German exploits on that front. The snow, light, feathery, but insistent, came silently down, filling the mountain passes, blocking the railroad, shutting off the invaders from their base. It was no time for fighting. The work of the army thus entrapped was to keep open its communications. During this interruption the relief forces sent by France and England to Italy's aid came up and on the last day of 1917 delivered a crushing blow on the invaders' front. The Allies were everywhere successful, and the offensive passed from the Teutons to them. During the weeks immediately following there was spirited fighting in the air, fleets of as many as twenty-five planes to a side being not infrequently engaged. But in the air, in

near its mouth. The movement was most menacing to Venice as it brought the enemy troops within twenty miles of that beautiful city—almost close enough for the Kaiser's guns to do what they had done to the cathedral at Rheims and the Cloth Hall at Ypres.

But the line of the Piave was not the only danger spot for Italy. In the north the foe was coming down the passes of the Dolomites and the Venetian Alps with the intent of taking the Italian Piave line in the flank and rear. The movement which culminated in the later days of November, 1917, was most menacing. The Teutons outnumbered the Italians by two to one—both in men and in guns. They suffered from but one weakness. For supplies and communications they were dependent on a single railroad to Trent and various highways through the mountain passes. A single snowstorm would interrupt supplies; a long period of stormy weather might be disastrous. Winter was upon them and the invaders pushed the fighting. During the week December 4th to December 10th, he at-

Italian guards protecting the entrance to a mountain tunnel

An Italian convoy halted at a particularly beautiful spot on one of the famous mountain roads

the flooded districts at the mouth of the Piave, and on land the advantage had now turned to the Allies and on the 8th of January, 1918, headquarters reported that all danger to Venice was now averted.

The year 1917 was notable, also, for the successful operations of the British in Asia Minor, particularly in the Holy Land and Mesopotamia. During the summer the British advance in those regions had been stayed by the entire collapse of Russian endeavors in the Caucasus and about Lake Van because of the Russian revolution. For a time the Turks and the Germans thought that, because of this abrupt termination of the Russian activities, the British would be either checked in their course or driven out of Mesopotamia altogether. They were sadly misled in their hopes. For without Russian or other aid the British, under the generalship of Sir Stanley Maude and Sir Edmund Allenby, pushed on brilliantly to as complete a vic-

© London *Daily Mail*

Italian Alpine troops known as the Alpini entrenched in an ice fort at Cadore, Italy

Jerusalem from the Mount of Olives. Marching troops now tread the quiet roads once trod by Jesus

tory as was won on any front. It was the only extended campaign of the war conducted by the troops of a single nation, and it was absolutely conclusive in its results.

In February, 1917, General Maude recaptured Kut-el-Amara, that had been taken by the Turks from General Townshend almost a year earlier. After this victory the British marched on to Bagdad, the ancient city of the Caliphs and the scene of the Arabian Nights Entertainments. This picturesque oriental town, brimming over with legends and history, was taken in March. Thereupon the season for campaigning closed, for in that latitude the scorching summer months put an end to military operations as did the winter months in Flanders and the north. It was, moreover, just at this time that Russia, which had been a helpful ally in the northeastern provinces of Asia Minor, was suddenly stricken with impotence and it behooved the British commanders to await developments before undertaking a new campaign.

Early in the fall, however, active operations were resumed and this time the advance of Sir Edmund Allenby from the Mediterranean coast engaged the attention of all observers. For while Maude had been fighting his way up the Tigris River and through regions famed in oriental tradition and in the books of the Old

The Church of the Holy Sepulcher where, according to tradition, the body of Jesus Christ was buried

Testament, Allenby's field included many of the most important cities known to Holy Writ, and comprehended much of the territory called by Christians the Holy Land. November 18th he captured Jerusalem for which Christians and Moslems had striven for twelve centuries, with the result of its having been left until now in the possession of the Mohammedans. It was matter of general comment at the time that had the Germans instead of the Turks been in possession of Jerusalem, and had been driven out, they would have destroyed all the sacred vestiges of scriptural times in their malignancy, as

637 and the Christian efforts for its recovery, known as the crusades, began in 1099 and were continued with intervals during the succeeding century. Poetry and romance have concerned themselves with its long history and the names of Godfrey de Boillon, Tancred, Saladin, and Richard Cœur de Lion are amongst those which have been immortalized with it. Now a British Army, aided by Arabs and East Indians, has redeemed the Holy City from the grasp of the infidel and it is unlikely that it will ever again pass into Moslem hands. In the course of General Allenby's campaign we read of his

© Press Illustrating Service

A market in the Holy Land to-day is exactly the same as was a market in the time of Christ

in France and Belgium they took special pleasure in wrecking churches and cathedrals. The Turks, however, respected these relics, and indeed throughout this war the English officers, who were brought into collision with the soldiers of the Sultan, were unanimous in their declaration that the Turk was no foul fighter but a gallant and honorable adversary.

For four thousand years Jerusalem has been a stake of war. No existing city has had so long or so turbulent a history. All the tribes and peoples recorded in the Old Testament fought for it, and as the power of Israel waned Persians and Tyrians, Babylonians and Macedonians, Greeks and Romans fought for it. The Moslems won it in A. D.

taking the Philistine city of Gaza, of which Samson carried off the gates in the scriptural story dear to every schoolboy, and in later operations Bethlehem and Nazareth fell for the first time in centuries into Christian hands.

The actual physical share in the war taken by the United States during the year 1917 was inconsiderable. It may be said that the moral effect upon the Germans of the knowledge that they had now to deal with a new, fresh, and powerful adversary must have been most discouraging. But if that were so no sign of the discouragement was then apparent. The leaders of German opinion insisted that the United States could never be a serious factor in the outcome.

They ridiculed our army, decried our plans for its development, insisted that there were not ships enough in existence to carry our troops across the Atlantic in season to save the Allies, and declared that even if the ships were built their submarines would sink them faster than they could be put into service.

To what extent the German people believed this, or indeed to what extent it was believed by the men who put these arguments out, is hard to tell. Certainly at the moment there were no signs of discouragement apparent among the German soldiers or the

United States, and the comparative condition of the belligerents at its close are likely to be studied with great care by historians. For nations are quite as vain as individuals—perhaps indeed rather vainer—and there is already a tendency among certain elements here in the United States to claim that but for the timely entrance of this nation upon the conflict the Entente Allies would have been defeated and Germany would have been left master of Europe, and in a position to make itself master of the world. This view is naturally hotly controverted by the spokesmen of the Allies.

British officers passing the municipal offices of Bagdad.   The German "Berlin to Bagdad" ambition ended when the British took Bagdad in July, 1918

German people. The army was well fed, and while the fighting of 1917 had gone slightly in the German favor, yet the final accounting showed the year's operations to have been about a set-off between the belligerents. Any person of intelligence must have recognized, however, the fact that any fighting at all was to German disadvantage since they had not the means of replacing their losses that were still left to the Allies. And the incoming flood of American troops more than made up any Allied loss without any further call upon the youth of France or Great Britain.

In time the records of this last year of the war before the active participation of the

It is a pity that any such controversy should have arisen, and it is more than doubtful if facts, to become known later, will support the contention of the American extremists. It is more probable that as the history of the war shall be fully revealed military students will come to agree with those German authorities, including the Crown Prince, who confessed belatedly that Germany lost the war when she lost the first battle of the Marne, five weeks after her invasion of Belgium. For that disaster instantly demolished the entire strategical plan with which she had begun hostilities. With it disappeared her last chance to crush France before Russia could act, and then to

The British under General Allenby enter Jerusalem, and the Holy Land, through the deeds of these modern crusaders, comes again under Christian control

crush Russia before Great Britain could create an army.

. There were other periods, later in the war, when the German chances of reaching Paris seemed as good as in that first fierce rush. But it was not taking Paris that in 1914 was expected to win the war. With the occupation of Paris at that time would have come the serious crippling of the French Army thus

In 1917, at any rate, there was no reason to despair of the allied cause even had the United States troops not been pouring into France. In the west the Germans had been beaten back to the Hindenburg line and were giving no indications of intending another drive. Italy had, it is true, encountered a grave disaster, but had at last stayed the enemy's advance and seemed able to recoup

General Allenby and his staff in front of one of the most ancient buildings in Jerusalem. The General's proclamation to the citizens of the Holy City is being read to them in Arabic

deprived of what was then its chief base. The transport of British troops to the continent would have been greatly interrupted, if not indeed absolutely shut off, for with Paris in German hands the channel ports could never have been retained by the French. But the first battle of the Marne averted all that and in the fullest sense prevented German victory, not only then but for all time. There were many dark days for the Allies thereafter, but not until the close of the war brought revelation of its secrets did we know how much darker they were for the foe.

her fortunes, as in fact she did. In Mesopotamia the British were wholly successful. The Russian débâcle was menacing but at the time no one knew, or even suspected, how thoroughly the revolutionary elements in that country were to come under German control. The situation in the Balkans was bad, but well-informed observers knew that the Teutonic strength in that region was wholly dependent upon German money and German manpower and both were rapidly being exhausted.

The moment indeed was such that the entrance of the United States should have

This was once the beautiful and prosperous town of Bapaume, France

been more instantaneously conclusive than it was. It would have been the part of wisdom for the Central Powers to take even more immediate and vigorous steps for ending the war than they in fact did. For even without this new adversary they were beaten to a standstill. While they might hope to avoid an ignominious surrender they could not hope for victory. But with the United States arrayed against them their cause was hopeless. All the men and money they sacrificed thereafter were wantonly thrown away; all the hurt they inflicted on their adversaries was as truly criminal as the murder done by a burglar attempting to escape after his crime has been detected.

President Wilson enjoying one of his brief respites from pressing national and international cares and responsibilities

CHAPTER VI

GENERAL PERSHING ARRIVES IN EUROPE—A TORPEDO ATTACK—TRAINING
SOLDIERS IN FRANCE—EARLY FIGHTING—BATTLE OF SEICHEPREY—HOW
AN ATTACK IS PLANNED—CAPTURE OF CANTIGNY—BOURESCHES, VAUX, AND
CHÂTEAU-THIERRY—THE MARINES AT BELLEAU WOOD

An American wrestling match in France. The fact that our boys were such good athletes helped them greatly as fighters.

THE dock front of Liverpool was gay with the entwined bunting of the United States and England, and a British general with a guard of honor stood awaiting, on June 18, 1917, the *Baltic* bearing General John J. Pershing and his staff —the Commander-in-Chief, fore-runners of the American Expeditionary Force to France. The occasion was one the historic significance of which could scarcely be exaggerated. For the first time in its national history the United States had become one of the participants in a general European war. For the first time her soldiers were to fight on European soil, and she had chosen for chief associates in the war—political considerations forbade the word "allies"—the nation which had been her first enemy, Great Britain, and that which had been her first friend, France.

But the ancient enmity had long since been forgotten. When a day or two after landing General Pershing was received by King George, lineal descendant of that George who pushed the American colonies into revolt, the monarch said, "It has been the dream of my life to see the two great English-speaking nations more closely united. My dreams have been realized. It is with the utmost pleasure that I welcome you at the head of the American contingent to our shores."

And a little later in Boulogne the American general, as he stepped for the first time on French soil, heard the veteran French soldier deputed to greet him say, "I salute the United States of America, which has now become united to the United States of Europe." All Paris was mad with joy as the little handful of American soldiers giving earnest of the millions yet to come, drove through its streets. Everywhere the tricolor and the stars and stripes were intertwined, and the Parisians did not fail to comment on the happy augury that the colors of the two republics were the same. "Vive Joffre who saved us from defeat!" cried an excited girl from a window on the Avenue de l'Opera, "Vive Pershing who brings us victory!" The American general was taken to the tomb of Napoleon and handed the great Emperor's sword to reverence—an honor prior to that moment never granted to any save a Frenchman. He was conducted to the House of Deputies where Ribot said, in the course of a speech of welcome, "The people of France fully understand the deep significance of the arrival of General Pershing in France. It is one of the greatest events in history that the people of the United States should come here, not to struggle, not in the spirit of ambition or conquest, but for the noble ideals of justice and liberty."

Shortly after this ceremony the general was conducted to the tomb of Lafayette in the Picpus cemetery, accompanied by the Marquis de Chambrun, a lineal descendant of the dead patriot. The ceremony was brief but stimulating. Holding an immense wreath in his hands the General stepped toward the tomb while all about him stood at attention. Visibly affected with generous emotion he laid the flowers on the bier with the fitting words "Lafayette, we have come,

King George decorating American soldiers for gallantry in action while fighting with the British

General Pershing inspecting a detachment of his troops newly landed in France

we are here!" and retired. The whole world the next day knew that the American leader had spoken precisely the right thought, when he made it appear that the American forces had come to the aid of France as France had a right to expect; that they were there to pay a long standing debt to Lafayette and to his country.

Much might be written about the international courtesies that attended the arrival of the American general. But he was there for a sterner purpose than the interchange of civilities, and it was only a day before he was plunged deep in the details of arranging for the arrival of the colossal armies that were being made ready on the other side of the Atlantic.

Before this war the civilian hardly grasped the idea of the enormous amount of work involved in the moving of the great masses of men that modern warfare calls into action. It was thought that we might need an army in France of 4,500,000 men, and we did in fact at the close of hostilities have there, or en route thither, no less than 2,053,347. Ships were lacking to carry this army. They must be built, or begged from England. This was no concern of the General, but it may be noted at this juncture that so rapidly did ship building proceed in the United States that, though destitute of a merchant

marine at the outset, we were able to transport more than 45 per cent. of our soldiers in our own bottoms. But not only ships were lacking, but ports for their entry. The ports of France along the channel, familiar to every American tourist, Boulogne, Havre, Calais, Dieppe, were crowded with English shipping, bringing over troops and munitions of war. Accordingly ports, not so well known nor so well equipped, were set aside for American use. These were four—Brest, already a great French naval station—St. Nazaire, Bordeaux, and LaPallice. Of these the first two were most used.

A considerable body of American special service troops had preceded the General-in-Chief to France, and on June 26th the first convoy of troop ships arrived at St. Nazaire. The voyage over had not been uneventful. The Germans were not to be caught napping, and Rear Admiral Gleaves, in command of the naval escort, reported that two submarine attacks had been made but that both had been beaten off. In each case the track of the torpedo was detected but the submarine itself could not be descried. An eye witness described the first attack as follows:

Hell broke loose. Our (the big ship's) helm was jammed over. Firing every gun available we swung in a wide circle out of line to the left. A smaller ship

© Paul Thompson

American troops in Paris on the Fourth of July, 1918, passing the "l'Hôtel des Invalides" where they were reviewed by
General Pershing and the descendants of the French officers who fought for the independence of the United States in 1776

slipped into our place and from what the lookout told me, I think one of her shells must have landed almost right above the submarine. But they are almost impossible to hit when submerged and the periscope is no target anyhow.

They fired three, if not four, torpedoes. It was God's mercy that they all went astray among so many of our ships. As you see our helm jamming was absolutely Providential.

Naturally the old —— acted quite differently from what the Boches expected; otherwise they might have got us. It was simply extraordinary. We drove right at them (really, I suppose the safest thing to do as the bow gives the smallest mark to shoot at) and it seems to have rattled Brother Boche considerably. After all, we draw enough water to smash a submarine at a level of the periscope, awash, and no doubt he did not care to wait for us. Or perhaps a lucky shot disposed of him. Anyhow, he disappeared and we saw no more of him.

The whole business lasted only about a minute and a half. But believe me it added more than that to my life. While the thing was happening I had no time for anything but to attend to my job. Afterward I found myself sweating and my breast heaving as if I had run five miles. The other boys told me the same thing, but we got a compliment on the rapidity with which the guns were served, so I guess it did not interfere with our actions.

American troops leaving Paris for the front on July 5th, 1918

Dawn had not broken when the American fleet steamed into the harbor of St. Nazaire. Leading the column was the ship *De Kalb*, which in more peaceful days had been the German liner *Prinz Eitel Friedrich*, and after a brief period as an armed commerce de-

American troops being reviewed by President Poincaré, General Pétain, and General Pershing

stroyer under the German flag had eluded the vigilance of the British fleet and slipped for sanctuary into the then neutral port of Hampton Roads. When the United States declared war she was seized, with other German ships, and by a fine stroke of fate was chosen to take the first body of armed men to France. They were a detachment of United States marines and what they did on the battlefield will be told elsewhere.

News of the arrival of "les Américaines" spread rapidly through the little town, and the wharves and waterfront streets were quickly filled with excited and enthusiastic French people. Where American flags had been found in that hamlet seemed inexplicable, but there they were by the scores and the people who had not the flag itself waved red, white, and blue streamers. Early as was the hour thousands were thronging the docks and shouting from every place of vantage, "Vive Les Etats Unis! Vive la France!" Steam whistles were blowing from the craft in the harbor, and the bands on the ships blew themselves hoarse with the Marseillaise and the Star Spangled Banner in alternation. There were formal delegations from the French Army and Navy there to greet the new allies, but the true greeting came from the populace who crowded the narrow streets as the men marched through to the great camp that had been prepared for their reception.

Frederick Palmer, veteran of American war correspond-

ents, says of this initial body of American troops in France:

The character of the ships which we had gathered as transports was significant enough of our lack of a merchant marine; a former German auxiliary cruiser, and sea-going and coast-going vessels of a plodding speed. Above the gunwales of their gray sides was a crowded mass of khaki spotted with white faces, and all the parts of the superstructure were blotted and festooned by khaki, freed of the long nights in the close quarters of the hold when no lights might be shown on deck, now out in the sunlight of a June day having their first glimpse of France, which was having its first glimpse of an American army. Nothing that these soldiers saw was like what they had left—boats, piers, houses, streets, people—and they were like no soldiers who had ever come to France before. Their talk had the rattling twang of the bleachers before the ball game begins, unmistakable wherever you hear it. Well, here they were. The "subs" had not got them. They

Men of the 42nd Division of the American Expeditionary Forces in a front-line trench in France

These American engineers were laying a road across the zone of combat near Verdun. They had been working steadily for three days in a drenching rain and under almost constant shell fire

wouldn't have to knock about deck in the dark, or be packed in the hold any longer. The sea was all right; let the navy have it. But give them the land; they were soldiers. When did they get ashore? And what next?

What was next was drill and more drill. Straight from the transports the men were sent to the camps in which they were to learn the art of war. General Pershing himself in his final report after peace had been attained tells briefly of this part of the training of a soldier:

Very early a system of schools was outlined and started, which should have the advantage of instruction by officers direct from the front. At the great school centre at Langres, one of the first to be organized, was the staff school, where the principles of general staff work, as laid down in our own organization, were taught to carefully selected officers. Men in the ranks, who had shown qualities of leadership, were sent to the school of candidates for commissions. A school of the line taught younger officers the principles of leadership, tactics, and the use of the different weapons. In the artillery school, at Saumur, young officers were taught the fundamental principles of modern artillery; while at Issoudun an immense plant was built for training caders in aviation. These and other schools, with their well-considered curriculums for training in every branch of our organization, were coördinated in a manner best to develop an efficient army out of willing and industrious

General Madolon of the French Army escorting General Wood of the American Army through a dugout

An American infantry company advancing and mopping up trenches which have just been captured in the Forest of Argonne, France

young men, many of whom had not before known even the rudiments of military technique. Both Marshal Haig and General Pétain placed officers and men at our disposal for instructional purposes, and we are deeply indebted for the opportunities given to profit by their veteran experience.

It is a curious fact that the precise points of American participation in the war were fixed by the location of the ports at which our men were landed, and the direction taken by the railroads leading inland from those ports. Except for a few slight skirmishes participated in by small bodies of our men who had been sent into the French trenches nearest at hand for training purposes, our fighting was all on the far east of the French line, in Lorraine, the Argonne, and the plains of Champagne.

Looking back upon the singularly precipitate end of the war, and the positions that the American armies had attained when Germany cried aloud for peace, a student of military strategy would see that this field of action which General Pershing in his report says was forced upon him by conditions of transport was in fact the most effective one for bottling-up the German armies in France and Belgium. Indeed our men had hardly got into action before their position so threatened the Germans' communication with their home country that the safety of their armies was seriously menaced. But of this more later.

In an earlier chapter I have told of the

first American deaths at the front. The men who then died were in trenches for training purposes, and not long after a group of engineers were unexpectedly caught in a British turning movement and dropped pick and shovel for rifle and bayonet, acquitting themselves so gallantly that even a German newspaper paid tribute to their gallantry though it questioned their comprehension of the issues which brought them to the battlefield thus:

There they stood before us, these young men from the land of liberty. They were sturdy and sportsmanlike in build. Good-natured smiles radiated from their blue eyes, and they were quite surprised that we did not propose to shoot them down as they had been led in their French training camp to believe we would do.

They know no reply to our query "Why does the United States carry on war against Germany?" The sinking of the American ships by U-boats, which was the favorite pretext, sounds a trifle stale. One prisoner expressed the opinion that we had treated Belgium rather badly. Another asserted that it was Lafayette who brought America French aid during the war of independence and because of this the United States would now stand by France.

But whether willing or not to tell the Boche why they fought, fight they did and so gallantly that the same German journalist credited them with making a "most desperate defense."

Skirmishes like these, however, while they helped to establish the American morale, are not to be considered as marking the true entrance of our forces upon the European conflict. General Pershing himself fixes the fight at Seicheprey, on the 26th of April, 1918, as the first serious participation of the American forces in actual battle. And even there our men were not acting as a unit. For late in March of that year, being spurred on by contemplation of the seemingly irresistible progress made by the Germans in the drive they began on the 21st, General Pershing had put the whole American Army at the disposal of General Foch, to be used either as a unit, or to be broken up among French commands that might need strengthening. It was an act of notable renunciation for the United States, and one which for the moment seemed to portend that we should never have our army operating as a coherent whole and winning distinctive laurels. But it was perhaps the culminating act of the war. For it made of the position to which General Foch had been chosen, after very serious hesitation on the part of the British, that of Commander-in-Chief in fact as well as in name, and the result proved not merely the wisdom of the choice but the fact that this unity of command had not been established one day too soon.

The Germans were then in the very midst of the drive. Nothing, it appeared, would stop them. They swept forward day after day, sometimes gaining as much as twelve miles in a single day, and sweeping before them all English and French opposition. The whole world held its breath as this fierce thrust at the Allied lines went on with apparently no possibility of check. April 20th they came for the first time into direct contact with the Americans at Seicheprey, in a sharp combat which may well be taken as our troops' first baptism of fire. At first our men were driven from their positions, a result which was naturally to be expected in the first clash of inexperienced troops with veterans. But almost instantly the American fighting blood was stirred. Sharp reaction came in the moment of seeming defeat and the troops, rallying, fought their way back to their original positions, inflicting upon the enemy a loss of several hundred men. Our own losses were for the first time heavy. Berlin reported the capture of 185 American soldiers and 25 machine guns.

Our men were now fairly launched upon the full tide of war. Day by day new divisions were sent into the French trenches, day by day more transports nosed their way into the French harbors and landed columns of khaki-clad men shouting for chances to get at the Boches. May came. Not the usual flowery French May, but a month of unseasonably cold and snowy weather. Ordered to the trenches in front of Montmedy,

A field gun on the edge of Belleau Wood effectively concealed from aërial observation

the men of our First Division under command of General Bullard came to know all that desperate chill, discomfort, and hardship of trench life which affects the soldier more than the sharper and deadlier clutch of battle. They stood athwart the Boches' path to Paris about 50 miles north of the city, and occupied a sector of the line with a French division on either side. Hardly had they arrived when preparations began making for an offensive. Before them in plain view was the town of Cantigny, perched on a hill and in possession of the foe. It was to be the job of the Americans to take it, and for long days they looked wistfully upon it over the parapet awaiting the moment to go over.

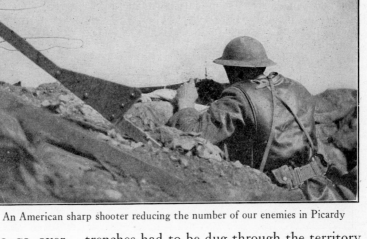

An American sharp shooter reducing the number of our enemies in Picardy

Assaults of this character in modern war are not made on the spur of the moment. All sorts of preparation are needed. Barrages are to be planned, the terrain carefully studied that the officers may know whither they are leading their men, runners must be drilled, and a complicated system of signals worked out. If all the details of such an offensive were set down in print it would make a very considerable volume. Manual labor was not stinted. Jumping-off trenches had to be dug through the territory pitted with deep shell craters. Ammunition and food had to be gathered for the men who were to participate in the assault. In this instance the men of the 28th Infantry who were selected for the perilous honor had each to carry 220 rounds of ammunition, two hand grenades, and one rifle grenade, two canteens filled with water, one shelter half (the technical name for part of a tent), four sand bags, one flare, and one shovel or pick. It was still cold but they were ordered to leave their blankets behind, although otherwise they were equipped for spending two days in the new positions, the winning of which none was permitted to doubt.

There had been quiet on the sector and in the Cantigny front for days. Nobody wanted to draw the Boches' attention to that neighborhood just then. But just about dawn on May 28th the big guns all along the Allies' line opened on Cantigny and on the Boche positions protecting it. No one could see the coming of the day, for the red light of the cannon flashes far outdid the glow that heralded the rising of the sun. The great guns crashed, the shells shrieked though the air

A wounded "doughboy" being carried to the rear on a stretcher

American troops between Château-Thierry and Verdun during a brief respite from fighting

and exploded with deep roars or with sudden sharp cracks according to their calibre. Of such another opening bombardment and barrage a soldier once said to the writer, "It was so deafening, so all-compelling upon every sense, that when it suddenly ended on the minute set and dead silence fell all along the lines the relaxation of strained senses was

This bridge across the Moselle is perhaps the best known war bridge in France. It marks the extreme eastern flank of the American offensive

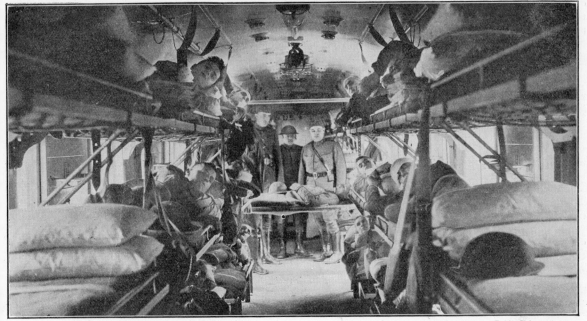

The interior of an American hospital train filled with wounded soldiers

such that every nerve end on our bodies sprang into angry protest, and our skins were covered with a sort of gooseflesh."

The first American offensive was wholly successful. Major Frederick Palmer, a veteran observer, writes of it in his excellent book "America in France":

At 6:45 in the early dawn of May 28th, as has happened many times before, the line of figures started up from the earth and began their advance. The formations were the same as those of the practice maneuvres and the movement was equally precise as it kept to the time table of the barrage. Each unit was doing its part, the tanks as they nosed their way forward doing theirs. Our shelling of the lower end of the town sud-

This was a village of France. The Germans destroyed three hundred and sixty thousand private homes in France alone

denly ceased, and then our men were seen entering the town exactly on time. Headquarters waited on reports, and they came, of prisoners taken, of the further progress of units—all according to the charts. We had passed through the town; we were mopping it up; and we had reached our objective in front of the town. Our losses to that point were less than a hundred men, with three hundred and fifty prisoners. A small offensive, as offensives go, but our own and our first.

Going over the top in a frontal attack had been almost tame, it was so like practice exercises. The fact that our practice exercises had been so systematically applied, that indeed we had done everything in the book, accounted for the perfect success of Cantigny. There was a glad proud light in the eyes of our wounded. They had been hit in a "real party." Nobody could deny that they were graduate soldiers now. But there was to be the reaction which always comes with limited objectives when you do not advance far enough to draw the enemy's fangs—his guns. Upon the road along which men must pass to bring up supplies, upon every point where men must work, or men or wagons pass, upon the command posts, he turns the wrath of his resentment over the loss of men and ground and in his rage concentrates most wickedly, most persistently, and powerfully upon the infantry which is trying to organize the new frontal positions.

The German artillery would show this upstart American division its mistake in thinking that it could hold what it had gained. Eight-inch shells were the favorite in the bombardment of our men who now had Cantigny at their backs as they dug in, while showers of shrapnel and gas added to the variety of that merciless pounding that kept up for three days. We suffered serious casualties now; but we did not go back, and we took revenge for our casualties in grim use of rifle and machine gun which, with the aid of prompt barrages, repulsed all counter attacks until the Germans were convinced of the futility of further efforts.

Of this initial endeavor of the United States troops General Pershing said in his final report, "Although local, this brilliant action had an electrical effect, as it demonstrated our fighting qualities under extreme battle conditions, and also that the enemy's troops were not altogether invincible."

While the guns were still roaring at Cantigny the Germans launched that drive upon the Marne and Paris which for a time seemed likely to regain for them all the territory that General Joffre had driven them from in 1914. In less than a week they drove forward against the best endeavors of the Allied forces for

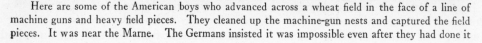

Here are some of the American boys who advanced across a wheat field in the face of a line of machine guns and heavy field pieces. They cleaned up the machine-gun nests and captured the field pieces. It was near the Marne. The Germans insisted it was impossible even after they had done it

American troops halted by the roadside in a picturesque French village on the Marne

a penetration of thirty miles. The rivers Aisne and Vesle were crossed. Noyon and Soissons were taken, and Rheims, with its sorely battered cathedral, was closely beleaguered. A great salient extended into Picardy toward Paris and once again German officers were gaily making dates to dine in the Café de la Paix. To the Allies the situation was a menacing one. Already their reserves were sorely depleted, so much so that for months they had been compelled to maintain the defensive, even when German dispositions invited offense. To some extent this was, of course, due to the fact that the Americans were coming up fast, and patience on the part of the Allies was certain to be rewarded in the end. Precisely the same reason impelled the Germans to keep ever and desperately on the attack. For however much they might belittle and ridicule the slowly swelling power of the United States at the seat of war, they knew well enough that the increase of that power meant their final defeat, and if they were to stave off disaster they must win their war before the full force of the American republic could have passed the seas.

That was the reason for the desperation and the gallantry of the German drive which brought their heavy artillery within range of Paris, and looking back upon it after the final Teutonic collapse it seems amazing that

a scant six months before their final abject surrender they could have nerved themselves to such a gigantic effort and have put into it such seemingly inexhaustible power.

It was due to American troops more than to any other single factor, or for that matter group of factors, that this fifth and last phase of the great German drive was blocked and rolled back. Not that there had been the slightest sign of weakening on the part of any of our Allies. But they had borne the heat and the brunt of conflict for more than four years, and the spectacle of the enemy at a moment when he should have been even more exhausted than they, coming up again to the attack in seemingly undiminished numbers and with certainly unaffected spirit was naturally to them discouraging. The Germans were indeed staking everything upon the issue of this conflict. It was shown later that in the Marne salient the Crown Prince had used 47 divisions, and between Rheims and the Argonne forest more than 40 more. In all, Germany brought into action on the western front from the beginning of the drive in May to its disastrous end in July 2,339,000 men. All Picardy was stripped of men, and from every point controlled by Germany whence new divisions could be called the stream of troops to the front was like the flowing of a mighty river.

Outnumbered at first, and still handicapped

French soldiers filling in a German "tank trap"—a hole covered with planking and camouflaged to look like the surrounding ground. The Allied tractors did not fall in as planned by the enemy

purpose to let this continue indefinitely. And as by act of the President of the United States and of General Pershing, he had the use of some tens of thousands of fresh and eager American troops ready to hand, with some hundreds of thousands too far away for immediate action, but speeding on their way as fast as ships could carry them, he determined to interpose a barrier in the Hun's path.

Accordingly, on the night of the 29th of May, the Third American Division, General Joseph Dickman commanding, which was getting ready to go into a quiet sector over toward Lorraine, received sudden orders to get under way for a station on the Marne in the thick of the fighting.

by operating on exterior lines, Foch stood long on the defensive finding profit in such small attacks as those at Cantigny and Bouresches, but while he took here and there a single village the enemy were taking them by the score. It was no part of the Foch Off they went in a mad rush. The motorized machine-gun battalion led the way, having its own transport, and not being compelled to wait for trains. Swiftly thereafter army trucks brought up the main body. While they were being concentrated the French High Com-

This scene is typical of every road back of the St. Mihiel salient during the American advance

The 26th Division, made up of New Englanders, who were said to have been the first Americans to enter front-line trenches

mand called on the Second Division as well—
a body still further advanced in war training
than the Third. All were rushed along at
topmost speed in crowded army trucks to
their lines at Meaux, Conde, and Martigny.
At dead of night the flying commands
would be halted on the road by French officers with orders to turn off here or there, and
go into the trenches which would be indicated to them. The roads were crowded
with fugitive peasants from the front. The
sky blazed with the fitful flashes of the great
guns and the earth shook with their shocks.
The air reverberated with the thunders of
the cannon, while from the passing crowds
of refugees rose ever the thankful cry "*Les
Americaines! Les Americaines sont ici.*"

It was clear enough to the men of the
Second and Third divisions that their prospect of a respite in a quiet sector had gone
glimmering. But their ardor was all the
greater as these signs told them that they
were on their way to a hotly contested
spot on the battle line. It was the Marne
for which they were headed—most famous
of rivers which the French nation should
certainly make holy for the part it played
in their national defense if there is any way
of canonizing a stream. The Germans
were now in force all along the northern side
of the river, but only at the village of Dormans had they crossed. At Château-Thierry
the stream runs through the town, and the

7th Motorized United States Machine Gun
Corps had dashed into that hamlet in time
to keep the enemy from getting across, while
the French retired across the bridge and
blew it up. First of all Americans to shed

Château-Thierry

A part of the so-called impregnable line which the Germans had held for four years and which the Americans took

their blood upon the banks of Marne were they.

Château-Thierry bulks large in our national traditions for it was there that our military forces first participated in a really great battle. It was there that the forces of the United States saved Paris and received credit for it from a world in arms. The machine gunners, first to arrive because of their motorized equipment, were holding the enemy at the bridges over the Marne, when with a rush up came the Second Division made up of regulars and a brigade of United States marines. Hard, disciplined, determined fighters were they. Mostly under the age of thirty, they had the physical fitness of youth, while long discipline had given them the cool determination of veterans. Along a line of twelve miles they dug in, and hour by hour more troops and ammunition came rolling up to fill the ranks and make ready for the demolition of the Hun.

The country which the Americans were facing had been fair to look upon before it had been distorted and lacerated by war. Broad open fields were interspersed by little clumps of woods and red-roofed villages. Both of these latter, however pleasing to the eye, were danger spots. In the villages, notably that of Bouresches, which the marines faced, the cellars were filled with machine guns and the stone houses common to that part of France were fortresses in a small

way. The woods, though cool and green in the June sun, were not less dangerous. Boche machine guns nestled in every thicket and back of every outcropping of rock, of which the woods were full. Artillery fire, however heavy, was ineffectual against guns so protected. It only cut down the larger trees making of them, intertwined with the underbrush, a barrier impenetrable to troops, but through which the bullets of the unseen machine guns sped with murderous certitude.

Bouresches was first to succumb to the cleaning up process. Our artillery pounded away at it until mere heaps of formless masonry covered the cellars in which the Boche machine gunners were ensconced. Then came the troops, infantry and marines both, through the desolated streets. They had to meet shrapnel and gas from German

A German cemetery just outside the town of St. Mihiel which indicates that the Germans thought they had come to stay

Headquarters troops of the 26th Division making a passageway for trucks through the wreckage of a French town

shells, and a rain of bullets from machine guns hidden in the ruins. But with heads bowed to the blast they went on, drove the enemy out of their cellars, with hand grenades and the bayonet, and established themselves there as a sort of forlorn hope. Their runners, speeding across a terrain swept by German fire, bore to headquarters the cheering news that the Americans were established in Bouresches and did not propose to be driven out. Twice the Boches essayed that task, but were blocked. Then for a time they put up a barrage of shell fire behind the Americans with the apparent idea of stopping all communication until they were starved into surrender. But the Yanks knew a trick worth two of that. They stripped both their own dead and those of the Germans of food and water, found some chickens, a cow and a pig or two which they slaughtered, and with this sustenance beat the enemy back in several fierce counter-attacks.

Meantime at Vaux, at Château-Thierry, and at Hamel the Americans had been fighting fiercely and victoriously. Vaux, a little

town on the Château-Thierry road down which the Germans passed on their way toward Paris, was completely obliterated in the fighting. Not a building was left standing. That was the result of twelve hours' pounding by our artillery, for while the town was that of a friendly nation it sheltered our joint enemies and had to go. Germans who had endured that fire described it as terribly efficient. A wounded German brought into our lines after the firing had proceeded for some hours said that the only places which were tenable in the town were the caves of which there were several score, and even into these the poisonous fumes from American gas shells had penetrated. But artillery alone could not clear up the town and our men charged through a wheat field and through a neighboring wood, preceded by a heavy barrage, in gallant style. The ruins of the town were quickly taken and their defenders slain with grenades or the bayonet, or made prisoners.

Most notable, however, of this series of actions was that fought for four desperate

An American fourteen-inch gun being fired. An airplane observer reported where the shell burst among the enemy in the Argonne Forest twenty miles away

days, mainly by men of the United States Marine Corps, in Belleau Wood. The spot was a dense thicket of trees and underbrush to the northwest of Château-Thierry, and directly on the road which the Germans were endeavoring to follow to Paris. It was on the 6th of June that the Marines began this attack to the northwest of Château-Thierry, and after their success at Bouresches made their way into the recesses of the wood that has become world famous. What they accomplished in that thicket so impressed the people of the neighborhood that they declared that the marines alone had saved Paris, and insisted on renaming the forest "the Wood of the Brigade of Marines." The battle was just a hard-fought, grubbing, gruelling advance through tangled thickets, and over rugged, cut-up ground heavily held by machine guns. There was no enemy line visible. His gunners, in clumps of from two to six, each with a spiteful machine gun, were hidden away behind impenetrable forest growths, in caves, or behind the outcroppings of limestone

A German gun captured by our troops in Belleau Wood

The 75th Battery, which was part of the enormous artillery concentration which was the dominant feature of the St. Mihiel drive

that are a characteristic of the section. It was, making allowance for the vastly more deadly quality of the weapons, something of the sort of fighting that our ancestors had employed against the Indians in our primeval forests and a knowledge of which enabled George Washington to save the remnants of Braddock's British Army at Fort Duquesne. The story is dear to every American school-boy. Here in France, as almost 150 years before in Pennsylvania, it was individual fighting, every man for himself and the officers in the thick of it with their men. There was no chance for other commands or tactics than "Up and at them." In a fight of this sort the American soldier, schooled to self-reliance and individual initiative, is at his best. So he showed at Belleau Wood, for with a determination and a pertinacity that would not be denied he forced his way through the thickets, climbed the rocky ledges, flung himself headlong into the caves, and beat down the Boches in a battle in which there were singularly few prisoners taken. The men who fought there had among them many who were themselves able to tell the story of such parts of the battle as they saw vividly. Here, for exam-ple, is the story of the part of the fighting in Belleau Wood which he saw as Private W. H. Smith tells it:

At four a. m. we went over or rather charged forward,

since there were no trenches to speak of and the fighting was all in the open or in the woods.

There wasn't a bit of hesitation from any man. All went forward in an even line. You had no heart for fear at all. Fight—fight and get the Germans was your only thought. Personal danger didn't concern you in the least and you didn't care.

Some of the dynamite which our troops discovered near St. Mihiel which was to have been placed under the road for the purpose of blowing them into eternity as they advanced

A winter's morning at a first aid dressing station just behind the fighting line. Here the first necessary dressings are made before the men are sent by ambulance to the evacuation hospital and on to the Red Cross hospital train.

There were about sixty of us who got ahead of the rest of the company. We just couldn't stop despite the orders of our leaders. We reached the edge of the small wooded area and there encountered some of the Hun infantry.

Then it became a matter of shooting at mere human targets. We fixed our rifle sights at 300 yards and aiming through the peep kept picking off the Germans. And a man went down at nearly every shot.

But the Germans soon detected us and we became the objects of their heavy fire. We received emphatic orders at this time to come back and made the half mile through the woods without hardly losing a man on the way.

German machine guns were everywhere. In the trees and in small ground holes. And camouflaged at other places so that they couldn't be spotted

We stayed for the most part in one-man pits that had been dug and which gave us just a little protection.

We saw one German a short distance before us, who had two dead ones lying across him. He was in a sitting posture and was shouting "Kamerad, Kamerad." We soon learned the reason. He was serving as a lure and wanted a group of Marines to come to his rescue so that the kind-hearted Americans would be in direct line of fire from machine guns that were in readiness.

Now isn't that a dirty trick? Say, it made me sore. Before I knew what I was doing and before I realized

An American listening post in No Man's Land only twenty yards from the German trenches

that everyone was shouting at me to stay back I bobbed up out of my hole and with bayonet ready beat it out and got that Kamerad bird. It seemed but a minute or so before I was back. But, believe me, there were some bullets whizzing around. They came so close at times I could almost feel their touch. My pack was shot up pretty much but they didn't get me.

After that I thought I was bullet proof, and didn't care a damn for all the Germans and their machine guns.

Soon we charged forward again. I saw one Dutchman stick his head out of a hole and then duck. I ran to the hole. The next time his head came up it was good-night Fritz.

Every blamed tree must have had a machine gunner. As soon as we spied him we'd drop down and pick them off with our rifles. Potting the Germans became great sport. Even the officers would seize rifles from wounded Marines and go to it.

The great battles of history, the decisive battles, are not necessarily those in which are engaged the greatest numbers of men. Belleau Wood was both a great battle and a decisive battle. It barred the Hun's path to Paris. Never again did the embattled forces of the Kaiser essay that road. As the French had stopped them finally, and for all time

Negro troops garrisoning Apremont which had been one of the strongest German positions

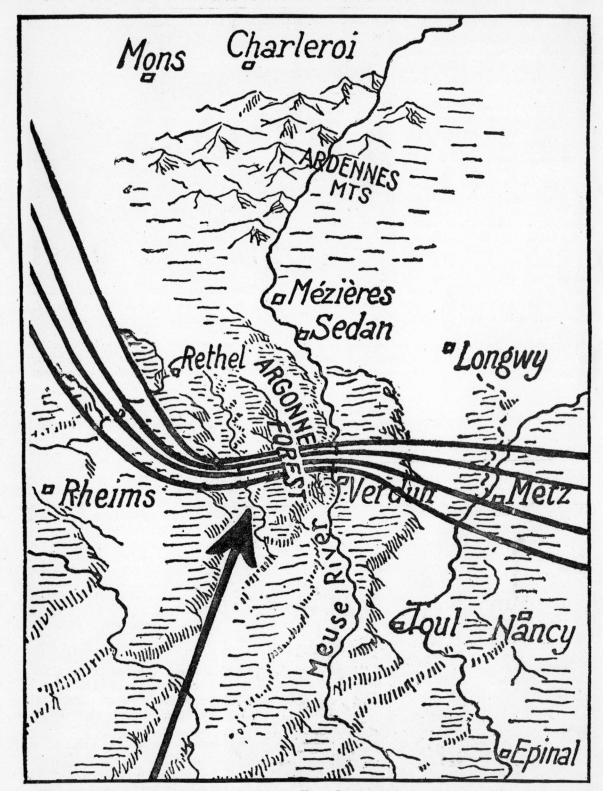

The German concentration our Army broke through. Up to September 26, 1918, the German defence lines were as indicated by the heavy black lines. In Belgium, Artois, and Champagne, the first, second, third, and fourth trench lines were considerable distances apart. In the Argonne sector, however, all four of them were practically together

American troops in the Argonne Forest. The field kitchen brought forward with great difficulty and danger has made this spot very popular

An actual gas attack in the Argonne Forest in 1918. The man in the foreground is choking with the deadly fumes and in his desperation has torn off his mask

A German general's headquarters captured by some dough-boys pushing their pistols through the windows while the general was entertaining visiting dignitaries

at Verdun, so the Americans put a rude stopper upon their ambition to tread the road to the French capital by way of Belleau Wood and Château-Thierry.

It was a great battle as well as a decisive one, not because it was hotly contested and afforded uncounted instances of individual valor, but because it for the first time brought into close and harmonious association the soldiers of the world's two greatest republics. Never will the Americans forget the French who fought by their side, and never will the poilus forget the cheery spirit of comradery and helpfulness shown by these men who came from far beyond seas to fight for France. A story is told of this battle, and on good authority, that illustrates this point:

A French officer was commanding a body of French troops in the wood, and had been fighting desperately for three days knowing that there, if ever, the Boche descent upon Paris must be blocked. To him appeared suddenly a body of Americans, rushing up, out of breath, and ignoring the storm of missiles hurtling through the trees. Their officer strove to explain their presence, though his French was not as good as his intentions: *"Vous Fatigués,"* he panted, *"Vous parti—notre job,"* "You tired—you get away—our job," was the import of his broken French. But it was understood and gratefully. The Americans did indeed make it their job and the enemy never saw the way through Belleau Wood.

CHAPTER VII

THE time had now come for the Allies to assume the offensive in what was destined to be the final great battle of the war. The Huns had been blocked at Château-Thierry and Belleau Wood. No longer was France in terror of their seemingly irresistible advance. Instead, under the generalship of the untiring Foch, the French and their allies were preparing themselves to take the active part and begin the work of driving the foe from France. Ludendorff and Hindenburg, though doubtless by this time aware of the desperation of the German cause, were still indomitable. They expected that the French would start a drive on the national holiday, July 14th, but when that day had passed without action on the part of their adversaries they rashly jumped to the conclusion that the French were demoralized and started a drive of their own. It was a fatal error, and the beginning of the end for the Huns. The French were more than ready. So, too, were the British and the Americans, and all along the wide front, from Fontenoy to Château-Thierry, the forces of the Allies not merely repulsed the Germans, but drove them, and followed them in what was destined to be a pursuit that should not end until the war ended.

It began July 18th, without the preliminary bombardment that had come to be looked for as the usual heralding of an assault. Just at dawn, with a heavy barrage preceding them, the Americans and French in the territory bounded by Soissons and Château-Thierry were out of their trenches, and rushing upon the foe. North of the Belleau Wood where our marines had already won enduring fame, the troops swept on and entered the little town of Corcy as thoroughly on time as if they had been guided by pacemakers. Belleau, Givry, Courchamps all fell in swift succession to the American arms. The fighting was of the fiercest. The Kaiser's famous Imperial Guards were in the division that came across the Marne to attack the Americans and fled back again before the foe that was so ready to be found. In the woods where the battle was hottest the bodies in spots lay three and four deep, and it was learned later that not less than 5,000 of the enemy had been slain there. In the defensive battle which preceded their charge the Americans held large numbers of machine-gun nests in the woods which the enemy had to destroy. The nests, or scattered coverts, each holding from two to ten men with one or more machine guns, are able to inflict enormous loss upon an advancing enemy, and as they are carefully hidden in the undergrowth or in gullies the charging foe not infrequently passes them in his rush, and is taken by their deadly fire in the rear. The fighting here was not unlike the Indian fighting of our pioneer days. So thick was the wood that men evaded the enemy and then turning behind him stole up on his rear throwing his ranks into confusion. In more than one instance American parties driven out of their own nests managed to steal around and capture guns from the foe for his undoing.

Prominent among the American divisions taking part in this battle was the Forty-second—the "Rainbow Division" as it came to be called. It was stationed in the neigh-

A panoramic view of Rheims taken before the Germans had partially destroyed the famous cathedral

King George on a visit to the Western Front with Marshal Foch, General Pétain, Field Marshal Sir Douglas Haig, and General Sir Henry Rawlinson and their staffs

borhood of Perthes, supporting the French line with orders that if the Germans should break through it should take up the conflict. Every man in that body of troops drawn from New York, Illinois, Ohio, California, and other populous states of the Union hoped in his heart that the break would come. Come it did. To their own bad fortune the Germans picked out that particular sector for their fiercest assault. Their guns rained gas shells until roads and woods and fields were saturated with the poisonous mists. From the sky their airplanes dropped death and destruction. The rattle of their machine guns was as the clamor of a ship-building yard in full operation. Their legions swept forward gallantly to the assault seemingly unwearied by four years of just such bloody service. Our men were ready to respond in kind. With roar of the 75's, borrowed from the French, for it is

a melancholy fact that for lack of early preparation we were forced to fight this war with artillery furnished by our Allies, we mowed down their advancing infantry. The French fought and fell back, after their elastic system which had for its purpose the saving of their own men, and the infliction of the great-

Americans helping a wounded German soldier on the Soissons-Rheims sector

British troops and transport passing through a French village during the last German offensive

est possible hurt upon the enemy. Our men rushed in to the positions thus surrendered. As the Germans came on in successive waves, after their accustomed tactics, they were cut down by our machine guns and rifle fire. Now and then in their impetuosity our men would not wait for the oncoming horde but rushing over the top would meet and overwhelm them on their way. At every point the assailants were repulsed, except in a patch of woods where they were able to drag up some machine guns into our lines, but even this triumph was short-lived, and, when the work quieted down on other parts of the line, our artillery took up this particular spot and drove him forth. It was a stiff day's fight but when it ended the enemy had been effectively stopped and our men of the "Rainbow Division" shared the glory of the victory equally with the French.

Elsewhere on the Marne other Americans had been in the battle. Part of the 28th Division, which as yet had not met the shock of battle, was near Dormans, where the Germans had some days before made their only crossing of the river. They were too few to stop the foe, but the fight they put up won them the admiration of the whole army. The 3rd Division, too, which now after its success at Château-Thierry had begun to take on the airs of true veterans, was in the thick of the fight. Its artillery blocked the enemy in determined efforts to cross the river, which at that point is but about 150 feet wide, and demolished the boats and the pontoon bridges with which he tried to effect the crossing.

With the German line thus effectively stopped the French and Americans in their turn attacked on July 18th on a 28-mile front reaching from the Aisne to the Marne. The tactical situation in that neighborhood showed a deep salient held by the German troops on which Château-Thierry was the southern apex with Soissons and Rheims as the other two points in the triangle. Each arm in the triangle was, roughly speaking, about 25 miles long. The determined German offensive which had ended a few days before, nominally directed by the Crown Prince but in fact under the command of General Ludendorff, had gained this territory, but, being checked, had left the Germans in a perilous position. A salient of this character, having a narrow opening, exposes the troops at its lower end to being cut off by a superior adversary attacking on either side. This adversary can, if his strength is equal to the task, push together the ends of the salient as one draws up the strings at the mouth of a bag, thereby enclosing all the troops which have been unable to slip out before the orifice is closed. This was precisely what General Foch attempted and with a great measure of success.

While the French and American troops were engaged at what has come to be known as the Rheims salient, other attacks were made by the British and French troops at two other points on the line. We may, for the present, defer discussion of these movements, although they were ultimately of the greatest value in effecting the defeat of the German Army, and confine our attention to those strokes which were delivered either by the French and Americans acting together, or by the Americans alone.

When the great Allied offensive of July 18th opened—the offensive which was destined not to be checked until it had forced the abject surrender of the entire German Army—the first blow was delivered by the army of General Mangin with French and American detachments against the right wing of the Crown Prince, under command of General Von Hutier in front of Soissons. The fighting had been hard there for days with the Ger-

mans on the offensive. But when at the shrill call of the whistle along the lines the Allied forces went over the top at daybreak on the day set, the struggle that followed dwarfed all previous battles. That was a Thursday. Not until Saturday was there the slightest let-up in the advance and in the fighting. Relief parties with food followed up the fighting line, and stretcher bearers, gathering the wounded, reported that they found hundreds of men whose injuries, however serious, did not pain them enough to keep them awake in the face of the complete exhaustion of the prolonged struggle. They slept soundly where they fell. The ground over which the Americans advanced was partly wooded and partly open fields of grain. The woods were cut to pieces by the tornado of shell fire, and the growing grain, just ripening at this season and so necessary to the starving world of Europe, was trodden down beneath the feet of the tramping and fighting thousands. Everywhere, through the fields and in the woods, were bodies alike of the assailants and of the defenders of the position. A correspondent who followed the troops tells of coming to a German machine-gun nest, sheltered by wicker work filled in with earth. In front lay three dead Americans, evidently part of the platoon that had charged the position. The gun was silent now and about it were piled the

The bridge across the Marne at Château-Thierry

French dragoons riding to meet the advancing Germans in the Battle of Picardy

bodies of the German soldiers who had manned it. All through the woods and in the fields were scattered nests of this character. Snugly sheltered in a pit behind a rampart two or three German gunners could mow down scores of the attacking forces before the men still left in line could sweep over the parapet and destroy them. In cases of this sort there was no quarter for the machine gunners. American soldiers reported that too often the enemy would operate his gun unflinchingly, shooting down scores of our men as they approached and then at the last moment, when capture was inevitable, appear smilingly on the parapet with hands up and the cry of "Kamerad!"

In such case, and it was the normal case, no mercy was shown.

In three days' fighting on this sector the French and Americans had penetrated the enemy's line to a distance of six miles, were established in front of Soissons, and had cut the enemy's line of communication to Château-Thierry. In the meantime, they had pressed the attack at the latter town, driving the Germans out of the northern section of it which they had held and penetrating the salient to the northward. On the American right flank English and Italian troops were coöperating to the southwest of Rheims. They were pressing into the salient and it was becoming only too apparent to the enemy that unless he desired to lose all of his army that was then in the lower end of that pocket he must not stop to fight but must get out, and stand not on the order of his going. To this policy indeed he had recourse. The Germans throughout the war demonstrated themselves to be trained strategists and seldom hesitated to retreat when they saw the safety of their army imperiled by continuing in a position that was seriously menaced. The salient, therefore, became the scene of a steady withdrawal of the Germans, who protected their troops by rearguard fighting and who never at any time permitted their retreat to be turned into a

A typical scene along a road leading to the front in France

A glimpse of the orderly British retreat before the advancing Germans during the Battle of Picardy

rout. It was not territory which lent itself readily to the needs of a retreating army, for it was interspersed with small streams which had to be crossed, and there was but one railroad that could be utilized for the transport of troops and that was cut early by the advancing Americans.

The action had hardly been in progress more than four days when it became evident to the soldiers fighting it and to the world that was watching them, that the Germans were beaten so far as that territory was concerned. They had indeed a great and powerful military machine. But General Foch and Pershing had forged a bigger one. It was a wonderful week in the world's history. At its beginning the Germans had hoped, and with apparent reason, that before its end they would be well on the road to Paris. Instead of that, baffled and beaten, they were retreating all along the line.

It was the good fortune of our American troops to take a most prominent and effective part in winning this victory. Their fighting at Château-Thierry was among the most gallant records of the war, and for years to come American tourists will go to see the remnants of that once beautiful river town, and study the streets through which our boys trod and the river banks on which they left their bodies. Edwin L. James, an American

correspondent on the spot, tells of the way in which a little village adjacent to this town was taken by the American troops:

Nothing more typically American could be imagined than the way in which we took a position yesterday afternoon north of Epieds. The Germans had intrenched along a roadway with a large number of machine guns. The terrain on both sides of the road was most difficult and seemed to mean certain death to infantrymen advancing up the road. Soon up that road came ten automobiles of a well-known American minor make. On each were one or two machine guns. Half a mile from the beginning of the German nests they got into action and went up the road at top speed, spurting streams of bullets on either side. The Germans stood until the cars were almost upon them, and seeing little

A forest full of dead Germans lay thus along the Oise--the price the German High Command paid for their brief triumph in the Battle of Picardy

French and British soldiers brigaded together, resting after a hard-fought battle

chance of "kamerading" to the cavalcade beat a retreat. The cars, returning, met the infantrymen going up to occupy the position they had cleared and to move on. The operation was completely successful, only two of the cars failing to come back. The American General at once christened the outfit "Ford's Cavalry." Stories of this exploit gave rise to an erroneous report that American cavalry had been used in action.

By the first of August the Germans had been pushed across the Ourcq with the Americans hard upon their heels, and the enemy was making as fast as possible for the banks of the River Vesle behind which he hoped to find a safer refuge. The fighting at the crossing of the first stream has been described by veterans as possibly unexcelled for bitterness by any during this savage campaign. On the German side were involved the veteran Imperial Prussian Guard who had been held to be the most formidable of all the Kaiser's fighters, and they did fight. We used to read, during the progress of the war, of German gunners chained to their guns lest they might run away, but our men who swept over the positions held by the Imperial Guard reported that these gallant soldiers of the Kaiser had to be killed at their guns for they would neither cease firing nor surrender. Just outside of Château-Thierry, on a hill known as Hill 200, stood a big heliograph tower—dating back to the time of Napoleon's

campaign and built by order of that great soldier. Here the Germans were guilty of a characteristic act of treachery. From the top of the tower waved a big Red Cross flag, but notwithstanding this appeal for immunity which was heeded for some time by the Americans, they mounted there two machine guns with which they opened fire on the American troops when they came within range. Having no artillery at hand the Americans detailed snipers to pick off the men who were serving the guns. This in due time was accomplished and when an American detachment charged the tower and mounted its stairs, the German gunners were found dead at the side of their weapons.

The character of the German defeat and the losses sustained by the enemy are well indicated in this story from the pen of an eye witness:

Saturday's withdrawal of the Germans before our never-lessening pressure took them at midnight across the river and into strong hilled positions on the northern bank. There they placed many hundreds of machine guns ranging on the river, and trained their artillery to lay down barrages on the stream. Two fresh Guard divisions were placed in front of the Americans, and the bridges were destroyed behind the fleeing foe. At midnight the enemy thought he had a new line. He had for a few hours. At 4 o'clock a part of the famed fighting unit stepped from the woods on the southern bank, leaped into the stream which is about two feet deep, and got to the other bank before the Germans were aware of it. But by the time all were over, the machine guns cut loose and the barrage swept them mercilessly.

They held twenty minutes and had to come back. But the Germans were all wrong if they thought the Americans were through. At 5:15 another dash was made, and after bloody fighting this, too, was driven back across the stream.

In the meanwhile our engineers brought up two bridges, with every piece of wood cut and fitted beforehand, and threw them across the stream. At 7 o'clock four companies made the dash. To say they stayed across makes a short story of valiant resistance. The Germans put down a barrage behind them along the stream and mowed them down with machine guns from their trees, from behind rocks, and from bushes.

While the situation was becoming precarious for these men big plans were executed behind them, and at 8 o'clock the grand rush started. It put thousands of Americans across the river by 10 o'clock. By this time our artillery was locating the Germans, and field guns on the south bank were shooting point blank into the Hun machine-gun nests. Our men got set on the northern bank and started for the hills lining the stream. After half an hour of the bitterest sort of fighting we got deep into these positions, and the enemy broke and ran down the northern side of the hills and over a valley to another series of hills near.

By this time Americans were across the river in a dozen places. By noon they had captured Sergy, and two hours later had Seringes. The Germans then began a withdrawal all along the line they had expected to hold. It was the first charge of the Americans which had broken them. The German machine gunners in the trees were killed and the others fled. We brought back a few prisoners. That the Germans intended to stand here is shown by pile after pile of ammunition we found where the guns had been hurriedly pulled out.

Never have the Americans done hotter fighting. Never did they show to better advantage. Never did the Hun fight nastier. It was not the deadly work of the machine guns in the trees and houses, and even in the

British heavy artillery being hurried forward to help check the German advance in the Battle of Picardy

churches, that awoke the wrath of our men. It was not the terrific barrage that angered them. But when they saw Hun snipers kill their wounded comrades then they saw red and made the enemy pay.

Time after time the Germans played machine guns on the stretcher bearers. I saw their wounded, and they told me. One overloaded truck came in with wounded and reported that a German airplane had swept low and dropped a bomb which destroyed an open truck carrying wounded. The driver and two wounded men were killed. Stretcher bearers wading

German guns captured by the British and being used against the Germans

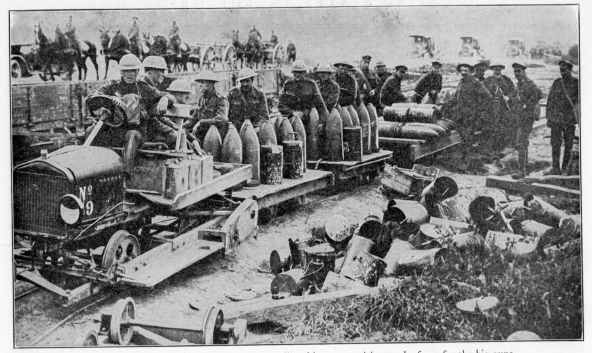

Carriages, cars, lorries, and light railways all rushing ammunition to the front for the big guns

the river with helpless wounded were fired on by German snipers in the hills beyond.

The Hun left nothing undone to make the Americans regret their audacious and gallant charge. He did not succeed.

Fère-en-Tardenois, Fismes, Château de Fère and all the territory between the Marne and the Vesle was taken by the French, Americans, Italians, and British by the end of the first week in August. The Germans by that time had been driven back of the Vesle, and obviously were going to be forced to continue their retreat beyond the Aisne. Their losses had been prodigious. They were able to move most of their men who were not disabled out of the salient, but they had neither time nor facilities for the removal of the enormous accumulations of military stores, which had been sent in to accompany what they had expected would be a triumphant march upon Paris. Mile after mile of ashes and débris of burned stores was passed by the advancing American troops. Food the Germans clung to with desperation, and had been able, for the greater part, to remove, but ammunition, guns, clothing, parts of wagons, trucks, and airplanes were all found heaped up and destroyed as far as time would permit. After the fashion of advancing armies in this day they had built a narrow-

gauge railway behind their front lines for the transportation of stores, and along this were distributed enough rails to extend the line as far as Bordeaux, and ties and other constituent parts of a railroad which showed that it was their purpose to widen it to standard gauge. Evidently the Germans had never expected to be driven out of this part of France once they had gained their foothold.

In this retreat the Germans showed great fertility of resource in concocting those cowardly and deadly devices for the murder of pursuing enemies, for which they became noted. It was nothing less than murder, for the men who laid the traps were out of reach of any attack from those who suffered. Ammunition was left piled and so arranged that it would explode two days after the retreating enemy had vanished. Infernal machines which would be touched off by the step of a man were in dugouts and buried under the highways. Wires over which an advancing soldier would trip were connected with explosives which would blow him into atoms. It was necessary for the pursuing troops to be always on their guard against deadly devices of this nature.

Thereafter the fighting of the Americans in what had been the Château-Thierry salient,

A huge French cannon on the Somme camouflaged from airplane observation by the structure of branches erected over it and by the ingenious painting of the muzzle

A French cannon on the Somme partially buried and concealed from enemy observation

but which had lost all the characteristics of a salient being thoroughly flattened out, was one steady series of victories. The enemy was driven successively beyond the Ourcq, the Vesle, and the Aisne. Our men took in rapid succession Morlaincourt, Juvigny, the highway from Soissons to St. Quentin, and forced a German retirement along a front of more than ninety miles. In a multiplicity of minor engagements which need no enumeration here the American forces were uniformly successful, as were the British and French on their flanks, for now had begun that great German retreat which the people of the Fatherland were assured was in accordance with plans and intended for strategic purposes only, but which in fact was the certain precursor of the collapse that followed.

For everywhere the Allies were winning. Though this volume is designed mainly to tell of the part played by the American armies in the war, a passing reference to the simultaneous operations of the other allies is necessary to make the story of the swift rush of the war to its end understandable.

To the west, then, of the Soissons-Rheims salient in which the Americans were doing most of their fighting, was at the beginning of August another, but more shallow, projection of the German lines into the Allied territory. Into this the British had been

edging their way in a series of small engagements that had attracted little attention until Sir Douglas Haig made a decided advance, driving the enemy back on a line extending from Montdidier to Compeigne, and beginning a forward movement which like that of the French more to the eastward was destined to proceed without serious check until the end. On beyond Arras the "Tommies" pressed, smashing into the Hindenburg line, capturing Bapaume, Albert, and the famous Queant switch, a notable German defensive work. The French, meantime, were keeping pace with them, and by the middle of September the battle line across France which had so long shown a menacing sag down to the south, toward Paris was straightening out, and began to parallel the Belgian border and at no great distance. True, still back of that line and in the hands of the Huns were cities and towns of strategic importance which the French earnestly desired to liberate. Lille was there, the martyr of French cities whose people were forced to endure such sufferings as no enemy short of an Apache Indian ever inflicted upon a helpless population. There too was Douai, a railroad centre of vital military importance; Cambrai, centre of the great French iron industry which it was the intention of the Germans now to steal as in 1871 they had

Seven hundred and fifty German prisoners captured by the French at Plessis le Roye when they came to the aid of the British

© Western Newspaper Union
A Canadian battalion led by Scottish musicians returning to camp after practice march

and shell craters, and other cross-fire from machine guns the other elements fought desperately against odds. In this and later objectives, from October 6th to October 18th, our 2nd Corps captured more than 6,000 prisoners and advanced over thirteen miles. The spirit and aggressiveness of these divisions have been highly praised by the British commander under whom they served."

While referring to this matter of praise from the veteran commanders of the European armies with whom our boys —all unused to war—were serving, it seems well worth while to reproduce the official tribute paid to them by General Mangin for their service in France during July and August:

stolen the iron fields of Briey; St. Quentin and Laon, the former a beautiful mediæval town which the Boches destroyed, the latter a railroad centre to which they clung with desperation.

But step by step the British and French lines moved forward until all these points and the territory back of them passed into Allied hands. In this progress the American army was not wholly unrepresented. The 27th and 30th divisions held the place of honor alongside the Australians of Haig's Army in a fierce assault at St. Quentin at a spot where the canal passes under a ridge through a tunnel. General Pershing says of these operations in his report: "The 30th Division speedily broke through the main line of defense for all its objectives, while the 27th pushed on impetuously through the main line until some of its elements reached Gouy. In the midst of the mass of trenches

Officers, Noncommissioned Officers, and Soldiers of the American Army:

Shoulder to shoulder with your French comrades, you threw yourselves into the counter-offensive begun on July 18. You ran to it as if going to a feast. Your magnificent dash upset and surprised the enemy, and your indomitable tenacity stopped counter-attacks by his fresh divisions. You have shown yourselves to be worthy sons of your great country and have gained the admiration of your brothers in arms.

Ninety-one cannon, 7,200 prisoners, immense booty, and ten kilometers of reconquered territory are your

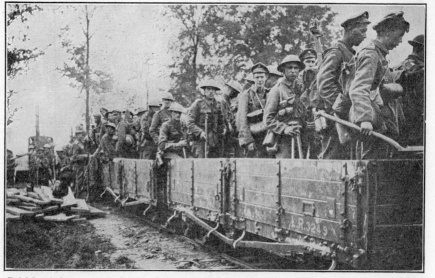
British reinforcements being hurried to the front on one of the light railways built by the soldiers themselves

British field guns hastily swung into position to hold up the German advance in the Battle of Picardy

share of the trophies of this victory. Besides this, you have acquired a feeling of your superiority over the barbarian enemy against whom the children of liberty are fighting. To attack him is to vanquish him.

American comrades, I am grateful to you for the blood you generously spilled on the soil of my country. I am proud of having commanded you during such splendid days and to have fought with you for the deliverance of the world.

At this time the Grand Cross of the Legion of Honor was conferred on General Pershing and personal congratulations were extended

British troops waiting in a support trench to repel the Germans in case they break through the front-line trenches

to him and his troops by King George, King Victor Emanuel of Italy, the Premiers of France, Great Britain, and Italy, and the Chief of Staff of Japan.

It is greatly to be hoped, despite all this well-earned compliment, that as the careful study of the progress of this war proceeds among our people they will refrain from exaggeration of the American part in it, and give due credit to the gallantry and devotion of the people of the nations that sustained its burden for four long years before we entered upon the conflict. Discussion of "Who won the war?" will always be profitless so long as there is an effort to make the answer confer especial credit upon any one nation. For if we look fairly at the record we shall discern the following facts that do not admit of contravention:

Upon France, of course, fell the heaviest burden and to France, beyond doubt, is due the greatest meed of glory. The blood of her devoted soldiers was shed without stint. Their courage inspired the fighting men of every nation, and their heroism fills a page of history that will long be glorious. The River Marne, the scene of two decisive battles, will bulk large in history

A big British gun surrounded by its ammunition known in French military slang as its "bait"

through all time to come, and though but a slender stream unvexed by commerce will hold its place with the greatest rivers of the world in the knowledge of men. But not even to France can sole credit for the overthrow of the Teutonic conspiracy against the world be given.

Had Belgium not resisted, at the certain cost of national martyrdom, the German invasion in August, 1914, France would certainly have been overrun by the enemy and the war won in the first three months according to the prearranged German plan.

Had not Russia—poor, betrayed, anarchy-ridden Russia—mobilized with unexpected speed and rushed her enormous armies into East Prussia and Galicia in the same month it would not have been necessary for General Von Moltke to detach several divisions from the army invading France, and the first battle of the Marne might not have been won by the French.

Had Italy stood by her alleged obligations under the Triple Alliance, had she even failed to give France early assurances that she would at least be neutral, huge French armies would have been tied up from the first guarding the Italian frontier, and France would

A row of French 155's being placed along a roadside to hold up the German advance in the Battle of Picardy

Irish troops in a captured German trench in the thrust toward Cambrai

ships bearing food, munitions, and reënforcements to the Allies the war would have unquestionably been lost.

And finally, had not the United States aided enormously with such money support as never before has been forthcoming from a single nation, with food, with explosives, with cannon, with deadly gas and all the other paraphernalia of war, and finally and above all with an army of such proportions as the world never believed

have been unable to hold back the Boches until Great Britain could organize armies and get into action.

Had Great Britain failed to revolutionize the precedents of centuries and become a great military power, and above all had she not thrown her indomitable and invincible navy into the struggle, keeping the seas closed to German commerce and open to all

we could raise, despatched to the scene of action with a celerity that amazed our foes and our friends alike, and rushing into battle with an impetuous daring that swept all before them—had the United States failed of all these things then indeed German autocracy would have overwhelmed the world and democracy would have perished from the face of the earth.

Cages filled with German prisoners taken by the British in the offensive of August, 1918.   These men were all captured in one day

British cavalry entering a recently captured village near Arras

After the naval battle off Santiago de Cuba in which the Spanish fleet was obliterated from the face of the ocean, and Spanish rule forever abolished in the islands of the West Indies, there arose an unfortunate controversy over the awarding of credit for the victory. Admiral Schley, who had been in actual command of the fleet in action, settled all this with the sensible remark, "There is glory enough for all." So in time we think history will determine that to no one nation, but to all working and fighting together for the triumph of the right and the defense of democracy, is due the final victory.

And so this volume, though in the main devoted to the story of American endeavors in the war, would be incomplete and fail to give an intelligent idea of the progress of the struggle if it did not at the same time briefly outline what was being done by our associated nations on the long battle line.

It became apparent very shortly after the forward movement that began at Château-Thierry had time to develop that the Germans were disheartened and pressed beyond their powers of resistance. Their retreat begun then was uninterrupted, though with no sign of demoralization. The grand strategy of General Foch, whose power as generalissimo was largely due to American suggestion and undoubtedly hastened the end of the war, was easily understandable to contemporary students of the war. In a general way, he

took the plan of campaign of the Germans on invading France, reversed it, and applied it to the task of driving them out. They had rushed through Belgium and into France in a grand left wheel, the pivot of their line being near Verdun and their right flank swinging around close to the western coast. It was as if a monstrous door was being swung open with its hinge at Verdun and its outer edge in Flanders. What Foch did was to swing this door back again though he set his hinge a little further to the east, in the Argonne region, and put in charge at that vital point the chief American army of whose deeds we shall tell in a later chapter. The door from the hinge to what we might call its centre panel was built up of American, Italian, and French soldiers,

A wiring party passing a big gun just outside Arras

British troops hastily digging trenches on the Somme

Of the scenes at Bapaume on the occasion of their second entrance Philip Gibbs writes:

So far as I could see, the only difference since the enemy sprawled back here and stayed a little while and then was flung back again is that many bodies of gray-clad men lie among the shell craters, and that the roads and tracks are littered with dead horses, so that the air is pestilential with foul odors, and everywhere among the old trenches and new, with their white, upturned chalk and the litter of barbed wire, are fresh German notice boards pointing the way to firing lines and observation posts and giving the directions of tracks—nach Mametz, nach Longueval, nach Ginchy. They had tried to camouflage some of their tracks by screens made of rushes, and had dug deep shelters under banks and in old trenches in order to escape from the harassing British fire.

In shell craters and ditches lie their helmets, gas masks, rifles, and equipment, and here and there is the wreckage of a field gun or limber, untouched but abandoned by the enemy in their flight, and strewn over all the ground are vast numbers of unexploded shells.

All this tumult of the tortured earth, all these pits dug by shells, all this wild destruction of places ruined in the first year of the war and mangled ever since were strewn with relics of German life and German death,

then began the joint lines of the French and British, then the British alone, and finally on the sandy dunes bordering the cold North Sea, in the little corner of their own country still left to them, the gallant Belgians.

As this line swung to the north and east the enemy were pressed closer and closer to the Belgian border, and in the far west King Albert and his men extended their conquest of their own territory until suddenly came the German appeal for peace.

Few of the British exploits were attended with more rejoicing than the recapture of Bapaume and Péronne. Both had been held by the British before and from both had they been driven out after desperate fighting.

© Underwood & Underwood

A mammoth British gun appropriately named, from the German point of view, "Kill Joy"

newly littered here. Their great
steel helmets punctured by bullets
or torn like paper by shell splinters
lay in thousands, with gas masks
and rifles and cartridge belts and
gray coats.

Along every mile of the way lay
rows of stick bombs, never used
against the British, and dumps of
unexploded shells, hideous in their
potentiality. A few dead horses
lay on each side of the tracks, as
they had gone trudging up with the
British transport before being shot.
Beside one horse lay a dead white
dog, the pet of the transport
column.

It was a moment of high and
justifiable exultation when
the British marched again into
these desolated places which
they had twice taken at the
highest cost of life and blood

Germans retreating in the fall of 1918 before the triumphantly advancing French,
British, and American troops

but which this time they knew could not be
taken away from them. Mr. Gibbs, most
graphic of correspondents on the spot, describes the scene thus:

It is utterly true to say that our men are going forward with gladness and exultation. They know the
risks ahead. There is nothing one can tell them about
the horrors of war. They know its fearful fatigues, the
beastliness of things, the stench and dust of the battlefield, the wicked snap of machine-gun bullets and the
howl of the high velocities.
But in spite of all that
they are marching forward
with a light in their eyes
and eager looks, and whole
armies are on the move
with a grim kind of joy.

It is an astounding pag-
eant, these hundreds of
thousands of men—Eng-
lish, Welsh, Canadians,
Scottish, and Australians
—all moving in a long,
reaching tide with horses
and guns and transport
along tracks over old battlefields, going forward
mile by mile very slowly
because of the surge of
traffic over narrow ways,
but never stopping.

Dust rises from these
moving legions in brownish
clouds which the wind
tosses above their steel
helmets, and through this
dust, in which the sun is

shining hotly, there is a vision of brown masses of men
with the glint of steel on rifles and helmets and twink-
ling colors, red and blue and green, of staff badges and
pennons.

Every man marches in a white mask of dust through
which his eyes shine. Dispatch riders are threading
their way through long lines of transport. The endless
columns of lorries, field batteries, and gun horses are
grotesque, like millers all floured from head to feet.
The horses are superb and in splendid form, as though
from an exhibition, and it goes to the heart to see

A field dressing station on newly captured ground. The wounded are being brought in by
German prisoners captured near Cambrai

These men, among the last of Germany's reserves, were on their way to Ham to reënforce the German lines

On the French front, where the advance was equally rapid and the succession of victories no less encouraging, the outstanding fact that impressed the observers with the armies was the barbarous and uncivilized determination of the fleeing Germans to work upon the country from which they were driven the utmost possible damage, and wherever possible damage that it would take years to repair, if indeed it could ever be repaired. Looting was to some extent the crime of the individual soldier, though there is not lacking evidence that it was encouraged by officers in authority. But the desolation of the country was ordered by high command. There was found an official message from the front declaring that the pursuing Allies would "find for winter only ground completely bare and devastated," and further that "the abandonment of this sector has been conducted with our customary care, and we have been able, without being interrupted, to take away from this region everything that would be of use to the adversary." And in an article written by a Colonel Gaedke was found this explanation of the German purpose: "A decisive struggle will

so many lying dead on the fields after the recent battles.

There is a great music of war over all this scene. Scottish battalions go forward to the fighting line led part of the way by their pipers, and across the battlefields come the wild cry of the pibroch and the drone of many pipes. The English battalions are marching with brass bands playing old English marching tunes, and, between whiles, merry bursts of ragtime. The crunching of gun wheels over rough ground, officers shouting orders to their men, the hooting of lorry horns and motor horns, and an incessant hum of airplanes overhead all make up a symphony which has a song of triumph in its theme.

Germany's last reserves being gathered together in St. Quentin in April, 1918, for Germany's last supreme effort

be made more difficult for the enemy by the devastation of the regions that now form a buckler before the German armies and will contribute to their successful defense."

Devastated they certainly were. From Ham the Germans took as loot everything of the slightest value, even loading army lorries with furniture for the "folks at home." When they fled they had filled the town with combustibles which they ignited over electric wires provided for the purpose, and the town was utterly destroyed, although it had survived the shellfire of actual war. Noyon, too, was destroyed, not in the course of its defense, but out of pure malignancy as the Huns fled. It had a town hall dating back to the Middle Ages, which they mined and demolished. In every town from Rheims to Ypres churches and cathedrals, especially those possessing antique beauty and therefore irreplacable, were the objects of German vandalism.

In the end, of course, all the cost of this systematic vandalism will be assessed against

The ruins of a French Red Cross warehouse which the Germans captured and looted of 50,000 francs worth of bandages and other supplies many of which had come from America

the German people. But those who ordered it, and those who committed the infamous outrages, will not be those who will pay. The charge will be borne by generations to come, but if the burden shall have the effect of teaching them the criminality and folly of provoking such a war as that from which the world has now slowly to recuperate it will not be wholly fruitless.

Some British Tommies dodging a big shell in No Man's Land

Drawn by Maurice Randall, from material supplied by the Coxswain of the *Shark*—courtesy British Bureau of Information

Commander Loftus Jones of the British ship *Shark* taking charge of the only weapon left in commission, the deck torpedo tube, after his leg had been shot away and after enemy torpedoes had hit his ship forward and smashed in her bows at the same time a shell blew up the forecastle

CHAPTER VIII

THE RUSSIAN REVOLUTION—CAUSES FOR THE REVOLT—GERMAN INTRIGUE
INVOLVED—THE SHIFTING CONTROL OF RUSSIAN AFFAIRS—KERENSKY,
LENINE, AND TROTZKY—SOCIAL CONDITIONS IN RUSSIA—RISE OF THE CZECHO-
SLOVAKS—THE ALLIES' SIBERIAN EXPEDITION—THE MURMAN PENINSULA—
POSITION OF THE UNITED STATES GOVERNMENT—THE OUTLOOK

THE story of the distinctively military events of the war may profitably be interrupted here to give some consideration to the amazing social upheaval in Russia which overthrew the throne of the Romanoff family, broke down the bureaucracy which had long ruled the land, swept away the corrupt and treacherous army officers who betrayed the stolid, brave, and cruelly deceived peasants to their defeat and destruction and brought down the whole Russian fabric in a *débâcle* from which it, at the moment of writing, shows no signs of recovery.

Volumes will be written in explanation of the reasons for the Russian revolt and still fall far short of giving the whole indictment against the men who governed and plundered in the name of the feeble and impotent Czar. Volumes will be written on the agonies of Russia in revolution, and still fail for many years to come in making clear the rights and wrongs of the situation in that hapless land, which is to-day without representation at the Versailles conference at which its fate will be settled, because there is no recognized government in Russia qualified to appoint delegates.

And yet the Russian people did their part for the Allies in the early days of the war. It was not the fault of the common soldier that the plans of his superiors opened convenient gaps in his lines of defense at the very points most convenient for the foe to attack. It was not the fault of Ivan that the ammunition for his cannon, when it reached the battlefield at all which was unusual, proved to be just a fraction of an inch out of the way to fit his guns, but by a queer coincidence fitted exactly the artillery of the pursuing Germans. Nor were the soldiers drawn from the farms responsible for the curious accidents by which sorely needed reënforcements seemed always to be sent to points where they were not useful.

The United States, which had been first to recognize the revolutionary government in Russia after the overthrow of the Czar, was destined to encounter in its friendliness to what had been hoped to be a popular government an endless amount of perplexity and peril.* For as has been already made clear, the Russian revolutionary administration passed by a series of military and political revolts into the hands of the most extreme of the revolutionary forces. It was greatly to the credit of our nation that it was early to recognize the endeavor of the people of Russia to establish for themselves a popular government. We could hardly have done otherwise, for it must be remembered that the United States itself is founded upon revolution, and revolt against constituted authorities cannot in itself constitute an offense in our eyes.

It is for that reason that, even after the Russian government had passed from the stage of an orderly endeavor to enforce democratic principles upon a turbulent people and had become a government founded wholly on force and maintained entirely by terror, the United States still held aloof from any efforts to interfere with the Russian

_____

*For an account of the early stages of the Russian revolution see "Nations at War," p. 241 et seq.

An American transport loaded to the gunwales with cheering, enthusiastic candidates for the Great Adventure

people in their efforts to work out their own political regeneration.

Perhaps nothing connected with the great war is so thoroughly enshrouded in mystery as has been the progress of the Russian revolution. The world has been fairly well able to cut away the fabric of deceit and disguise with which the Germans have endeavored to envelop the question of responsibility for the original outbreak of war. Day by day facts have been brought out which have fixed that responsibility clearly where it belongs upon the German Kaiser and the militarists by whom he was surrounded. But over suffering and bleeding Russia hangs an impenetrable pall of secrecy. That this is so is as much due to the nature of the Russian people as it is to the rigid censorship with which those responsible for the anarchistic conditions now prevailing have surrounded and concealed the facts. The enormous proportions of Russia, the prodigious distances between its towns, its wide steppes thinly populated by people not used to self-expression, the comparative lack of organs of public opinion, and the rigid rule which has long since blotted out any sem-

The same crowd, none the worse for their voyage, about to land on French soil

Russian soldiers during the original revolution going to the Duma for a patriotic demonstration carrying banners bearing the inscription "Down with monarchy! Long live the democratic republic!"

blance of independence among those existing made any clear understanding of the Russian situation almost impossible to an outsider. Even such matters as the continued existence or the assassination of the Czar and his family, which it might have been thought would have been duly recorded, are left at this writing in some doubt. All that the world knows of Russia is that after the treaty of Brest-Litovsk, the circumstances attending which have been already described, the internal condition of the country went from bad to worse, while it ceased to be for foreign nations a government to which any attention could be paid.

Germany thereafter looked upon Russia merely as a fat goose ready for the picking. Her authorities discarded the creed upon which they had entered upon negotiations with Russia—"No annexations and no indemnities"—and

straightway set themselves to plunder the country which they had deprived of any organized defensive force. In their dumb and inarticulate fashion the masses of the Russian people manifested their resentment

Czecho-Slovak soldiers going up a river in Siberia on a naval launch

of this German plan of spoliation. But the Bolsheviki were thoroughly intrenched in power, and their principal leaders, Lenine and Trotzky—real names, Ulyanov and Braunstein—were either the paid tools of Germany, or were ready to concede all to Germany in order to secure German aid in maintaining their own power and securing the complete destruction of all that had constituted the Russian state or the orderly Russian society.

they at once found that as they had opposed others while they were out of power, now they were in turn opposed, being in power. And their answer to this situation was a repudiation of all of the more ethical ideas which they had been preaching. The brotherhood of man disappeared in a series of the most cold-blooded massacres. Socialism, which is an ideal state of strictly ordered relations between its people, vanished in true anarchy. A fundamental complaint of those

Some Russian soldiers who have joined the Czecho-Slovak army engaged in the peaceful occupation of peeling potatoes

What the Bolsheviki stood for can be summed up in a few words. For many years the essence of their preaching has been "a dictatorship of the proletariat and the peasantry." They are utterly opposed to any compromise between the working classes, industrial as well as agricultural, and that great middle class which the French call the *bourgeoisie*. They are communists and syndicalists of the purest water. Along these lines they had worked out in theory the remedy for every social and economic ill, and now being established in power they purposed putting these theories to a practical test, no matter what the difficulty. But

who first overturned the Russian government was the prevalence of the death penalty for political offenses. The Bolsheviki, while still protesting against the death penalty, revived it in the form of assassination or wholesale massacres ordered in star-chamber council.

Theoretically, they proposed the most absolute democracy. The army was to be controlled not by its officers, but by committees of its soldiers. Industries and financial institutions were to be managed by the employees. All government was to be vested in a central body called the Council of Workmen's and Soldier's Delegates, or more briefly the Soviet.

What happened was that as Lenine and Trotzky controlled the Soviet they controlled the whole government, and no czar, nor any despot of history, ever inflicted upon a suffering people a more tyrannous personal rule than theirs.

There was left to Russia no semblance of a responsible government. Neither for the remnants of the old régime nor for the revolutionists themselves was there protection for life or for property. Assassination had been the weapon of the despots. It now became the defense of the down-trodden. Repeated efforts were made upon the life of Lenine and other members of the administration. To defend themselves the rulers made the possession of a weapon by an individual ground for his immediate execution without trial, while to criticize the government was reason for immediate imprisonment. Gross oppression, of course, sprung from the existence of such a law. The agents of the government, and they were innumerable, who desired to plunder a man, had but to accuse him falsely of having a weapon in his possession, in order to kill him with impunity; or, in rarely merciful moments, by alleging that he had criticized those in

authority to send him to a distant concentration camp, and work their will with his property and his family. The trials of those accused of sedition were farcical. Seldom was there an acquittal. Permission to put in a defense was frequently denied. Though in theory the accused were entitled to a jury trial, in fact on many occasions the judge would take the verdict out of the hands of the jury and himself condemn the accused to death.

Largely because of the absence in Russia of any such solid middle class as in France finally put an end to the Terror, the worst forms of Bolshevism increased and spread throughout the country until the whole land became a mere seething sea of anarchy. Meantime, the Germans were doing as they chose with the sections in their immediate front. On one pretext or another they ignored the provisions of the treaty which they had forced at Brest-Litovsk. They imposed upon subject provinces enormous penalties which were exacted in gold and which went far toward paying the German war expenses. Russia was deprived of at least one fourth of its area in Europe, and territory containing one third of its population was erected into

A barge armed with machine guns, captured by the Czecho-Slovaks from the Bolsheviki, on the river north of Vladivostok, Russia

An exact reproduction of a Bohemian village built in this country in connection with the Czecho-Slovak recruiting campaign

normally independent states which were in fact under German control, and in which Germany at once began to enforce conscription for its armies. The details of this

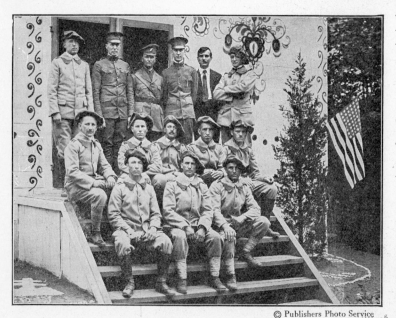

The officers of this Czecho-Slovak recruiting camp and their guests

treaty ceased to be of anything except merely historical interest when the forces of Germany were defeated and compelled to sue for peace in November of 1918. For the first act of the Allies in granting the armistice at that time was to declare that this treaty would not be recognized. Undoubtedly many features, such as the recognition of Ukrainia as an independent state, will remain in effect but not because of their existence in the Brest-Litovsk convention. That died when German power was crushed. But from the moment it was signed the relations existing between the de facto Russian government and the belligerent nations, notably the United States, became so strained as to be hardly existent. The Germans pressing into Russian territory so menaced Petrograd that the capital was removed to Moscow. This seemed to be a

"A HIT"

The American plane on the left has made a hit. His shots have perforated the enemy's gasoline tank and set his plane afire. One wing has broken away and the German aviator is about to jump

© Publishers Photo Service

A section of Camp Borglum, the headquarters of the Czecho-Slovak recruiting station

sufficient precaution against foreign interference, but soon domestic violence and outlawry proceeded to such an extent that the ambassadors of foreign nations refused longer to remain at the capital where their persons could not be protected. The British Embassy was sacked, in the absence of the ambassador, and the officer of the army in charge of it was killed. Ambassador Francis of the United States, who clung to his post last of all of the foreign representatives, finally withdrew after expressing some caustic opinions as to the character of the government which failed to govern Russia. The town of Volgoda, to the east of Petrograd, was for a long period the seat of the ambassadorial activities.

History knows of no such collapse of all forces of organized society as that which befell Russia. The French revolution was readily understandable, in comparison with the inextricably interwoven abuses and remedies, ambitions and catastrophes which have attended what the whole

A section of the American Army in Siberia with their beef accompanying them on the hoof

world hopes may be in the end the birth of a Russian democracy. The world, of course, knows that for more than half a century the fires of revolt against the Czar, and the autocracy which he typified, had been smouldering in Russia and every now and then breaking out in flame. In all probability had this final outbreak come at a time when peace prevailed in Europe it would have been suppressed by outside aid, probably German aid, to the established monarchy. But it came at a time when Russia was absolutely

they embarked upon an ambitious socialistic programme. All forests, mines, waters, and landed estates with their livestock, buildings, and machinery were declared the common property of the people. The principal of socialization of all factories, and state control over all production and distribution was re-affirmed. All national loans issued under the Imperial, or the succeeding Kerensky government, were repudiated—this affected the outer world very materially as the Russian national debt aggregated several billions

Czecho-Slovak troops under General Simionov drawn up in front of the railroad station in Vladivostok, Russia

isolated. The entrance of Turkey upon the war on the Teutonic side had closed the Dardanelles to Allied ships and to Russian ships. The latter could not go out to sell the enormous quantities of wheat and other foodstuffs which Russia produced, and which all Europe needed; the former could not enter the Black Sea to carry to Russia the munitions of war and the leadership which she craved. The only neighbor accessible to her was Germany—her enemy. The men desiring to seize upon Russian government saw their profit in making peace with Germany and thereby securing their elevation to power.

In their effort to administer internal affairs

mostly held abroad and much of it in the United States. All the banks were nationalized, the final result of which was that their assets were seized by Lenine and Trotzky. The old army was demobilized and a new "red" army organized. The immediate result of this was that a "white" army, enlisted by the opponents of the Bolshevist régime, made its appearance and civil war raged. All church property was sequestered; all private property rights in city real estate exceeding a certain maximum value were abrogated. The existing judicial system was overthrown and revolutionary courts established. A universal eight-hour day was

Landing an American officer's horse at Vladivostok, Russia

instituted with a minimum wage. Every conceivable relation of man to man and to the state was regulated and the Bolshevist council capped the climax by making marriage obligatory, and providing conditions under which partners for life could be forcibly selected without the acquiescence of both parties, and the arrangement ratified by state authorities.

All these and a host of other forms of regulation invasive of what had been always considered the rights of individuals were seriously enacted by the Bolshevist government in the name of liberty. What proportion of them can ever be enforced the world has yet to learn.

Meanwhile, the world looked on at the situation in Russia perplexed, amazed, and not a little horrified. To the great masses of the people it appeared that the whole nation was going down in blood-red chaos. This apprehension was due to the conflicting character of reports from the scene of this great social and economic struggle, and from the fact that the forces in power

Colonel Marrows superintending the unloading of the above transport

Admiral Knight with marine and foreign officers reviewing American troops in Vladivostok

there by their rigid exercise of the censorship had caused the rest of the world to utterly distrust as prejudiced and untrue all information coming out of Russia. Even the State Department of the United States had to admit a lack of precise information, and to report that for weeks at a time no word came through from Ambassador Francis while even such messages as came from him were deprived of great importance by the fact that he was not in touch with the government of the country to which he was accredited.

Some outline of the social condition in Russia is given in the following extracts from a letter by a Russian woman long prominent in diplomatic society in Washington:

It was bad enough before the March revolution, when our unhappy, half-witted Emperor, under the influence of his German wife, seemed to do everything possible to make people lose patience. But now we have a thousand anonymous potentates, the top ones paid by Germany, and the lower ones lured into supporting them by money, money, and money.

The present Government has abolished all laws, all courts, the police, land ownership, all private real estate

American Marines guarding the American Consulate in Vladivostok

American Army passing in review in Vladivostok before the Russian, Czecho-Slovak, Japanese, and British soldiers and sailors of our associates in the war

Major General William S. Graves, the commander of the American forces sent to Siberia to help to protect that country for Russia against the Germans from without and the Bolsheviki from within

The congested water front of Vladivostok with 35,000 bales of cotton set on fire by the Bolsheviki burning on the hillside in the background

A Y. M. C. A. club car used by the Czecho-Slovaks at the front in Siberia

in towns, all distinction of castes and grades in the army and navy. They have seized all the banks, are opening all the private safes, and confiscating all gold and silver found therein, though it had never been said before that it was criminal to have it. Of course, everything they "decree" is so mad that it is quite sure not to last forever, but the chaos they make will take centuries to forget. The country is going back to a savage state. And we will not live to wait for better times. . . .

On the pretense of equality they abolish all grades in the army and navy and make all posts elective by the simple soldiers. In most places it is understood as complete extermination, lynching of the officers, who, for being better educated, are under suspicion of being "counter-revolutionary." The highest posts are occupied by elected soldiers who very often can hardly sign their names, and the former officers are made simple soldiers, with a soldier's pay of $3.50 a month, and ordered to the lowest tasks, cleaning of the barracks, cooking food, taking care of the horses.

Our great country could only exist when all the wheels of the Government were working in harmony. Now everything is a perfect chaos. Everybody was willing to throw over the Czaristic Government, but not in order to change it for this one of loot, anarchy, and treason toward our allies! Ah, the shame, the disgrace, and the folly of it!

The army, which now consists of young boys (the regular one is long ago killed), without any sense of duty, morals, and discipline, see their acquired "freedom" in the freedom to go home when they want to. And so all the trains, all the stations, are attacked and destroyed by this horde of savages, who kill engineers, if it seems to them the train goes too slowly, who martyrize the railway agents who tell them of the impossibility of starting their train, for there is another one coming toward them on the same track. As this human flood goes home without any organization, everything is looted and destroyed.

Life in Petrograd is horrible—all the criminals, all the workmen, and demoralized soldiers rob the few cars that still bring some kind of products. In the very heart of the city, in daytime, you have your clothes taken off your back literally. Just think that there is no police, nobody to call for help, for those

who would like to help have had their firearms confiscated, even the officers, even the highest generals. All the soldiers, etc., are armed and have become highwaymen. At any moment you can expect a number of them to come into your private lodging and, under the pretense of "perquisition," take away all your

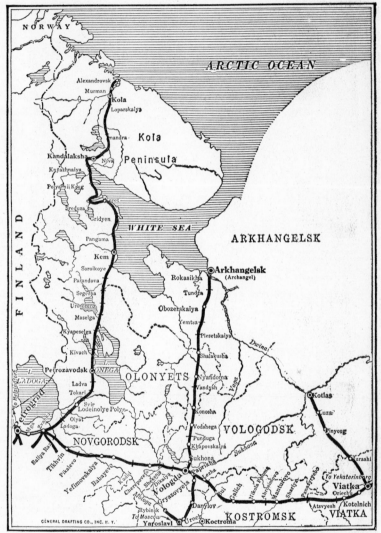

© 1918 by the *World's Work*

The Murman Coast and Archangel. An Allied expedition of British, French, and American troops is holding the Murman Coast and part of the railroad line south of it, chiefly to prevent its use as a naval and commercial outlet by Germany. Alexandrovsk is an open port the year round, due to the influence of the Gulf Stream. Archangel is accessible only in the summer

money and valuables.

Maxim Gorky who is perhaps the most distinguished Russian to join the Bolshevists in the Russian daily paper *Novaia Zhizn* (New Life) which he edits, he, the novelist who above all Russian writers of this period was able to speak with precise knowledge of the peasant class and their

Prof. Thomas Masaryk, President of the Republic of Czecho-Slovakia, of which the temporary capitol was Washington, D. C., and whose permanent capitol is Prague in Bohemia

consumed the entire grain supply, including the seed. In other districts the peasants are hiding their grain underground for fear of being forced to share it with starving neighbors. This situation cannot fail to lead to chaos, destruction, and murder.

There are numerous reports to the effect that the soldiers are dividing among themselves the military property of the country and committing unspeakable acts of violence. Wild rumors are current about the troops returning from Asia Minor. It is said that they have brought with them into the Crimea a large number of "white slaves" and that there is in Theodosia a veritable slave market. The supply is so great that the price has fallen from 100 or 150 rubles to 15 or 30 rubles apiece.

The Bolshevists, however, were not able to maintain their dictation without very determined opposition both political and military. Always there was a party in the Soviet opposed to them and at times it narrowly approached control. Indeed, despite the veil of secrecy that was thrown about Russia, the evidence was complete that the dominant power was not able to maintain its authority by the normal methods of political agitation and the exercise of military force, but was obliged to resort to massacre and assassination. Switzerland and Finland became centres of conspiracy. Every now and then some new aspirant for power would set up a government of his own in some distant section of the country, and indeed Russia was far extended enough to permit

aspirations, appeared an article in which the following paragraphs gave a graphic idea of the situation prevailing among the peasants, and the rank and file in the army:

All those who have studied the Russian villages of our days clearly perceive that the process of demoralization and decay is going on there with remarkable speed. The peasants have taken away the land from its owners, divided it among themselves, and destroyed the agricultural implements. And they are getting ready to engage in a bloody internecine struggle for the division of the booty. In certain districts the population has

the establishment of very considerable independent states within its borders and out of easy reach of the government established at Petrograd. The Germans were not averse to encouraging these movements of secession from the general Russian state. Nothing would suit German purposes better than the destruction of the great power which in more orderly times had menaced her Eastern frontier, and the substitution therefor of a number of small and weak independent states, many of which she could control through diplomatic astuteness. Accordingly, the creation of Ukrainia was followed by the erection of Esthonia, Lithuania, Livonia, Courland, Finland, and states which were to be formed out of Russian territory and under the dominion of either the Czecho-Slavs or the Jugo-Slavs.

The story of the former nation—for it has been recognized as a nation by the Government of the United States—is an interesting one. The Czecho-Slavic people are to be found, in the main, in Hungary and Western

plies, forced to live upon the country through which it marched, confronted by a journey of nearly 3,000 miles across Siberia, may well be doubted.

But the Czecho-Slovaks were not destined to pursue their initial plan very long. They were making progress in the campaign they had mapped out for themselves, finding here general sympathy from the Russian people and securing many recruits; or encountering there the hostility of Bolshevist forces to which they had to give battle. But as the

The Bolsheviki rule Russia with machine guns and every form of brutality and terrorism

Russia. At the time of the downfall of the established Russian Government a very considerable army, composed almost entirely of these people, was serving under the Russian flag. When its officers discovered that the revolution was going to play into the hands of the Germans they promptly revolted against Russian rule, and started on a march to the East, intending ultimately to reach the Pacific Coast at Vladivostok, and thence be transported in the ships of the Allies to the fighting fields of France. It was an amazing conception. Whether it could have been carried out by an army without any home government, with no base of sup-

time wore on, their leaders saw more and more clearly that German influence was becoming dominant in the Bolshevik camp and that if they were to fight for their own nationality they must fight the forces that were then dominating Russia. Their leaders were possessed not merely of military genius but of a clear political vision. It is not probable that at the moment this wandering army broke from Russian control and started eastward it had any preconceived idea of establishing a nation of its own. But as the break up of Russia became more and more apparent this idea did occur to the leaders of the army, and to political leaders in the territory whence its members had been drawn, and in Switzerland, Holland, and in the United States. At our national capital Professor Thomas G. Masaryk proved an able diplomat and a wise counsellor. The conception of a great Czecho-Slovak state which should be carved out of the portions of Russia, and of Austria-Hungary peopled by these people was enforced upon the world's consciousness. It fitted in admirably with that doctrine that the organization of nations and their boundaries should be a matter of the self-determination of their people, and that a nation should be racially a coherent whole. President Wilson enunciated this theory to Congress. Professor Masaryk pointed out that his people afforded the best possible opportunity for giving it a practical test. Never had they been contented under the dominion of Russia or of Austria-Hungary. Their men had served in the armies of these countries under protest and were now serving as an independent force against these two governments. The exploits of their army in the field had aroused general public admiration, and greatly reënforced the arguments of their diplomats in the world's capitals. They were recognized

as a militant force even before they attained political recognition as a state. The Allied governments, seeing in them the only force combatting German influence in Bolshevik Russia, sent to their aid an expeditionary force made up of Americans, Japanese, British, French, and Chinese troops which was landed at Vladivostok early in August, 1918. Our own detachment consisted of two regiments under General William S. Graves which had been serving in the Philippines. It was to be the task of this expedition to fight its way westward along the Siberian Railroad, open communication with the scattered bands of Czecho-Slovaks furnishing them with arms and munitions, and proceed onward toward the heart of Russia. By the end of the year these forces had attained a position in the neighborhood of Tomsk, the railroad behind them was clear to the coast, and the country in which they had been operating virtually pacified.

In September of the same year the United States Government formally recognized the Czecho-Slovak National Council as a de facto belligerent government. Its reason for granting this recognition was that the forces of this Council were waging a war

The American Army under General Graves landing at Vladivostok, Russia

This a unit of the one-time splendid Russian army which through Bolshevik fanaticism and treachery was surrendered to the Germans—Russia's implacable foes now as always

against the common enemy, the Empires of Germany and Austria-Hungary. Great Britain and France soon thereafter followed suit. The event promises to be one of great importance in the history of the world, for it as truly marks the birth of a nation as did our own Declaration of Independence. The area of the countries represented by the Council that was thus legitimatized approximates 48,000 square miles, and in it reside rather more than 10,000,000 people. Territory and

people are both drawn chiefly from Austria-Hungary, although at points the boundaries trench upon German and Austrian soil. Before the year had ended, a tentative constitution had been prepared and formal notice given to the world of the fact that the new state would be a republic.

Northern Russia saw another invasion, not wholly unfriendly, by a joint Allied expedition in the last year of the war. It will be remembered that Russia is largely desti-

Czecho-Slovak soldiers drawn up along one of the principal streets of Vladivostok, Russia

tute of ports on her western coast that are not subject to ice blockades in winter. Petrograd and Riga are icebound fully six months in the year. Archangel, on the White Sea, although far north of either of these ports, has a longer open season but for certain periods during the winter can only maintain navigation by the use of ice-crushers whose most powerful endeavors are not infrequently futile. Curiously enough, far to the north of Archangel, and on the Arctic Ocean, is a port which is practically free from ice the year round. Presumably some warm ocean current sets in toward this port of Kola and keeps it open when the more southerly harbor of Archangel is frozen. While Russia was still an active belligerent, Kola was made into a base for the supply of the Russian armies, a railroad running south from it to Petrograd. This road runs either through, or immediately adjacent to, Finland, and Finland in its eager-

ness to break away from Russia fell under German influence and in the latter months of the war was necessarily regarded as a pro-German force. Enormous quantities of food, clothing, and munitions of war were stacked up on the walls and in the warehouses in Kola and held there for a long time by the Allies because the Russian Government to which they were consigned had been overthrown and the new government was not recognized as friendly. It became apparent that the Germans, who were sorely in need of precisely this sort of material, were planning a descent upon this base and the seizure of the stores. Finland, though nominally neutral, would put no obstacle in the way of the passage of German troops through her territories. Accordingly an Allied force was landed and proceeded down what is known as the Murmansk Peninsula with a view to protecting the railroad to Petrograd.

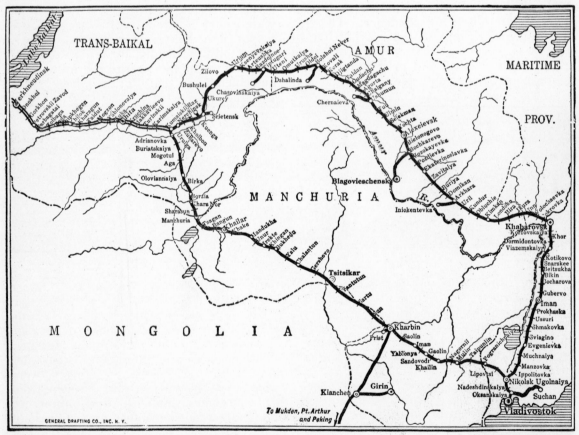

© 1918 by the *World's Work*

The Trans-Siberian Railroad from Lake Baikal to Vladivostok. This section, except for Vladivostok and Kharbin (Harbin), is largely controlled by the Bolsheviki and will have to be taken from them by the Allied expedition and the Czecho-Slovaks. The direct line from Kumaiskii Raz to Vladivostok is the Chinese Eastern Railway, and is used by the expedition with the consent of the Chinese Government. The line along the Amur River, by way of Khabarovsk, was only recently completed

At the beginning a detachment of American Marines constituted our contribution to this force, but it was presently followed by two regiments of infantry made up of men from the United States who were able to speak Russian or, in some instances, French, and who, prior to coming to our country, had resided in arctic climates. They made their way to Archangel where they were reviewed by Ambassador Francis, and greeted with the utmost enthusiasm by the populace.

every point. Russians and inhabitants of Finland, who were opposed to the extension of German authority in that country, formed organizations which came to be known as "The White Guard" and coöperated with the expeditionary forces. At the end of the year 1918, the Murmansk Peninsula was wholly in their control and it seemed altogether probable that they would presently extend their march to Petrograd when peace was declared.

Czecho-Slovak soldiers and American bluejackets going on guard duty together in Siberia

Although this expedition had been undertaken in a spirit of the utmost friendliness to Russia, and wholly with the purpose of preventing German acquisition of the stores, which had been intended for the Russian Government, the Bolshevists who had seized control of that government made of it an occasion for once again showing their complete subservience to Germany. They declared this relief expedition to be in fact an invasion of Russian territory, and demanded that the troops be withdrawn. As the Allies refused to give any heed to the demand, Bolshevist forces, or as they came to be known "The Red Guard," attacked the expeditionary troops, but were defeated at

Naturally, however, Russia as a factor in the determination of the war had ceased to exist. If her influence had any bearing upon the outcome of the conflict it must be regarded as favorable to Germany, because conditions in the new states, carved out of her territory and recognized by Germany, were such as to enable the Germans to secure from them enormous enforced contributions of money and a number of men for the German armies running far up into hundreds of thousands.

In considering the Russian situation it is fair to keep in mind the long years of tyranny to which the people of that country had been subjected. For centuries their resentment

Annanefe soldiers, orientals from the French protectorate in southeastern Asia. These men were among the best of the Allied troops

had smouldered and when it broke out into successful revolt the natural result was a reign of violence. It may be doubted, however, whether all the worst atrocities accredited to the Bolsheviki exceeded in inhumanity the deeds committed throughout past years by the governments of successive Czars. To talk of a "reign of terror" in Russia under the revolutionary rule is but to resort to the commonplace. All government in Russia for three hundred years has been a reign of terror. The difference to-day is that a different class of society is suffering. The utter unreasonableness, the seeming barbarity of political persecutions under Lenine and Trotzky is no greater than it was in earlier days under officials devoted to the maintenance of the empire.

It is therefore too early to pass upon the ultimate worth of the Russian revolution. But the temporary conditions bred of it aroused in all other civilized nations a very serious dread lest the Bolshevism that had captured Russia should spread to other lands. Particularly was this the case with Germany in the days immediately succeeding the estab-

lishment of the armistice. Always in Germany the socialistic element had been strong, and as the overthrow of the Imperial Government followed almost instantly upon the restoration of peace it was apprehended that the socialists would seize the government and establish even a more radical form of socialism than they had theretofore been preaching. Those who dreaded such an event placed their chief reliance upon the existence in Germany of a large and powerful middle class, such as was entirely lacking in Russia, and which wherever it is found is a check upon extreme radicalism.

But the world was nervous. Of that there could be no doubt. Supporters of the Bolshevist régime in Russia declared that as a result of this nervousness the reports of turbulence and chaos existing there were grossly exaggerated. This is not improbable, and yet the evidence is irresistible that life, liberty, and property were deprived of all protection under the Bolshevist régime, that industry was struck down, commerce destroyed, and ruin and starvation forced upon the people. The United States Government, which had been first to extend a hand of friendship to revolutionary Russia, was forced into an attitude of protest, and said in a formal communication to the Allies:

This Government is in receipt of information from reliable sources revealing that the peaceable Russian citizens of Moscow, Petrograd, and other cities are suffering from an openly avowed campaign of mass terrorism and are subject to wholesale executions. Thousands of persons have been shot without even a form of trial; ill-administered prisons are filled beyond capacity, and every night scores of Russian citizens are recklessly put to death; and irresponsible bands are venting their brutal passions in the daily massacres of untold innocents.

In view of the earnest desire of the people of the United States to befriend the Russian people and lend them all that is possible of assistance in their struggle to reconstruct their nation upon principles of democracy and self-government, and acting therefore solely in the interest of the Russian people themselves, this Government feels that it cannot be silent or refrain from ex-

pressing its horror at this state of terrorism. Furthermore, it believes that in order to check the further increase of the indiscriminate slaughter of Russian citizens all civilized nations should register their abhorrence of such barbarism.

As a result of this situation it was felt at the time of the Peace Conference that it might be necessary to keep American forces in Europe for some time, in order to combat the powers of anarchy which seemed to have grown to menacing proportions in Russia. What the outcome of the situation may be none may tell, but there is reason to hope that just as the Terror **brought** the violent period of the French revolution to a close and left the ground prepared for the erection of a stable government, so the red fury of Bolshevism is preparing the way for a popular government which shall give a people long oppressed by tyrants a government of their own for their own good.

German, Austrian, and Bolsheviki prisoners being brought into Vladivostok by the Czecho-Slovaks

Jugo-Slav horsemen going into battle during the irresistible Allied offensive of September, 1918, in the Balkans

Recruits for the Russian Women's Battalion of Death being reviewed by their commander Maria Botchkareva and Mrs. Pankhurst of Great Britain

CHAPTER IX

WHERE TEUTONIC DISSOLUTION BEGAN—THE WAR IN THE SOUTHEAST—
BULGARIA SURRENDERS—THE DOWNFALL OF TURKEY—BRITISH VICTORIES
IN PALESTINE—ITALY REGAINS HER WAR STRENGTH—FIGHTING ON THE
PIAVE—THE SMASH-UP OF AUSTRIA-HUNGARY—ASPIRATIONS OF SUBJECT
PEOPLES—REMAKING THE MAP OF EUROPE—SOME OF THE MORE PERPLEXING
PROBLEMS

TO THE ordinary observer it appeared that the great war was won in France. There from its earliest days the fighting was most constant, and it was there that the great French general was in command to whom, at the last, the German appeal for an armistice was referred. It was France that the Teutonic hordes sought to overwhelm, and France, with aid of course from her Allies, that beat them back. It was in the main the ruined cities of France, the desolated homes, and the cruelly torn and lacerated families of France that most stirred the compassion of the world, and roused that wrath against the Hun that nought but complete victory could appease. And so it was fitting that the last act in the tragic drama should be staged as it was in France.

Nevertheless, an important part of the work of beating the Hun was done at a great distance from France, and the story of the sudden German collapse, which we have yet to tell, will not be comprehensible unless preceded by some account of the military actions in Macedonia, Albania, Bulgaria, and along the Italian-Austrian border that made the surrender of Germany on French battlefields inevitable.

The successes won by the Allies in the eastern theatre of war at the beginning of its fifth year came as a surprise to the world, which had heard little from that section except continued reports of the victories of the Germans, or of their Balkan allies. Indeed there had grown up a certain belief that even if Germany was to be beaten in France she would prove invincible in the Near East, and would build up for herself an empire there that would atone for the failure to win any territory on the western front. It was recognized that the dream of a Pan-Germanic empire that should extend from the Baltic or the North Sea to the Persian Gulf was to a great extent the animating purpose of the German declaration of war, and the success of German diplomacy and the German arms in the Near East seemed for a long time to justify the fear that this ambition would be attained. When the United States entered the war the situation looked hopeless for the Allies in the whole theatre of war east of the French border. Italy was slowly recovering from a monumental defeat. Rumania and Serbia had been overwhelmed and forced to make treaties of peace that amounted to abject surrender. So far as the world could see Turkey was in a condition that promised continued service to the German cause. For while her armies in Mesopotamia and Palestine had sustained a succession of defeats at the hands of the British under General Stanley Maude and Sir Edwin Allenby, the collapse of Russia had relieved them from all pressure on the Caucasus side, and the steady massacre of the unhappy Armenians was progressing under the approving eye of Christian Germany. The world, outside of the war councils of the Allies, could see nothing in the Balkans to encourage hope.

Yet the element of weakness was operating

A narrow escape for some British fighters in Mesopotamia. With characteristic British scorn of danger one of these men
commented, "A close one that held us up a bit"

very effectively in the enemy's ranks although
scarcely suspected.   South of the Dardanelles
the British progress was very like a triumphant parade, and the repeated Turkish defeats
aroused political revolt in the capital in the
course of which Enver Pasha and Talaat Bey,
adventurers who had seized control of the
government and had effected the diplomatic
agreement with Germany, were overthrown.
Revolts broke out among the Arabs in various
provinces of Asia Minor, and the British
forces operating in that section soon found
that their activities were largely reduced to
accepting the surrender of enemy armies who
had no longer any desire to fight.   The
enemy's resistance collapsed completely.   An
official correspondent with the British troops
in Palestine describes one scene of rout
thus:

More than 260 guns have been located in our lines,
and possibly more will be found.   Artillery ammunition
in vast quantities has been found everywhere.   Some
of the depots are acres in extent.   As the Turks only
manufacture small arms ammunition, if they try to
raise new armies to take the place of these destroyed,
they must call on Germany for every gun, transport,
and instrument of war required.

To-day saw one of the most remarkable sights which
a soldier ever gazed upon.   From Balata, where the
road from Nabulus falls through craggy hills and narrow
passes to Wadi Farah, there is a stretch more than six
miles long covered with débris of the retreating army.
In no section of Napoleon's retreat from Moscow could
there have been a more terrible picture of hopeless,
irretrievable defeat.

In this area alone were eighty-seven guns of various
calibres, fully 1,000 horse and oxen drawn vehicles,
nearly 100 motor lorries, cars filled with kitchens,
watercarts, and a mass of other impedimenta.   The
road was black with the carcases of thousands of
animals and bodies of dead Turks and Germans.

This was the work of the Irish, Welsh, and Indian
infantry.   The artillery pressure behind the indomitable British and Australian airmen in front of the
infantry had forced the enemy over the hills into the
road, and just as the guns began to shell the retiring
transport airmen swooped down to 200 feet and bombed
the head of the column.   Once that was accomplished,
time only was required to finish the job, and this was
done with surprising thoroughness.   One flight after
another took up the work, until the whole column was
one vast, broken mass.

The enemy troops, seeing escape with the vehicles
was impossible, fled to the hills.   Some who had
endeavored to find an outlet up the Beisan road fell
into the hands of cavalry waiting for them.   Others,
accepting the inevitable, sought refuge in our lines.

British troops outside the Jaffa Gate guarding the end of the line of communication to Jerusalem, forty-one miles away

A camel transport near the Suez Canal during the British campaign in Egypt

However dire the state of the Turkish armies in the field, and however great the political

An arrested Arab sheik volubly protesting his innocence to his impassive captor, a British Tommy, who doesn't understand a word of his language

unrest in Constantinople, the government was not precipitate in giving up the struggle. This was mainly because whoever was in nominal power the real power in Turkey was at that moment Germany. The German ambassador was virtually in control, and his word was backed by the German battleships, *Goeben* and *Breslau*, which had been nominally sold to Turkey but were still commanded by German officers. The Turkish armies, too, were largely under German control. Accordingly in the face of dire disasters in the field the Turkish Government made no overtures for surrender.

But the successes of Allied troops north of Turkish territory and the reverses that befell the Bulgarians in the fall of 1918, ultimately put the Turk out of action. In September of that year General Franchet d'Esperey, in command of an allied force approximating 400,000 men, British, French, Serbian, Montenegrin, Italian, Russian, Jugo-Slav, and Greek, a truly cosmopolitan force, began an attack on the enemy's forces in Serbia. It was a movement that had been expected by the Allied world for months, perhaps for years. It had long been delayed by distrust of Greece under her pro-German monarch, King Constantine. But with the intriguer driven from the throne, and the Greek Government practically in the control of the Allies the danger of a fire in the rear was done away

The First Christian Nation. Six Turkish vilayets in the northeastern part of Asia Minor constitute Armenia. The Armenian nation is one of the oldest in the world; the Armenian church is the oldest state Christian church in the world. There are about 2,000,000 Armenians in these provinces—a little island of Christians surrounded by people of hostile race and hostile religion. For five centuries their lives have been one continuous martyrdom, their agony reaching its most terrible stage in the spring and summer months of 1915

with. Moreover, the enemy troops in front of d'Esperey were weakened just at this time, for Austria and Bulgaria had responded to German demands for more troops on the west front, and had sent some divisions thither. Accordingly, September 16th, the Allied offensive was opened on a ten-mile front in the region between the River Vardar and Lake Doiran. It was expected to be the precursor of an extended operation but it is not probable that the commanding general himself knew how suddenly it would develop into a triumphant pursuit of a retreating and demoralized army. For within two days French and Serbian troops had advanced five miles and had taken such strategic points as made the interruption of the enemy's retreat most improbable.

While heavy blows were being dealt on this sector Italian troops in Albania were pounding that part of the enemy's line that extended into Albania while French and Serbians were attacking his centre. Within ten days from the commencement of the offensive the Bulgarians were in retreat all along the line, burning their stores and

leaving great bodies of prisoners in the hands of the pursuers. As usual a cry went up from the failing nation for German aid, but this time there came no response. Germany was having troubles of her own. King Ferdinand, of Bulgaria, "the Fox of the Balkans," who had forced his people into the war on the side which most of them hated, saw his kingdom in revolt and seizing all the treasure he could lay his hands on abdicated and fled. With his abdication came the unconditional sur-

A pressure pump in the Desert of Arabia for obtaining water by friction

Indian lancers, who substantially contributed to the British and Allied triumph in the Holy Land, entering Haifa

render of Bulgaria—the first of the Kaiser's accomplices to leave him in the lurch. It lacked but nine days of three years since Bulgaria had cast in her lot with the Teutonic alliance, and was a tragic ending to a story of royal intrigue and indifference to the wishes of a people.

The surrender of Bulgaria was recognized everywhere as assuring the early retirement of Turkey from the war. For the Moslem nation was now cut off from the source of all its strength, and isolated from the power which had coaxed it into war and supported it in the moments of greatest trial. Bulgaria and Serbia being lost to the Germans, there could be no longer an uninterrupted commerce between Berlin and Constantinople. The Hamburg-Constantinople express that had been inaugurated with such pomp and had been expected to be one of the permanent features of German imperial expansion was rudely switched off. No more German officers, German munitions, nor German money could be sent to the city on the Golden Horn. The Allied troops busied themselves for a while clearing out of Serbia, Albania, and Montenegro the remaining enemy forces, serene in the certainty that Turkey would be forced to quit with-

Wounded Turkish prisoners being carried on camels in the Desert of Arabia out any further fighting on their part. If more force should be needed the British armies pressing north through Palestine might be trusted to apply it. Meanwhile, they cleared all Germans, Austro-Hungarians, and Turks out of Bulgaria. They were given a month to leave, and their going was greatly expedited by the process of bundling them all, officers and soldiers together, into freight cars and shipping them to Vienna while the roads were crowded with motor trains carrying such material of war as the defeated foe was permitted to take. As fast as the enemy retired from Serbia the allied forces pressed on his heels and by November, Belgrade, on the boundary line of Austria-Hungary, was reached. Serbia, the hapless country that had been made the pretext for this most barbarous war, was purged of the barbarians that had forced it upon her. The final reply to the Austrian ultimatum, dictated from Berlin, which precipitated the war, had at last been made.

But before this time Turkey had laid down her arms. October 31st the armistice was signed which in the hope of all civilized people means the final expulsion of the unspeakable Turk from any part or place in European civilization. The surrender was unqualified and included Turkish domains in Asia Minor as well as all to the north of the Bosphorous. It will be for the Peace Conference at Versailles to determine the future of the Turkish domain, but it is certain that the Dardanelles will never again be the property either of Turkey or of any other power with authority to close them to the commerce of any nation. It is assured that Constantinople will not continue under Turkish rule, and that Jerusalem, and indeed all of the Holy Land, will be redeemed from Moslem domination. What is left of the Armenian people after wholesale massacres and persecution

baffling description—and for which Christian Germany was more responsible than the Moslem Turks—will be assured freedom from the damnable tyranny under which they have suffered, and an opportunity in the coming ages to build up that prosperous and civilized Christian nation which they are eminently able to develop and maintain. Enormous as has been the cost of the Great War, and terrible as have been the sufferings that it has entailed, it is possible that in the age-long balance sheet it may be shown that all has been more than paid for by this final expulsion of the Turk from power at the eastern end of the Mediterranean.

So Turkey and Bulgaria dropped out of the war. It was then the moment for the world to foresee the immediate fall of the two Teuton empires. The southeastern empire that

Kaiser Wilhelm visiting in Sophia, Bulgaria, his fellow conspirator, King Ferdinand of Bulgaria. The Kaiser is wearing a Bulgarian uniform while the King is wearing that of a Prussian Field Marshal

A rifle bomb barrage on the Serbian front.   This is characteristic of the beautiful country which was so defiled by Austrian, German, and Bulgarian outrages

Prince Alexander of Serbia, who has been Prince Regent since the retirement of his father, King Peter

time was needed to restore it. Time was needed, too, for the Allies to make amends for their earlier neglect, and furnish those supplies the lack of which had been one of the causes contributing to Italian disaster.

When the passes were opening it was Austria that struck first, and the blow recoiled on her to her utter destruction and final undoing. On the 15th of June, in response it is said to an order from the Kaiser to Emperor Charles that he "put the Italian armies *hors du combat*" the Austrians struck both in the mountain regions of the Veneto and on the Piave. On the former front the Italians were helped by both British and French forces, and a small number of British were also on the line of the river. At both points the Austrians were first held, then beaten back disastrously. The Italians were but briefly on the defensive, then rallying their forces rushed into an offense that never was checked until the Austrians themselves suffered the fate the Kaiser wished them to inflict upon their foes. In a month's time the Austrian casualties were estimated at between 270,000 and 300,000 of whom about

Germany had sought to establish was gone. The supplies of wheat, of oil, of foodstuffs that she had thought to draw from Mesopotamia, from Russia via Odessa, from Roumania and Bulgaria were suddenly shut off, and most menacing of all the great ally Austria-Hungary sore beset on every side, racked by internal political dissension, beggared, starving, and freezing, was on the point of collapse and did in fact give up the struggle on November 3d, three days after Turkey had laid down her arms. But the downfall of Austria was compelled by events that occurred outside the Balkans, and on the Italian frontier. They constitute a most glorious chapter of Italian history, and indeed one of the most stirring records of all wars.

In an earlier chapter we left the Italian armies, at the beginning of 1918, standing on guard on the line of the Piave and at the mouths of the mountain passes leading down into the Venetian plain. Here they stood throughout that winter, and until the snows were well out of the passes in summer. Their morale had sustained a severe shock, and

A typical headquarters of a Serbian commander on the Balkan front

During the capture of Douze-cent-Douze this Serbian battery of 75's was harnessed and on its way to an advanced position in less than twelve minutes

In the Balkan Mountains there were no motor ambulances for the wounded. This is the kind of comfortless transport they had to endure

A group of Serbian soldiers, known as rifle bombers, ready to attack the cruel German-Austrian invaders of their country

Monastir, Serbia, looking north from a minaret. This town changed hands several times during the war and was one of the chief bones of contention between the nations

60,000 were killed, and 20,000 taken prisoners. Along the Piave the fighting was truly amphibious. Torrential rains that began to fall during the first days of the Austrian attack put that low-lying country wholly under water. All the bridges across the river save two were swept away, and these were speedily demolished by shells dropped from airplanes by British aviators. The upper part of the river flows through a narrow gorge with steep walls, and here it was a rushing mountain torrent which nothing could pass, and after the destruction of the bridges the German General Boroevic was only able to feed those of his troops that had crossed before the bridges went down by resorting to the use of airplanes.

Lower down the river spreads out over broad and shallow flats, and here the scene was a frightful one. The outlet into the Gulf of Venice was obstructed by great masses of floating timber, the débris of structures destroyed by Italian artillery higher up, splintered boats, and the corpses of animals and men that came floating down in increasing numbers to bear ghastly testimony to the savagery of the battle on the upper waters. In this fighting a small American pioneer corps took an active part. They were in the assault at Montello where the Allied artillery was turned on dense masses of Austrian troops, caught on the danger side of the Piave with all bridges down behind them. Artillery and the ceaseless fire from aircraft which hovered above making deadly play with machine guns and bombs, spread death and panic in their ranks. American aviators, though flying foreign machines, were in the flocks of aërial fighters and did magnificent service. From the uplands of Montello down both banks of the river to San Dona the country was one great cemetery in which, however, the dead lay unburied. Below the latter point the river

widens out, and here the fighting continued long after the Austrians had been put out of action farther up the stream.

It was difficult country for modern military methods. The soil was too moist for trenches to be dug, and the fighting men of either side, hungry for some form of protection, turned every farmhouse, wall, or mill into a small fort. The banks of the innumerable canals were the only pieces of solid ground to be found and these were thickly lined with machine guns, while the muzzles of the same deadly weapons peeped from every tree strong enough to support them. Floundering in the bogs, swimming canals and breasting torrents, the fighting foes gave many instances of picturesque tactics. The Italian arditi equipped themselves with long leaping poles such as boys use at play and descended upon the enemy behind his ditches as from the air.

Enver Pasha, the Turkish Minister of War and tool of the Kaiser's, who accumulated a vast fortune made out of the sufferings of the people during the war

American soldiers, representatives of the newest great army in the world, marching through the central square of one of the oldest towns of northern Italy

King Victor Immanuel of Italy and his staff inspecting the American regiment which fought on the Italian front

American and Italian aviators jointly occupying one of Italy's beautiful aviation fields

The anniversary of the entrance of America into the war being celebrated in the Colosseum at Rome. One of the greatest events of the world to-day being observed in one of the greatest monuments of the past

Austrian prisoners in an Italian detention camp behind the Italian front

American soldiers in Italy being taught by Italians how to cross a river in Italian boats

Courtesy of the American Numismatic Society

Distinguished Service Cross   The Congessional Medal of Honor   The Distinguished Service Medal
Authorized in 1918   Authorized in 1862   Authorized in 1918

The Philippine Congressional Medal   The Naval Medal of Honor (centre)   The West Indian Naval Campaign Medal
Authorized in 1861

A group of American officers who saw service on the Italian front. They are left to right: Lieutenant Colonel Boyers, Captain Scandland, General Treat, Major McCraw, Major McKinney, and Captain Hiller

One Austrian command that fought well and was practically wiped out was the famous Viennese "Company of Death," composed of volunteers, uniformed in black sweaters embroidered on the breast with a white skull. There were but few of these rather melodramatic costumes known in this war. But among them was the uniform of the command favored by the German Crown Prince, with skull and cross-bones embroidered on the front of its headgear. It is not recorded that this terrifying insignia added particularly to their efficiency in battle, and the Crown Prince, by running away immediately upon the German smashup, saved exposing himself to the death which the decoration seemed to typify.

The most savage fighting in this renewal of activity along the Italian front was that on the Piave. But to the west on the Italian line, where it ran along the mountains that separate Italy from Austria and guarded the passes through which the enemy had once swarmed down upon the Venetian plain, the Italians had pressed forward for heavy gains, and had secured several strategic points against the moment when they should launch their great objective. This came October

9th. In France the Allied advance was at its fullest tide of success. The Americans had just broken the Kriemhilde line, the Germans had evacuated Lille, Ostende, Ghent, and Bruges; at every point the signs of German disintegration were apparent, and in the Argonne and along the lines of the Meuse the Americans were relentlessly pressing on toward Sedan and Mezieres with the purpose of cutting off the retreat of the German armies that were facing defeat.

The moment was propitious for final Italian victory. From Foch, the all-seeing Generalissimo on the western front, came speeding the order to attack. The men under Diaz were speedily under way. They smote the Austrian invaders in the mountain passes about Asiago and on the marshy reaches of the Piave. Just a year earlier, at Caporetto, the Austrians, with the aid of treachery, had overwhelmed the sons of Italy, but now vengeance was taken to the fullest.

Fifty-one Italian divisions, three British, two French, and one Czecho-Slovak division and one American regiment participated in the movement, begun October 24th, which finally put Austria-Hungary out of the war, and to present appearances put that double-

American soldiers constructing defenses along the Piave in Italy

headed monarchy out of the list of nations. Within twenty-four hours after the battle begun the Italians had captured 3,000 prisoners, and had taken the enemy's strongest positions in that quarter. On the Piave the overthrow of the Austrians was not less complete. In what seemed to be but a few hours of fighting the arrogant enemy which but a few days before had felt certain of capturing Venice, and was talking of sweeping down from the mountains on to the plains of northern Italy and opening a back-door for the invasion of France from the southeast, was in full retreat. Up again through the mountain passes which they had won with such infinite pains two years earlier, only to be expelled again, the Italians made their way. The mountain peaks were passed again. The head waters of the Isonzo again witnessed the triumphant flaunting of the Italian colors. Back through that rocky and desperate country though which once before they had dug and blasted and fought their way the Alpini, the Bersaglieri, and the other picturesque units of Italy's fighting force ascended irresistibly, for it was all uphill fighting. At last they stood once more in the outskirts of Goritzia. In a month Austria had lost all the territory upon which the armies came into contact,

400,000 prisoners, 7,000 cannon, and a body of dead and wounded which could hardly be computed. There was nothing left for the Austrians except surrender and on the 1st of November they asked and received terms of an armistice. While her acceptance was still under consideration the Italians pushed the fighting with such good effect that before the final surrender of Austria three days later their armies were in both Trent and Trieste and *Italia Irredenta* was redeemed.

During the period of the final smash-up of the Austrian armies ill fortune attended the ships of that nation as well. Italian bluejackets showed a dash and gallantry worthy of the nation that gave to the world Columbus, Amerigo Vespucci, and a host of less famous but still adventurous seamen. November 1st, the very day of the surrender, the great Austrian superdreadnaught, *Viribus Unitis*, was torpedoed and sunk by an Italian naval tank steamer—a most ignoble end for a deep-sea fighter.

While the final acceptance of the armistice was still in doubt the Italians were unrelenting in their ferocious attacks, and the Austrians seemed quite incapable of recovering their morale or the ability to make any sort of a stand against their pursuers. The re-

General Eben Swift of the American forces in Italy detects James H. Hare, photographer for *Leslie's Weekly*, in the act of taking his picture

from an officer who was with the correspondents. When asked if they knew about the armistice, they said: "We want food. Food is the only thing we are interested in. We are indifferent to war and peace and death—everything but food."

It is estimated that nine Austrian divisions were taken with their staffs. Thirty-nine divisions were partially disorganized and fifteen, although in bad condition, are retreating from the advancing Italians. These troops, while equipped for their retreat, are without orders, and go travelling here and there like droves of sheep.

While the Austrian armies were being thus cut to pieces on the battlefield the Austro-Hungarian empire itself was being broken to bits at home. Revolution menaced in the streets of Prague, of Buda-Pesth, and of Vienna itself. Late in October, while his armies in the field were still recoiling before the irresistible onslaught of the Italians in mountain passes and on the turbulent reaches

treat of the defeated armies through the steep and narrow defiles of the Alps could for its scenes of horror be compared only with the famous retreat of Napoleon's grand army from Moscow. A correspondent who witnessed it writes:

Great masses of men wait for long hours to move a few feet or a few hundred yards, to halt anew on a road littered with the carcases of horses, pieces of shells, pistols, rifles, broken-down auto trucks, and machine guns. Many Austrians are dying from sheer fatigue and starvation and not wounds. The Italians are doing all they can to hurry up food supplies. This is difficult, and in the meantime dead horses are eaten, the flesh being cooked by the roadside by fires kindled by the soldiers.

Large bodies of Austrians are helpless. The correspondents passed between Overto and Trent, a distance of sixteen miles, an unending column of men marching none knew whither. They asked orders

American reserves in Italy going to the assistance of hard-pressed comrades in response to signal rockets

American soldiers on the Piave with their rapid-fire guns loaded and ready for the enemy

Signor Fogazzaro's home in the foothills near the Italian mountains which was ruined together with many other beautiful
homes as well as many humble ones

Marshal Foch, Commander-in-Chief of the Armies of the Allies, as he looked after he had defeated the greatest military power in the world and saved civilization

The work of the Austrians at Roveretto, near Trent in Italia Irredentia which was taken by the Italians just before hostilities ceased

American soldiers operating one of the famous Lewis guns on the Piave in Italy

A powerful Italian submarine chaser operating on the beautiful Gulf of Venice

of the Piave, Emperor Charles appointed a "liquidation ministry"—to business men the term is most suggestive of bankruptcy. The duty of this body was to arrange terms of surrender and to take over the reins of government until it should appear what form of state the people would erect to take the place of the one that had brought upon them this unbearable burden of calamity and woe. Word was swiftly sent to the trenches, and toward evening of October 29th the Italian lookouts near Seravalle, in the Adige Valley, saw an Austrian officer bearing a white flag advancing across No Man's Land. Several officers who went out to meet him found that he was a captain who claimed to be authorized to discuss terms of an armistice. At that moment there was nothing about which Italy was less concerned than an armistice. Her troops were everywhere driving the Austrians back, capturing their positions, taking guns by the hundreds and prisoners by the thousands, and inflicting on the ancient enemy losses from which he could not hope to recover in decades. As the messenger of peace was found but imperfectly provided with papers to show his authority, he was sent back with instructions to have an officer of higher rank and more thoroughly accredited come in his stead. Meanwhile, the word went to every Italian battle line to press the assault with renewed vigor. The next day

came a more formal peace embassy, headed by General Von Weber, and composed of army and navy officers, diplomatic and

The type of gas masks worn by the soldiers of Italy

Italian soldiers in the Plaza of Trent on November 2, 1918, just after they took possession of this long-coveted Italian city which had so long been held by the hated Austrians

This was the first Italian cruiser to reach Trieste after its occupation by the Italians.   J. H. Hare, *Leslie's* photographer, was on board

King Victor Immanuel of Italy being officially welcomed in Trieste on November 10, 1918

Capodistria, a beautiful spot in the reclaimed territory of Italia Irredentia

other civil officials, and a full staff of secretaries and stenographers. With suitable ceremony the party was taken in automobiles to a château near General Diaz's headquarters. Here, after due deliberation and telegraphic communication with the Allied War Council then in session at Versailles, the terms of an armistice were agreed upon and signed.

This armistice marked the end of the Austro-Hungarian empire as the world has known it. It marked the final downfall of the House of Hapsburg, which all the world had long predicted could not stand the test of another European war. It restored to Italy all the territory which under the name of *Italia Irredentia* she had mourned as France mourned for Alsace-Lorraine. It demobilized the Austrian armies and surrendered the Austrian navy but this was of the least importance for there was left no longer an Austrian Imperial Government to direct the operations of either. Most important of all to the coming development and history of the world is the fact that this armistice set free several great peoples that had long been aspiring to independence and national self-determination. Czecho-Slavs, Poles, German-Austrians, Rumanians, Jugo-Slavs, and Hungarians had all been tied together in the bonds of the dual Empire, and

practically all had found those bonds burdensome. Now all were put at liberty to order their future national lives as they might see fit—or as the Peace Conference of the triumphant Allies might direct, which may possibly prove a very different matter. Of all these nationalities only one, the Czecho-Slavs, had taken such a part in the war as to draw from the established nations any official recognition of its national existence. Yet each of the others possesses enough of racial coherence persisting throughout past ages to justify it in insisting upon its right to form its own government and state. The Jugo-Slavs form perhaps the most numerous people, and the one whose claims are likely to arouse the greatest menace to the future peace of Europe. For their territorial aims clash inevitably with those of Italy, which the latter set up prior to her entrance upon the war, and acquiescence in which is believed to be part of the price the Allies promised to pay for her support. The Jugo-Slavs racially dominate Albania, Serbia, Montenegro, and the southern provinces of Hungary. Nearly 12,000,000 people are numbered in this race, all inhabiting regions so contiguous that they can well be erected into an independent state with borders that comply with natural physi-

Some Italian torpedo-boat destroyers lying in their docks. In this vital department of modern war the Italians are excelled by none

cal boundaries. But the aspirations of the Jugo-Slavs include the incorporation into their territory of the city of Trieste, and the long line of small islands along the eastern shore of the Adriatic known as Istria.

Trieste, as part of *Italia Irredentia*, has been marked by Italy for her own, and has doubtless been conceded to her by some agreement among the Allies that had not been made public at the close of the war. The Adriatic Islands, or at least a greater part of them, are claimed by Italy as necessary to her national protection. For they abound in harbors and in spots fitted for fortified naval bases while the Italian shore is low lying and with few of these necessary adjuncts to national development. It is the insistence of Italy that with the east shore of the Adriatic in the hands of a foreign power, her own shores are at the mercy of that power. A certain portion of the seacoast she is willing to leave to the proposed Jugo-Slav state that it may not be wholly cut off from the sea, but the greater part of the islands, even though their population is but to a slight degree Italian she proposes to hold for her own.

What may be the determination of the Versailles Peace Conference on this question cannot at this moment be determined. It is apparently the most difficult question affecting any of the new nationalities that is likely to arise. But there are other mooted points, arising from the Austrian *débâcle*, that may give trouble. Among these is the question of the future of the German sections of Austria. These provinces are almost as German as Germany itself and it has been due to the influence they exerted in the dual Monarchy, an influence very disproportionate to their population, that Germany was so long able to dominate that nation. Immediately upon the dissolution of the empire of the Hapsburgs it was suggested that these provinces should be incorporated with the new Germany. That would indeed be the logical disposition to make of them in a remaking of the map of Europe in a fashion designed to keep peoples of the same race under the same government. But the circumstances of the inception of this war no less than the manner of its prosecution and certain things attendant upon its conclusion made the world very suspicious of Germany. Amazing as it may seem after so bitter and costly an experience and so conclusive a defeat there were not lacking signs in the German attitude of a willingness to begin at once organizing for another attack upon civilization. All the work of the Peace Conference will be directed toward the end of making this impossible. But to enable Germany to annex from the ruins of Austria provinces that in wealth, population, material resources and military potentialities would more than make up for the loss of Alsace-Lorraine would be to strengthen rather than weaken the nation which is regarded with such grave suspicion. For this reason the German-speaking people of the late Austrian empire entered upon that conference with grave doubt as to what was to be their future in the family of nations.

It was accepted as a matter of certainty that in some fashion a new Polish nation would emerge from the ruins of present-day Europe. But how it should be created was a problem to puzzle the wisest. The Poles were a homogeneous, coherent race who at various periods in the world's history had possessed their own government and independent nationality. They constituted when the war began a considerable part of the population of Russia, Austria, and Germany, and any Polish state to be created would necessarily be taken from all three of these nations. But in creating a new Poland the proposed new Czecho-Slovak state, the only new nationality to which all the Allies were definitely committed would have to be drawn upon heavily, and the lines of demarkation between the two peoples would be difficult to draw.

The break up of Austria-Hungary more than any immediate outcome of the war precipitated upon Europe the decision of all these delicate and perplexing reorganizations of races, state boundaries and governments. For Austria-Hungary had been but a loosely bound bundle of rival peoples nearly all of which had fervently believed that they would be better off under some other rule. The long life, and the astute policy of Emperor Francis Joseph had been the tie that bound the whole together so long, and his death, in the fourth year of the great war, was looked upon everywhere as the certain precursor of national decomposition. His successor, the Emperor Karl, succeeded to a tottering throne and a hopeless war. Like the other absolute sovereigns of Europe he went down in defeat, and his abdication followed fast upon the armistice. Even before that the people in the principal cities were in open revolt against the further domination of the house of Hapsburg. Students and workmen in front of the Parliament building in Vienna denounced the Hapsburgs, and officers in uniform went about urging their fellows to remove their cockades and other badges of authority.

Kaiser Karl of Austria-Hungary with his Chief-of-Staff. This picture of the last ruler of the ancient, cunning, cruel, and once mighty House of Hapsburg was taken shortly before his downfall

CHAPTER X

WHILE the war was thus being lost irrevocably to the Teutonic alliance in the southeastern fields fighting was proceeding with its accustomed desperation in the theatre of France and Flanders. But it was to some degree a new sort of fighting. The old deadlock of the trenches was past and gone. A new and more mobile style of action had taken its place. To a great extent this was due to the perfection of the system of artillery preparation and the barrage which first cut down the barbed wire, then levelled the parapet of the trench, and finally made the remaining ditch untenable for those who would defend it. Even more instrumental in effecting this change in the character of the fighting were the so-called tanks which like land battleships could carry an advancing force unhurt up to the very line of a trench and, in cases, perch astride of it and rake its length in both directions with machine-gun fire. It took six or eight months of the war to bring trench warfare to perfection, and nearly three years more to devise a way of beating it. But the latter was accomplished before the American forces reached France in any great numbers. We like to think that it was the gallant impetuosity of our men that did away with the deadly monotony of the long deadlock between opposing trenches, but it

was in fact the British tank, and our men reached the scene of war just in time for the new style of warfare—to which indeed they showed themselves peculiarly adapted.

Examination of a map of the western theatre of war during any period after the initial rush of the Huns into France will show at the eastern end of the battle line a sharp triangle reaching into French territory with its eastern end at a little town called Pont-a-Mousson, on the German border just south of Metz, its apex at St. Mihiel; and the other leg of the triangle reaching off to the northwest behind Verdun. This salient had been created at the time of the initial invasion of France. It had persisted throughout the long and savage battles for Verdun. The French had repeatedly sought to iron it out but without avail. Now, as the railroads from the American bases on the channel ran directly toward that spot and as the largest American concentration camp was at Toul just south of the salient, it seemed to offer itself very prominently for American attention —and presently it received that attention.

In his official report General Pershing says that the reduction of the St. Mihiel salient had early been planned as the first independent American offensive action on a large scale. The disposition of troops in preparation for it began as early as August 30th, and before its completion entailed preparations which the General describes thus:

The preparation for a complicated operation against the formidable defenses in front of us included the assembling of divisions and of corps and army artillery, transport, aircraft, tanks, ambulances, the location of hospitals, and the molding together of all of the elements of a great modern army with its own railheads, supplied directly by our own Service of Supply. The concentration for this operation, which was to be a surprise, involved the movement, mostly at night, of approximately 600,000 troops, and required

Some American soldiers detailed to help operate a French tank under French officers

for its success the most careful attention to every detail.

A correspondent of the Chicago *Tribune* who was present during the preparation and the assault itself goes a little more into detail and some quotation from his description of the infinity of detailed preparation which precedes a modern battle will be of interest.

In order to take 152 square miles of territory and seventy-two villages, captured in the crushing of the St. Mihiel salient, the American Army first issued 100,000 detail maps covering in minutest detail the character of the terrain of the St. Mihiel salient, includ-

ing natural defenses, and telling how each was manned and by what enemy units. These maps were corrected in some instances as late as the day before the battle opened, and were supplemented by 40,000 photographs. These were for the guidance of the artillery and infantry, and were scattered among the officers of the whole army a few hours before the zero hour.

Five thousand miles of wire was laid in the St. Mihiel salient and on its borders before the attack, and immediately after the Americans advanced 6,000 telephone instruments were connected with these wires throughout the battle zone.

When the battle opened on the morning of September 12, 1918, trucks started northward at a speed of seven miles an hour, unreeling wires across No Man's Land until they reached points where the reels had to be carried by Signal Corps men afoot.

Such work made it possible for an American officer whose troops had flanked the foe's trenches to telephone back, informing the artillery of the exact location of the enemy trenches and in a few minutes bringing a deluge of metal on the Boche.

Telephone squads carried these lines up to the fighting front on Thursday morning and soon in the triangular battle ground there was a telephone system in operation that would have been adequate to handle the telephone business of a city of

An elaborately camouflaged tank ready to be felt but not seen

British Tommies on the Fampoux Road in France attracted by a stranded monster which tried to negotiate too big a ditch for even a tank

Some Yankees are serving with the British as members of the crew of this land battleship

100,000, and it was going at top efficiency. The branch lines were connected with the main axis, which was established through the middle of the salient. Ten thousand men were busily engaged in operating the system. Many of the phone exchanges were on wheels. Several thousand carrier pigeons supplemented the Signal Corps.

The kind of a tank which can wander over a shell crater as large as the excavation for a good-sized house without inconvenience

In the midst of the battle other Signal Corps men took more than 10,000 feet of movie film depicting war scenes and many thousands of photographs.

Extensive hospital facilities were arranged, including thirty-five hospital trains, 16,000 beds in the advanced areas, and 55,000 others farther back. Happily, less than 10 per cent. of the hospital facilities were needed, and therefore our surgeons and nurses were enabled to give the finest care to our wounded and sick, and every attention to the German wounded.

In the course of the operation our guns fired approximately 1,500,000 shells. Forty-eight hundred trucks carried men and supplies into the lines. They were assisted by miles of American railroads of standard and narrow gauge, and the cars were pulled by engines marked "U. S. A."

Formidable as all this preparation sounds it was more than justified by the facilities for defense possessed by the enemy. After the victory was won Thomas Johnson, a well-known American correspondent, went over the ground our boys had taken and describes its nature thus:

The French cemetery at Pont-a-Mousson which the Germans shelled during a memorial service, thereby killing and maiming many women and children

The further one goes the stronger becomes the impression of how strongly fortified was this whole place. It abounded in dugouts deep and strong and well built, while in all villages and many other places were the famous steel and concrete German pill boxes. American officers and soldiers were eating German food and drinking German beer in the captured dugouts.

To get the full flavor of the victory the best way is to go over the battlefield from our old front line starting at Seicheprey, where the Americans had their first real fight with the enemy last April. Passing Remières Wood on the right one rides through our old trenches, then goes into No Man's Land and across to Lahayville, Sainteaussant, and Richecourt—villages that thousands of Americans have looked at longingly since Jan. 18, when the first American force took over the sector facing them. One trip over the ground is enough to show that the defenses the Americans went up against here were as strong as those on the Somme, Chemin des Dames or any other famous battle sectors of the west front.

The greatest fortress of all was Montsec itself, and nothing that has ever been said about that solitary peak can convey an idea of how it dominated and looked down upon our old trenches around Seicheprey, Xivray, Beaumont, Rambucourt, Bouconville, and all those other towns that one is able now for the first time to name as having held the Americans ever since January. The only way to get an idea of it is to climb to the top of the Woolworth tower. It dominates New York no more than Montsec dominates its surroundings.

From there the Boche could see every single American who walked in the road or in a trench for ten miles on a clear day. That's not the only reason why Montsec

Major Hyatt of the American Army standing in the mine crater which the Germans exploded just too soon to kill several thousand Americans

A comparatively concealed battery position from which an American barrage fire suddenly burst upon the enemy

seemed a great goal. It was a symbol of the future, for they knew that when they could take it it would mean the time of the fulfillment of their promise had come. Seeing Montsec, one realizes what a veritable fortress it was, not only because of its steep wooded sides, but because of its dugouts, which were not really dugouts but subterranean chambers capable of holding thousands of men. They were made of steel, concrete, stone, mortar, brick, forty or fifty feet within the mountainside. Some built in 1915 are ornamented with the German coat of arms. They are littered with maps, papers, clothing, knicknacks, showing they were furnished in great comfort with beds, chairs, and pictures.

The Germans had four years to do it in. These dugouts, facing north and so difficult of observation by the Allies, had fine porches, pretty tables with a splendid view across to the Meuse heights, and it was there the German officers used to drink their beer. One of them had a hammock slung under the trees and another had an open air bath tub, but great gaps showed where our shells had crashed in upon them and one big dugout, by name "Villa Minna," had completely caved in. The occupants lay on their faces on the floor. In another dugout lay a dead German Officer, while beside him lay a dog silently watching his dead master. He wouldn't make a responsive sign to coaxing or whistling.

It took but thirty-six lines in General Pershing's final report to tell the story of the victory at St. Mihiel as its important phases appeared to the Commander-in-Chief. But the general reader will ask something more than this succinct summary that emanated from the mind of a soldier unused to writing, and who seemed to think that gallant fighting was all in the day's work:

After four hours' artillery preparation, the seven American divisions in the front line advanced at 5 A. M. on Sept. 12, assisted by a limited number of tanks manned partly by

A heavy gun "planted" and held in silence until the German defenses had been destroyed by an American barrage which the prisoners later described as the most terrifying and deadly they had ever known

These American soldiers and their horses are snatching a brief respite from the thrilling but exhausting occupation of chasing the fleeing Germans

Americans and partly by French. These divisions, accompanied by groups of wire cutters and others armed with bangalore torpedoes, went through the successive bands of barbed wire that protected the enemy's front line and support trenches, in irresistible waves on schedule time, breaking down all defense of an enemy demoralized by the great volume of our artillery fire and our sudden approach out of the fog.

Our 1st Corps advanced to Thiaucourt, while our 4th Corps curved back to the southwest through Nonsard. The 2d Colonial French Corps made the slight advance required of it on very difficult ground, and the 5th Corps took its three ridges and repulsed a counter-attack. A rapid march brought reserve regiments of a division of the 5th Corps into Vigneulles in the early morning, where it linked up with patrols of our 4th Corps, closing the salient and forming a new line west of Thiaucourt to Vigneulles and beyond Fresnes-en-Woevre. At the cost of only 7,000 casualties, mostly light, we had taken 16,000 prisoners and 443 guns, a great quantity of material, released the inhabitants of many villages from enemy domination, and established our lines in a position to threaten Metz. This signal success of the American First Army in its first offensive was of prime importance. The Allies found they had a formidable army to aid them, and the enemy learned finally that he had one to reckon with.

The American Army was disposed somewhat like a pair of pincers and right sharply did the enemy get pinched. One tip of the pincers was near Pont-a-Mousson, the other just south of Verdun on the Meuse. The pivot between the two was at St. Mihiel and

The famous church of Jeanne d'Arc standing on the commanding eminence of the solitary hill of Pont-a-Mousson, with a statue of Jeanne d'Arc on top of its steeple, which was shelled by the Germans all through the war, but never hit

The French fortress of Pont-a-Mousson on the Moselle River.   The peaceful and beautiful scene of desperate and hideous fighting

American military police guarding a German gas warning
station after the capture of Thiaucourt in France

each arm of the pincers was about ten miles long. After the artillery had made play for some four hours these two arms began coming together, not at all slowly but irresistibly. From one claw-tip to the other was about thirty miles.

It took two days to bring the two together, but it was accomplished and thereby about two hundred square miles of French territory was wrested from the Huns. When the closing movement began this bit of land had held about 100,000 of the enemy but he slipped away with all the speed he might. The hardest fighting took place on the southern leg of the salient, running northward toward Thiaucourt. The terrain there was low and marshy and the field before the advancing Americans was swept by fire from the French forts. The very hardest fighting occurred on the west side of the salient on a hillside called Les Esparges. This had been assaulted by the French repeatedly in the past but to no avail. Now after vigorous artillery preparation French and Americans together swept up the slope in a rush that never stopped until they had reached the top of a series of elevations that extended almost to St. Mihiel and that, because of its commanding height had been of the utmost strategic advantage to the Germans. Barbed wire, dense thickets of underbrush, and innumerable nests of machine guns had to be met and overcome, but the assailants were equal to all. The American artillery practice was credited with playing a great part in the victory. The hail of shells cut the barbed wire and mowed down the trees and bushes that impeded the path. It is not altogether gratifying to our national pride, however, to learn from General Pershing's report that while the gunners were ours the guns belonged to the French —we were not yet able to equip our troops with this most essential arm.

It may be doubted whether any victory of equal proportions during the great war was so speedily won. Within two days the Germans were driven out of the salient, while those who were slow to go had been captured. At one point a whole Hun regiment was surrendered in a body with all its officers, and to expedite matters, after the men had been relieved of their arms, the regiment was marched to the rear under command of its own chiefs, and with a few American cavalrymen riding alongside like stockmen riding herd. Everywhere were stacks of abandoned munitions and supplies. At one point a big American shell had exploded on a railway just in time to stop the progress of a retiring train with twenty-two cars loaded with machine guns, big guns, and ammunition.

bells, statues, water pipes, kitchen utensils were seized and sent back to Germany. And when they were finally whipped, and every responsible officer must have known that the war was ended, they fled destroying practically everything that they could not carry away. This was one of the reasons why American soldiers listened with cynical in-

The bust of Jeanne d'Arc on the front of this house was carved by a French soldier in a quarry at Thiaucourt within one thousand feet of the German lines

Unhappily no such fortunate shot stopped the thievish enemy carrying away loot. It is said that at few places along the battle-lines did the Germans give fuller play to their destructive and thievish proclivities than at Thiaucourt which they had occupied for four years. The banks had been plundered first by "requisitions" and at the last moment by the simpler process of breaking open their vaults and taking all that was there. Metal of every sort, church

difference to the cry for aid which the Germans set up twenty-four hours after the armistice was signed. The welcome of the liberated population of St. Mihiel to the incoming Americans, among whom was Newton D. Baker, Secretary of War, was one of the most pathetic spectacles of the whole long conflict.

With the St. Mihiel salient thus obliterated the work of the American armies did not slow up in the slightest degree. Before them to the north lay three objectives, each of great importance.   Within range of our great guns lay Metz, the rich and populous capital of Lorraine, and a German fortress of the highest rank.   Beyond Metz, only a few miles, were the coal fields of Briey, the real reason for the seizure of Lorraine by Prussia in 1871 and without the possession of which the great Krupp works and the German Army

A glimpse of what the Germans did to the noble cathedral of Arras

could not have been kept going throughout the war.   And straight up the valley of the Meuse lay Sedan, a mere village the fields about which had been the scene of the fatal defeat sustained by the French armies in 1870.   Its importance now lay in the fact that through it ran one of the chief railways connecting France with Germany.   With this railway cut one of the two great avenues for the supply of the German armies at the front would be closed, and one of the lines of retreat, should those armies meet with disas-

ter, would be shut upon them.   And off to the west the forces of our Allies, and our own men too, were pressing the Huns with such vigor that already they were in full retreat and their need for all the available routes back to the Fatherland was becoming very evident to them.   The importance of the American operations north of Verdun was sufficiently clear to the enemy, and our commanders were prepared to see the strongest German commands hurried to that point of danger, as indeed happened.   Of our initial advance General Pershing has this to report:

On the night of Sept. 25 our troops quietly took the place of the French who thinly held the line in this sector, which had long been inactive.   In the attack which began on the 26th we drove through the barbed wire entanglements and the sea of shell craters across No Man's Land, mastering all the first-line defenses.   Continuing on the 27th and 28th, against machine guns and artillery of an increasing number of enemy reserve divisions, we penetrated to a depth of from three to seven miles and took the village of Montfaucon and its commanding hill, and Exermont, Gercourt, Cuisy, Septsarges, Malancourt, Ivoiry, Epinonville, Charpentry, Very, and other villages. East of the Meuse one of our divisions, which was with the 2d Colonial French Corps, captured Marcheville and Rieville, giving further protection to the flank of our main body.   We had taken 10,000 prisoners, we had gained our point of forcing the battle into the open, and were prepared for the enemy's reaction, which was bound to come, as he had good roads and ample railroad facilities for bringing up his artillery and reserves.

In the chill rain of dark nights our engineers had to build new roads across spongy, shell-torn areas, repair broken roads beyond No Man's Land, and build bridges. Our gunners, with no thought of sleep, put their shoulders to wheels and drag-ropes to bring their guns through the mire in support of the infantry, now under the increasing fire of the enemy's artillery.   Our attack had taken the enemy by surprise, but, quickly recovering himself, he began to fire counterattacks in strong force, supported by heavy bombardments, with large quantities of gas.   From Sept. 28 until Oct. 4

American cavalry advancing to the capture of Thiaucourt

All that is left of a large and flourishing French railroad station in the war zone

British cavalry on the St. Poe-Arras Road

Germans used to bring in the wounded at an advan

British cavalry on the French front waiting in n

...ance resting after a long and hard ride

...ritish dressing station at the front in France

...racking idleness for the order to go forward to the attack

These loaves of bread were brought one morning by army truck to this desolate spot in the Argonne Forest. In a drenching rain they were thrown off in this pile for our doughboys

we maintained the offensive against patches of woods defended by snipers and continuous lines of machine guns, and pushed forward our guns and transport,

seizing strategical points in preparation for further attacks.

The Forest of the Argonne, in which the fiercest fighting of this period occurred was itself admirably fitted for defensive purposes. It was dense with underbrush, cut up by gullies and outcroppings of limestone ridges, with but few roads, dark and almost impenetrable. It is such a region as the Wilderness in which the armies of Grant and Lee grappled in our Civil War. Through it extended in sinuous and sinister course the western end of the famous Hindenburg line—the *Kriemhilde Stellung*, the Germans called this part of it, with an allusion to the Wagnerian opera. No ordinary defensive work was this, but a network of trenches, big and little, guarded in front by wire enough to fence in a whole nation, concreted, and provided with bombproof dugouts, some of which attained a degree of comfort amounting to luxury, thanks to the neighboring homes which the Germans had despoiled of the furniture and even pictures. Some had electric lighted tunnels reaching far back into the streets of a neighboring town whereby the defenders might go out to seek rest and amusement in safety. Much of the line was constructed of solid masonry, reënforced with bars of steel. The defenders had foreseen that their assailants

This is what happened to 360,000 of the homes of France

The four fighting sons of a fighting father—left to right: Archie Roosevelt talking to Theodore, Jr., at Plattsburg; Quentin
Roosevelt, who was killed in France (upper right) and Kermit Roosevelt marching at Plattsburg

would rely largely upon tanks in the attack and had made preparations for them. Walls were built across all roads of masonry sufficiently heavy to withstand even the forceful push of a tank. Traps dug deep in the earth were cunningly concealed by a surface layer that would give way immediately upon feeling the weight of a tank. Barbed wire was everywhere and back of this wire were machine guns innumerable that started up with their murderous crackle the instant the wire

gun from a tree on the other side of the wire. Then another and another, and twenty machine guns are going.

Their aim is poor, and their flashes give our rifles a chance. Our doughboys pile through that wire fence and through the underbrush and stack up against another fence ten feet farther on. The range has been telephoned back to the boche batteries and shells begin to fall all around.

They cut that barbed wire and then stumble on to concealed wire entanglements covered with brush. They climb these. All the time, from the dark, German snipers

The wreckage which was the French town of Vaux

was touched. And back of it all were not less than 350,000 of the best German troops whose numbers were steadily increased as the battle progressed.

The accounts of some eye-witnesses of this struggle may be fitly quoted to round out General Pershing's official account:

Turn your attention to the all-night fighting in the Argonne Forest, writes Edwin L. James, in the New York *Times*, and realize what our men are going through. It is raining and there is inky darkness. The boche is shelling heavily and pouring gas into all the valleys. Our men must travel on the hills. Those hills are being raked by thousands of German 77s.

The Americans in the advance hit the barbed wire. Rifles are slung across shoulders and pliers are pulled out. Busily our men cut wire after wire. The noise they make brings the nasty rat-a-tat of a Hun machine

and machine gun men, always with time enough to fall back, are taking their toll. Now our line comes upon a broad trench with more wire. In the dark our boys leap across it; some fall into it. Others get over at the first attempt and pull out their pliers to cut more wires.

All this time it is raining and cold, very cold. The inky blackness there in the forest is broken by streams of fire from machine guns and the intermittent flash of some German sniper, seeming to taunt the youthful Americans struggling against such devilish odds.

It takes stout hearts, it takes real men to stand this. But it was over two and a half miles of this sort of terrain that one American division tore its way through the Argonne Forest. This was the worst part. Farther on the wire was less frequent, and our men in the Argonne, having crashed through the Bois d'Apremont, are now reaching a zone where the roads are good, and the advance is easier.

Since the French tried vainly to take it in 1915 the

The spinning room of a weaving and spinning factory on the River Oise in France which was systematically ruined by the Germans because it was not convenient to steal it and take it to Germany

A sugar factory on the River Aisne in France deliberately destroyed by the Germans without the slightest military excuse

Germans had used the Argonne Forest as a rest area—a sort of recreation ground for their war-worn troops, and had built such defenses as they thought would defy all attempts frontally. For three years the Argonne has been a kind of pleasure resort for boche fighters. It is worth years of any one's life to see what they had built there on the pretty wooded slopes and through tangles of verdant beauty.

There were underground palaces with electric illumination and with hotel ranges to cook for the officers. On a slope just a mile back of the front line there is an

fight. Differing little in character from the earlier fighting it continued until October 10th when the wood was wholly cleared of the enemy.

It was during this period of the battle that occurred the incident of the "lost battalion" that stirred American emotions as did few occurrences of the war. A party of Americans,—largely "Yiddishers" from the east side of New York—led by Major Whittlesey,

American soldiers in the ruins of the town of Vaux in France

enormous cave fronting north. Its front was built of brownstone, on which had been chased pillars and other carvings. Above its big portals was the word "Offizierhaus," and above that an enormous iron cross. In this club there were a large dining hall and perhaps ten rooms. The inside was lined with concrete and wooden floors had been laid. At the dining table were mahogany chairs, filched from some nearby French château. Over the General's place hung an electric call bell, and electric lights were strung down the middle of the table. It represented the luxury of war. This was just one of hundreds and hundreds of these dug-in and scientifically made dwelling places.

The progress of the Argonne-Meuse offensive is divided by General Pershing in his report into three parts, and between his accounts of these he diverges to tell the story of the work of the Americans on the more western battle fronts. We may, however, proceed with the Argonne story to its completion. October 4th began what the general calls the second phase of the Argonne

had pressed onward into the depths of the forest until suddenly they found themselves out of sight or hearing of any of their fellows. This in itself was not extraordinary for the thickets were such as to make it difficult for supporting bodies to keep in touch with each other, but presently it was discovered that they were surrounded by Boches. A runner was sent back to tell of their plight, and curiously enough the commander to whom he reported proceeded to send him on to New York so that the first news that he had of the really desperate condition of his former comrades was when he reached home and the reporters came thronging about him with the story of the lost battalion.

Meantime efforts were being made to relieve the beleaguered battalion. Their position was well enough known to their friends, but so large a body of Germans had got in behind them, in a deserted trench that it seemed

Admiral Mayo, Commander of the Atlantic Fleet

Admiral Sims, who commanded the Overseas Naval Forces of
the U. S. in the World War

Major General O'Ryan, Commander of the 27th Division

Major General Lejeune, Commander of the Marines in France

Some doughboys and transport drivers in the Argonne Forest comparing notes on German trophies

Stragglers from many units organized into reserves which were sent forward in time to help counter-attack

"LAFAYETTE, WE ARE HERE"

© *Brown Brothers*

Marshal Joffre applauding the words of General Pershing at Lafayette's Tomb on the Fourth of July, 1917.
These simple words travelled instantly around the world and became imperishably famous

for a time impossible to get help to them. In all nearly 500 men were thus cut off, and the question of food soon became serious. Attempts to relieve them by attacks upon the enemy failed, but had value because they prevented the foe from annihilating the little band. Relief by air was tried. Fourteen airplane missions were sent out dropping

their fortunes seemed at the lowest ebb a blindfolded man appeared among them coming from the enemy's lines. He proved to be an American who had been taken prisoner and he bore a note reading:

"Americans, you are surrounded on all sides. Surrender in the name of humanity. You will be well treated."

Major Whittlesey hesitated not a moment.

"Go to hell," he cried in a voice so loud that the Germans hidden in the thickets must have heard him, while the men around cheered loudly even in their weakness. It might have been their death warrant they cheered, but it was not, for relief came in a few hours.

The third phase of the Argonne-Meuse struggle immediately preceded the German surrender and is thus described by General Pershing:

The bridge on the Marne at Château-Thierry. It was twice blown up and the river was choked with German dead

With comparatively well-rested divisions, the final advance in the Meuse-Argonne front was begun on November 1. Our increased artillery force acquitted itself magnificently in support of the advance, and the enemy broke before the determined infantry, which, by its persistent fighting of the past weeks and the dash of this attack, had overcome his will to resist. The 3d Corps took Ancreville, Doulcon, and Andevanne, and the 5th Corps took Landres et St. Georges and pressed through successive lines of resistance to Bayonville and Chennery. On the 2d the 1st Corps joined in the movement, which now became an impetuous onslaught that could not be stayed.

two tons of food and considerable ammunition at points where it was hoped they could be reached. Homing pigeons were also dropped by parachute in their lines so they could communicate with the main body. To a great degree all these efforts at relief had to be made by guess as the forest was so thick our aviators could see nothing of the missing men. A final and desperate attack on the enemy at last broke through and the men were saved on the brink of starvation. While

On the 3d advance troops surged forward in pursuit, some by motor trucks, while the artillery pressed along the country roads close behind. The 1st Corps reached Authe and Châtillon-Sur-Bar, the 5th Corps, Fosse and Nouart, and the 3d Corps, Halles, penetrating the enemy's line to a depth of twelve miles. Our large-calibre guns had advanced and were skillfully brought into position to fire upon the important lines at Montmedy, Longuyon, and Conflans. Our 3d Corps crossed the Meuse on the 5th and the other corps, in the full confidence that the day was theirs, eagerly cleared the way of machine guns as they swept northward, main-

© Underwood & Underwood

General Edwards bestowing the Congressional medal of honor upon Lieutenant Colonel Whittlesey who commanded the "Lost Battalion" in the Forest of Argonne

A bag of German prisoners taken by the Americans during the fighting of September, 1918. They would not look so contented
if they were treated as our men were treated when captured by the Germans

This is the road and the place where the American Marines first came into action against the onrushing German hordes
in their great drive toward Paris in the summer of 1918. The Marines held, and here started the great Allied offensive which
ended in victory.

taining complete co-ordination throughout. On the 6th, a division of the 1st Corps reached a point on the Meuse opposite Sedan, twenty-five miles from our line of departure. The strategical goal which was our highest hope was gained. We had cut the enemy's main line of communications, and nothing but surrender or an armistice could save his army from complete disaster.

Such is the comparatively cold and colorless account of what was in fact the most savagely fought battle of the war. Whether the enemy knew that his surrender was near at hand or not, he fought as though nothing were further from his mind. The menace that lay in the advance of the American Army upon his best line of retreat was very evident to him and he hurried to the threatened spot troops from every part of his battle line. From Flanders, from Cambrai, from St. Quentin they were brought, even while those places themselves were menaced by other Ally forces. General Pershing did not in anyway underestimate the strength of the force thus being aligned against him. His best troops were put into the advance and fresh divisions hurried up from the great camp at Toul as fast as motor lorries could carry them. Before the troops could get near the Mezieres-Sedan railroad, their first objective, the big guns began work upon it with a view to mak-

Brigadier General Douglas McArthur talking to a group of his boys of the famous Rainbow Division. The Division gained its name from the fact that the men came from a large number of different States

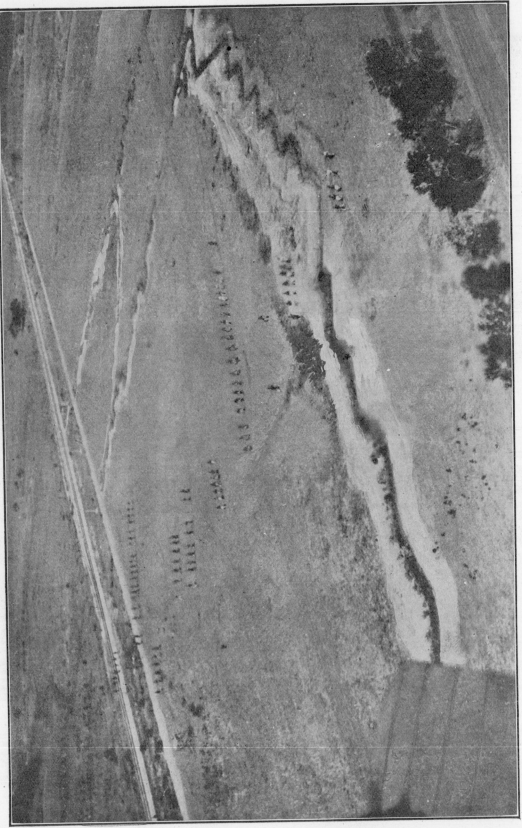

Wave upon wave of infantry following the attacking wave across No Man's Land to reinforce it

A breakfast of iron rations in the Forest of Malancourt, one of the fields which saw the hardest fighting between Dead Man's Hill and Montfaucon in France

ing it useless to the Germans. Great naval 14-inch guns had been brought by rail to the battlefield, and mounted on flat cars were pushed forward as fast as the lines were advanced. Blue-jackets from the American navy manned them and if those who stayed on the sailors' proper element failed to get a shot at the Boche afloat these land going gunners had plenty of opportunity to show their skill.

The rest of the story of the American push for Sedan is simply a record of steady progress, which in time developed into a complete piercing of the German lines and the pursuit of the enemy as he fled frantically for any sanctuary. It reached the point at last at which the Yankees mounted on huge trucks, shouting scores of them, dashed madly up roads and byways chasing down the retreating Huns. Sedan was in sight. On another part of our line Metz was so near that our great naval guns might have done for it what the German cannon had done for scores of picturesque Flemish towns, save that Americans had no desire to shine as vandals. One after another the foe's most cherished positions were taken. The volume of prisoners became so great as to be embarrassing. In six days from the beginning of General Pershing's third phase they had smashed the German Freya line, liber-

Colonel Edward M. House, President Wilson's adviser and one of America's five Commissioners to the Peace Conference

The barrage fire has just been lifted and these men are charging across No Man's Land to strike the enemy

ated hundreds of French villages and thousands of the French people on the bank of the Meuse, taken Sedan, cut the railroad and were fired with such confidence bred of these successes that nothing could have been asked of them which they would not have cheerfully undertaken.

Meanwhile in the battle sectors farther to the west Americans were playing their part, though not as single detached armies, with a definite task to be performed alone. They were with the British in the victorious attack upon Cambrai. They fought shoulder to shoulder with the French at Laon and at Conflans. They marched into Belgium with a portion of the Belgian Army, and thus gained the inestimable boon of being able to participate in person in the redemption of that martyred nation from the bondage she had incurred in the service of civilization. Ostende and Zeebrugge, badly smashed by the persistent work of the British Navy, had been occupied by the Belgian Army on October 20th, and the Germans began their retreat from the remainder of the country they had so barbarously misused. The Belgians and French followed fast upon their heels, whipping them on the Lys River, and

driving them out of Ghent. The British pushed over the border between Valenciennes and Tournai, and shortly thereafter captured the former town in an assault led by Canadian troops with notable gallantry. To the east of Valenciennes the field was left to the French under General Mangin who drove the fleeing Germans beyond the Belgian border, taking Mauberge, which before this war unsettled all military values had been esteemed one of the world's greatest fortresses. Still farther to the east the French and American lines were in liaison on the front between the Aisne and the Meuse. Here both of these allies were pushing forward indomitably with the foe recoiling before them, not in disorder but in hopeless retreat when suddenly from the General Headquarters came the message, not wholly welcome, to suspend all attacks as an armistice had been signed.*

At the moment the Germans were thoroughly beaten on every front. The morale of their armies had been shattered and although demoralization had not yet set in,

*A more detailed account of the operations of the Allied armies, as distinct from that of the United States will be found in "The Nations at War."

veteran military observers agree that had the campaign continued for another ten days the orderly retreat would have degenerated into a frantic rout and that the armies of the Kaiser would have been utterly destroyed.

The world hardly expected German surrender at that moment. The masses of the men fighting in the Allied armies certainly did not apprehend it, and if the general commanders knew they had held their peace. Everywhere it was expected that the Germans would hold out until winter might bring them a respite from the savage attacks of their enemies and a chance to recuperate and fight for better terms in the spring. But nothing that had been done by the German high command from the day of its precipitate entrance upon the war to this moment of sudden and ignominious surrender showed more cool, if ignoble, intelligence than this action. For the German fight was irrevocably lost. She was left without allies, the surrender of Austria-Hungary having opened a back door into her domain that she had no adequate means of closing. It was all very well to say that in earlier years campaigning had been stopped with the first sign of winter. But who could tell what these Americans would do? And they were coming over in such prodigious numbers despite all the figures of the German professors showing that they could never get enough ships to serve for their transport, and the promises of Von Tirpitz that his submarines would speedily dispose of them. Even if winter was to quiet things down there was still remaining at least six weeks before winter's arrival. Sorely pressed the German armies could feel no certainty of living out that six weeks. If they tried it the Americans in the Argonne were certain to prevent them from any possible escape in the hour of disaster. So the High Command that had so bravely ordained the crushing of little Belgium, and attempted the destruction of France, less by military

prowess than by treacherously violating a treaty, turned abject suppliants and begged like whipped children for the stoppage of hostilities.

The armistice which brought this greatest war of all ages to its end was not completed without prolonged diplomatic negotiation. Austria and Germany both turned to the United States in the moment of their extremity, thinking probably that they had less to fear from this nation than from any of the other belligerents toward whom they had been guilty of the most indescribable barbarity and savagery. It was a distinction accorded us by the world's greatest criminal which most Americans would have been glad to have escaped. However, the position of first recipient of the Huns' plea for mercy was ours whether desired or not. In the course of a world-wide discussion of the purposes of the war President Wilson had enun-

General Tasker H. Bliss, one of the five American Peace Commissioners

ciated Fourteen Points on which he said the United States would insist. Austria opened the peace negotiations by proclaiming her willingness to accept these conditions and asking for an armistice that peace in accordance with them might be discussed. Germany speedily followed suit, and, upon the suggestion of the President that the German government had shown itself to be one with which no nation could treat with any confidence, declared that the form of that government had been amended in a way to make it more nearly coincide with the democratic principles which the President sought to establish, and that the men guilty of the long record of perfidy which had sullied Germany's annals had been deprived of power. How far this plea was in accord with fact is yet to be established. But after due submission of the German propositions to an Allied War Council sitting at Versailles, terms of an armistice were prepared and submitted to the German Government. In this council Col. Edward M. House and General Tasker H. Bliss represented the United States.

Meantime the work of the armies continued with unremitting vigor. All the time the council was holding its sessions our soldiers in the Argonne Forest, on the bank of the Meuse, around Conflans and Laon and on the Freya Line were pushing their attacks and meeting with uninterrupted success. Our allies were gaining at every point and the demoralization within the German lines was spreading daily. There are not lacking those that hold that the granting of the armistice was premature and unfortunate, and that a fortnight more

General Liggett and General Edwards on the battlefield of Château-Thierry. Evidently this was not a serious moment

of war would have done more for future peace, by utterly crushing present German strength, than can any provisions to be made by the final peace conference, however drastic the latter may be.

But there was no desire for delay in the German ranks. Promptly on learning that they would be received the German delegates, two Generals and an Admiral in uniform, and two civilians representing the government crossed the lines under protection of a white flag and sought General Foch's headquarters. They were received with chill courtesy, and the conditions of a truce were read to them by the Marshal himself. Neither amendment, nor even debate was permitted. The Germans might take what was offered, or go back to continue the fighting. For the latter they had no stomach, and, facing the presence of defeat and knowing that delay would add only to the severity of the terms, while perhaps resulting in the devastation of their own country as they had devastated France and Belgium they surrendered. At eleven o'clock on the morning of November 11th— the eleventh hour, of the eleventh day of the eleventh month— the signatures of the German Delegates were attached to the terms of the armistice and the four years of piracy, murder, theft, and rape which the Teutonic nations had prosecuted and called war ended in ignominious surrender. Within a few hours the Kaiser was a fugitive seeking refuge in Holland, to be followed by his eldest son, the degenerate Crown Prince and the government of Germany had gone down before a revolutionary movement the end of which it is impossible now to foresee.

CHAPTER XI

THE NAVY IN THE WAR—ITS RAPID GROWTH—THE GREAT TRAINING CAMPS—
THE DESTROYERS—LOSSES OF FIGHTING SHIPS—THE AVIATION CORPS—
THE FLEET IN THE NORTH SEA—THE FIGHTING MARINES—SURRENDER OF
THE GERMAN FLEET

IN ONE great respect the Great European War was a surprise to all observers. Though in it from the first were engaged as antagonists the two greatest naval powers of the world, no decisive sea battle was fought and the naval activities of the hostile battle fleets were confined in the main to keeping careful watch upon each other. The world can hardly tell yet what estimate the German people are putting upon the quality of their navy which, after long years of boasting of what it intended to do did in fact surrender ultimately without a fight. It is probable that nothing contributed more to getting the German Empire and Great Britain into a position that compelled war than the mad desire of the Kaiser for sea-power. When he first declared to his people "Our future is upon the sea," and began the construction of a mighty navy he challenged Great Britain as she had never been challenged before. And when he curtly rejected the diplomatic suggestion of a British ministry for a limitation of naval armaments, and instead began a race of naval construction he virtually served notice upon the British, long before any specific cause for a clash arose, that at some time he intended to contest Britannia's rule of the waves.

All the world knew for years before the outbreak of war of the regular function in the ward rooms of German men-of-war at which a toast was riotously drunk to "Der Tag," meaning thereby the day on which a German fleet should give battle to one under the white ensign of St. George. All the world found it hard to believe, until a certain misty morning off the Firth of Forth in December, 1918, that all this after-dinner lust for combat would end in abject surrender. But so it was. The war tested to the fullest the value of the British Navy. It showed the worth of our own in many ways. But it did not in its entire course put the actual fighting power of the ships of either to the supreme test because they confronted a foe who was quite willing to take the opinion of naval statisticians that he was hopelessly outclassed and let it go at that, without an effort to try the matter out by gage of battle. For him the sneaking submarine and finally the supine surrender.*

When the war storm broke upon a terrified world the United States and Germany were regarded as about equal in naval strength. Some of the harsher critics of our state of naval unpreparedness insisted that we lagged far behind the nation, in which only a few at that time thought we were likely to find a foe. Instantly upon her embroilment Germany, of course, began building new ships, how many or of what character it was impossible to learn during the progress of the conflict. And as the United States hardly woke up to the imminence of her own entrance upon the conflict before she was fairly in, it happened that we rushed into armed conflict with a nation which was superior to us afloat, and immeasurably so ashore. But we had the British Navy as ally and it alone was

---

*The story of the naval operations of the war prior to the entrance of the United States is told in the "Nations at War"

The American Atlantic fleet on the high seas. The ships are the *Wyoming*, *Nevada*, *Utah*, *Oklahoma*, *Florida*, *Arkansas*, *New York*, *Texas*, *South Carolina*, and *Michigan*

sufficient to keep the capital ships of the Kaiser in their sanctuaries.

This was a situation not at all to the liking of our naval officers. A war without a battle was not a pleasing prospect to men of the service that produced Paul Jones, Farragut, and Dewey. For them were eighteen months of the most wearying, nerve-racking service imaginable without the stimulating excitement of battle, and in nearly all cases with the foe unseen, but doubly dangerous for that reason. For the fight upon the undersea boats the men of the United States Navy had been

© International Film Service

American destroyer patrolling the North Sea

© Kadel & Herbert

The forecastle of the U. S. S. *Missouri* showing shells ready for the 12-inch guns

eager ever since that day in October, 1916, when American destroyers tied from truck to keelson in the bonds of a pale neutrality were forced to ride idly on the surges of the Atlantic off Newport and watch the German submarine *U-53* destroy one after the other six ships, two of them neutral and one having Americans on board. All that our bluejackets could do at that moment was to rescue the survivors. But the wrath and indignation which our men were then forced to suppress found ample expression later, for every officer on the watching squadron of destroyers then became active in the warfare upon the under-sea vipers of the German Navy. For, indeed, the first squadron to be sent abroad by our Navy Department was one made up entirely of destroyers. It reached Queenstown on May 13th and upon reporting to Admiral Bayley of the British Navy the commander was asked "how soon can you be ready for business?"

Supplies being taken aboard an American battleship just before her sailing for the war zone in Europe

First among the duties that the navy had to perform was the furnishing of trained gunners for American merchant ships. This work was begun even before the declaration of war, and put a heavy strain on a small navy none too well provided with marksmen. The larger merchant ships were furnished with two guns, usually 4-inch calibre, mounted fore and aft. Many instances of successful resistance to submarines were reported, but the nature of the submarine boat made it difficult to tell just how successful the armed merchantmen had been in actually destroying these pests. One of the first of these combats was between the freighter *Mongolia* and an unknown submarine in the war zone. The freighter was unusually well armed, carrying three guns, two of them 4-inch and one 6-inch, and a naval crew of nineteen men. The "sub" was sighted dead ahead lying in such a position that she could not effectively launch her torpedo. Before the *Mongolia*'s guns could be brought into action the enemy sunk gently from sight,

"We can start at once, sir," was the answer. There was some surprise on the part of the British officer, to whom explanations were made that all preparations for active service had been made in the course of the voyage across. As a matter of fact, however, it was found that one quite essential preparation had been overlooked. The American Navy had always been a warm weather navy, the ships going south for fleet practice as soon as winter set in. When assigned to duty in the chill waters of the North Sea our men were found to be entirely destitute of suitable clothing, and were obliged to solicit the friendly aid of the British in procuring it for them. Hereafter our navy will be fit to serve anywhere as its vessels have been on duty all the way from Pola, on the Arctic Sea, to the southern extremity of the South American continent.

and thereupon all hands turned to scanning the waters for a sign of her reappearance. Soon the periscope broke water, and almost instantaneously the 6-inch gun spoke. There was a great up-rush of splinters amid the geyser of water where the shell struck, and as the *Mongolia*, at full speed ran over the point at which the periscope had been, in hope of ramming the boat, a great patch of oil, and débris on the surface told of disaster to the unseen enemy. It was never easy to tell with certainty whether or not a submarine had received its fatal stroke, but in this instance the record was thought to be unquestionable.

It is worth noting that the navy men who served as gunners on our ships prior to the declaration of war took an added risk because of the German contention that they were in irregular service and not entitled to the

Stocking the American fleet with every kind of provisions and supplies before its departure for the war zone in Europe

The American submarine squadron, the advance guard of the Atlantic fleet, lying at anchor in the Hudson River at the time of its review by the President, just before starting for the war. They sailed for Europe a month after we declared war

The U. S. merchant ship, *Philadelphia*, with her stern gun and her gun crew ready for self-defense during the brief period of our armed neutrality before we entered the war

treatment accorded to prisoners of war if captured. Already a British merchant sailor, Captain Fryatt, who had gallantly defended his ship against torpedo attack had been put to death by the Huns when captured, and our own men had this possibility to consider every time they went into action. But the thought never deterred them nor as a matter of fact did the enemy ever repeat in the case of one of our men the inhuman act of which they had been guilty in the case of Captain Fryatt.

As the greater part of the service of the American Navy throughout the war was in the campaign against the submarines it will be worth while to give some account of the methods and results of this service before taking up the work of the larger units.

All the vessels on foreign station, and not a few scattered up and down our own coast, were detailed on this service. The torpedo patrols were made up in the main of two types of craft—the regular destroyers, and converted yachts, or swift power boats built especially for the purpose. The latter were significantly enough called the

Loading a torpedo on to the American submarine *K-5*

The converted yacht, *Druid*, the first armed merchantman to leave this country in conformity with President Wilson's policy of armed neutrality. She sailed for Cuba with a rapid fire gun forward

"Suicide Fleet," although in the end no dire disaster attended their record to give aptness to the phrase. Nevertheless the yacht *Alcedo* while escorting a convoy off the French coast was torpedoed and twenty of her crew were killed or wounded. The submarine that launched the torpedo came to the surface to inquire the name of the ship she had destroyed, but submerged again without manifesting any interest in the fate of the survivors who floated in an icy sea for fifteen hours before being rescued.

In December, 1917, the destroyer *Jacob Jones* encountered a submarine which let fly a missile striking the American directly amidships, and abreast of a fuel oil tank. In eight minutes the ship went to the bottom. All the boats and rafts were launched that time would permit, but the ship went down so speedily that the commanding officer ran along the decks ordering the men to leap overboard and trust to being picked up by the boats already in the water. Two men were picked up by the submarine which came to the surface long enough to gaze on the destruction it had wrought, then disappeared with its captives.

Considering, however, the dependence the Germans placed upon submarine warfare and the extent to which they had developed this branch of their navy the United States suffered but little from submarine attack. Not

© Underwood & Underwood

The fire room of a battleship where some of the hardest and most patriotic work was done during the war

American destroyers escorting a convoy across the Atlantic during the war. Not one American soldier was lost on an American transport on the way to Europe

Lieut. Bruce Richardson Ware, Jr., in charge of the gun crew on the *Mongolia* which sank a German submarine on April 19, 1917

one American troopship on the way to France was torpedoed, and but three in all were lost from this cause—the *Antilles*, *President Lincoln*, and *Covington*, all of which were sunk on the return voyage. Besides the *Alcedo* and *Jacob Jones* the only fighting ships lost were the cruiser *San Diego*, sunk by a mine off Fire Island, and the coast guard cutter *Tampa* which was lost with all on board, 111 officers and men, in Bristol Channel. The collier *Cyclops* vanished utterly from the face of the waters and nothing has ever been learned of its fate.

The actual losses to our navy were most gratifyingly small when the number of our men engaged in naval service is considered. We had in commission not less than 2,000 craft of every sort, while naval aircraft plied the skies, and marines and shore parties of blue-jackets were engaged in the most hotly fought battles of the European fronts. The navy's 14-inch guns were

dragged from the coast to the Argonne, and with their seamen crews took part in the victorious battles there. As for what the Marines did that has already been told in the story of the battles of Belleau Wood, Château-Thierry, and the Argonne.

When the declaration of war upon Germany

A torpedo just starting on its deadly errand

A fleet of transports on their way to France at the time our "ocean ferries" were carrying over more than three hundred thousand men a month

© Committee on Public Information

U. S. S. Vidette. Converted yacht used as submarine patrol and convoying ships along the French coast and in the English Channel

was signed the total personnel of the navy amounted to 65,777 men; the day the armistice was signed it had increased to 497,000 men and women, for in the clerical work ashore women were enlisted with the grade of yeowomen and served efficiently thoughout the war. A patriotic feature of the navy's rapid growth was the rapid increase in the number of Naval Volunteers, the organization which in war time supplanted the old Naval Militia. At the time the war ended more than 290,000 young men had voluntarily offered themselves for this service.

To train this enormous body of men, to supply properly equipped officers, and to furnish seamen as they were needed not only for the navy but for the great merchant marine which we were determined to establish, was a task of no small proportions. The educational section of the Navy Department became one of the great features of American life. In almost every college was a school for naval instruction, and at countless places were schools for certain specialized features of naval service. Just north of Chicago the Great Lakes Training Station that had been established for some years with a capacity

© International Film Service

The *Henley*, torpedo boat destroyer, just before she made her fine war record

View from the mast-head of an American transport unloading her cargo at American built docks in France

for training 6,000 seamen was swiftly enlarged so as to take care of 40,000—and the whole 40,000 were there with considerable pressure for places for more. Another station of like capacity was at Pelham Bay on the northern border of Greater New York. In all these schools the utmost care was given to the enrolled men. Their health, their comfort and their morals were all watched over with the utmost solicitude, and their pleasures were not neglected. They had their own bands and theatrical com-

panies, their athletic teams and their social organizations. To many boys it furnished the joy in youth which college life gives to those

This shell fired by the Germans at this British torpedo boat didn't hit anything except the ocean

Lookout in crow's nest of the skeleton mast of a U. S. cruiser anxiously scanning the waters during the war

foreign aviators, or at best upon Americans flying foreign machines for this vital service to a modern army. It may, perhaps be as well to dismiss here the whole matter of American aviation during the war. Although the airplane is distinctly an American invention, owing its inception to the vision of Professor Langley, of the Smithsonian Institution and its perfection to the Wright Brothers, our nation lagged far behind in the construction of successful war flyers. Our appropriations for this purpose were prodigious, our preliminary boasting of what we intended to do was

who are fortunate enough to enjoy it. Not all, perhaps only a small fraction of those who had this training, saw actual service in the navy. How many will make their way into the merchant marine it is yet too early to say. But it is certain that no youth who was fortunate enough to put in the prescribed time at one of the training camps failed to gain there something of value in the formation of character and a serviceable training for whatever walk in life he might later elect.

The navy also had its aviation service. According to the report of the Secretary for 1918 there were incorporated in this branch of the service 828 naval aviators, while about 2,052 student officers, and 400 ground officers with about 12,000 enlisted mechanics were under training at the various aviation camps. Neither in the flying service attached to the navy nor in that department of the army did the United States win much glory for itself. The delay in the construction of machines necessarily led to delay in the training of aviators. In the hotly contested battles of St. Mihiel and the Argonne our troops were obliged to rely upon

The *K-5*, one of the newest and most powerful submarines in the U. S. Navy, going at full speed

A scene on board the *President Lincoln* shortly before she was sunk. Every soldier has his life preserver on and is ready for the then unexpected catastrophe

An American cruiser helping the British Navy in its tireless patrol of the North Sea during the war

An American battleship in the act of firing an enormous torpedo

The fourteen-inch guns on board the U. S. S. *Texas* warming up for the Germans

© Brown & Dawson

Firing a thirteen-inch disappearing gun at one of our coast fortifications. You will note the gunners are protecting their ear drums against the fearful concussion

nauseating, our actual accomplishment was contemptible. Earlier in the war the very flower of our youth had formed the Lafayette Escadrille to fight in the air for France. When the United States came into the war every possible obstacle was put in the way of such of these gallant youths as still lived and desired to enter the service of their own country. In the greater work of supplying the necessary machines the country

failed abjectly. To some extent this was probably due to the failure to create a single responsible head for the aviation service. It was divided between the army and navy departments and neither Secretary was willing to sacrifice his share of the power to the creation of an absolutely new department. As a result the war ended with the achievements of the United States in the air trivial, while about the expenditure of hundreds of millions

Nets protecting an important harbor on the New England coast during the war

The fourteen-inch guns on the *Arizona*. Some naval guns such as these were landed in France and used with great effect in the Argonne

of dollars for no perceptible results there hung an atmosphere of scandal which had not been cleared away when the Germans had been cleared out of France.

But to recur to the navy:

The greatest fact of the war was the marvelous increase in the size of the fleet. When war was declared the United States had 197 ships in commission; in December, 1918, there were 2,003. Many of these were of course converted merchantmen, for modern men-of-war are not built in a few weeks—a fact which it is hoped Congress will remember hereafter. But yards all over the United States were busy building destroyers, the type of ship which it was evident would be most serviceable in this war. Ninety-three ships of this class and 29 submarines were launched in 1918. The destroyers were used not only on patrol work but in convoying troopships and other craft necessary to the maintenance of our armies in Europe. Not only did we carry 2,000,000 men across the ocean to fight for democracy but we had to maintain a steady procession of ships over and back carrying the huge quantities of provisions and ammunition needed to maintain them in the field of action. Not all of this work was done by United States ships of course. A little more than half of our army was transported under the British flag. But the convoying ships

were almost all American cruisers and destroyers.

In supreme command of our American naval forces in European waters was Admiral Sims, while Rear Admiral Rodman commanded the battleships serving with the British Fleet, Vice Admiral Wilson the naval forces in France and other rear admirals were in command of minor operations.

Commanding a battleship squadron with an enemy who persistently avoids battle is a task which may well grate on the nerves of a navy sailor. But Admiral Rodman's report of the operations of his fleet makes it clear that if there was a lack of the perils of battle there was a plethora of hardships and of nervous strain.

"There was no liberty or leave worth mentioning; no one allowed away from the ships after dark, nor for a period longer than four hours and then only in the immediate vicinity of the ship, in signal or telephonic communication subject to recall."

If there was no great battle there was ever present danger.

In our operations in the North Sea we were frequently attacked by submarines and our battleships had numerous escapes often only by prompt and skilful handling. On one occasion a submarine rammed the flagship *New York*, dented the bottom and demolished the starboard propeller. But there is every reason to

The great collier *Cyclops* which was lost at sea during the war

A mine layer tied up to the dock waiting to take on a load of the mines lying on the deck

Recruits who have just arrived at the Naval Training Station at Newport, R. I.

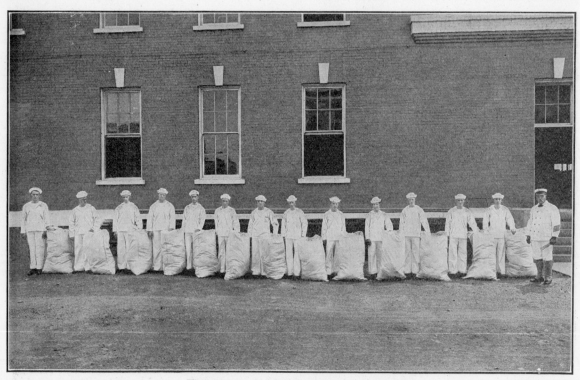

The same recruits one hour after their arrival

Recruits standing at attention in squad formation on their second day at the Newport Naval Training Station

Recruits formed in a company square. This formation is used particularly in quelling riots or civil disturbances of any kind

believe that the blows from the propeller sank the submarine. En route to dry dock, and to make repairs and instal a new propeller three torpedoes in rapid succession were fired at her by hostile submarines, but again she avoided them by rapid clever manœuvring and escaped. Once when guarding or supporting a convoy of thirty or forty vessels on the coast of Norway in midwinter a bunch of hostile "subs" fired six torpedoes at us. Again only our vigilance and instantaneous manœuvring saved us, but by a very close margin.

Some idea of the hardships to which the men of the fleet were exposed may be derived from this paragraph from Admiral Rodman's statement:

It would be superfluous to go into the details of our

lance of the whole fleet to put to sea on all but instant notice.

One branch of the United States Navy, however, saw plenty of fighting ashore while the bluejackets afloat were eating out their hearts in vain waiting for the enemy to offer battle. This force was the United States Marine Corps, an ancient branch of the service, members of which like to recall that historically it existed even before the Navy Department was organized. In an earlier chapter the work of the Marines in France has been described. Some facts drawn from the report of the Secretary of the Navy will be

© N. G. Moser

The crew of a five-inch gun on the Flagship *Pennsylvania* rehearsing for their hoped-for shot at the German fleet

operations in the North Sea, or to mention the rigorous climate, when the latitude is north of Sitka, in Alaska, or about equal to that of Petrograd, in Russia; or the terrific weather, the cold, sleet, snow, ice and heavy seas; the arduous and dangerous navigation, the continuous cruising in close formation at high speed, without lights, where the winter nights lasted eighteen hours, or the dangers of mine fields—our own, sometimes, as well as those of the enemy—or the repeated attacks of hostile submarines on our battleships, before mentioned, and the never ending readiness and vigi-

of interest as showing further how great a part this corps d'elite played in the brief participation of the United States in the World War.

The Marines were not a large body. Only 8,000 of them took part in the battles in France and of that 8,000 there were killed 69 officers and 1,531 enlisted men, while 78 officers and 2,435 men were wounded badly enough to have their hurts reported by cable. A casualty list aggregating nearly fifty per cent. of the men engaged is something seldom seen in war and speaks volumes for the fighting character of the Marines, whom their enemies came to call "devildogs" in recognition of their daring.

It is not usual for the head of a great executive department of the government to set forth in his annual report anything except the most matter-of-fact account of the work done by those under his authority, but Secretary of the Navy Josephus Daniels honored the Marine Corps by a graphic and stirring

Sergeant in command; but the attack did not falter. At 9:45 o'clock that night Bouresches was taken by Lieutenant James F. Robertson and twenty-odd men of his platoon; these soon were joined by two reinforcing platoons. Then came the enemy counterattacks, but the Marines held.

In Belleau Wood the fighting had been literally from tree to tree, stronghold to stronghold; and it was a fight which must last for weeks before its accomplishment in victory. Belleau Wood was a jungle, its every rocky formation containing a German machine-gun nest, almost impossible to reach by artillery or grenade fire. There was only one way to wipe out

American naval aviators learning their dangerous trade on Lake Michigan

account of its service, and we think, honored himself by abandoning in such a cause the traditional official restraint to give proper expression to the admiration the work that these soldiers of the sea aroused. A short quotation must suffice here:

The Marines fought strictly according to American methods—a rush, a halt, a rush again, in four-wave formation, the rear waves taking over the work of those who had fallen before them, passing over the bodies of their dead comrades and plunging ahead, until they, too, should be torn to bits. But behind those waves were more waves, and the attack went on.

"Men fell like flies," the expression is that of an officer writing from the field. Companies that had entered the battle 250 strong dwindled to 50 and 60, with a

these nests—by the bayonet. And by this method were they wiped out, for United States Marines, bare chested, shouting their battle cry of "E-e-e-e-e y-a-a-h-h-h yip!" charged straight into the murderous fire from those guns, and won!

Out of the number that charged, in more than one instance, only one would reach the stronghold. There, with his bayonet as his only weapon, he would either kill or capture the defenders of the nest, and then swinging the gun about in its position, turn it against the remaining German positions in the forest. Such was the character of the fighting in Belleau Wood; fighting which continued until July 6, when after a short relief the invincible Americans finally were taken back to the rest billet for recuperation.

The time came when the great gray ships that had lurked so long behind the stronghold

German sailors on the dock at Wilhelmshaven learning how to wig wag.   In the background is the *Westfahlen*, taken by the mutineers in the first mutiny in the German Navy

© Underwood & Underwood

Admiral Meurer of the German Navy is here stepping on board Admiral Sir David Beatty's flagship to arrange the terms of the surrender of the German High Seas Fleet

of Heligoland, or in the ramparted fastnesses of Kiel or Wilhelmshaven were to come out, without flags, stripped of ammunition and with their great guns turned inward to make abject surrender to the navies of the triumphant allies. They were given up without a fight, and to more than one of the officers who received the surrender that seemed worse than defeat itself. Defeat on land had forced upon the Germans this surrender by sea. But if to the tars of our navy it seemed that they were reaping the glory won by soldiers ashore let it be remembered that among those soldiers, the most timely in their victories were the amphibious men of the Marine Corps.

The surrender of the German fleet was provided for in the terms of the armistice dictated by General Foch. Much has been written of it, for this abject surrender of a powerful fleet unscarred by battle was both pathetic and picturesque. But perhaps best of all men to judge its significance was Admiral Hugh Rodman, who was present as commander of the American battleship fleet. With the quotation of a part of his description of the scene this brief study of the part of the United States navy in the World War may well be ended:

And so, after four years of war for the Grand Fleet, and after we had been a part of it for the last year, there came the débâcle, the last scene of the great drama. Not as we had all expected, as the successful termination of a great sea battle, but as an ignominious surrender without firing a gun.

Surely no more complete victory was ever won, nor a more disgraceful and humiliating end could have come to a powerful and much-vaunted fleet as that which came to the German High Seas Fleet. Let me try to describe it to you.

The Commander-in-Chief of the Grand Fleet demanded and received what actually amounted to an unconditional surrender of the whole German navy. Under his orders, the enemy's ships were disarmed, ammunition landed, torpedo war heads sent ashore, breech blocks and fire-control instruments removed and every offensive utility rendered innocuous.

Then with reduced crews, under the command of a German Admiral, in one long column, the heavy battleships leading, the Hun fleet sailed for a designated rendezvous, to arrive at a specified time just outside of the Firth of Forth in Scotland, where the Grand Fleet lay at anchor.

Before daylight the Grand Fleet was under way and proceeded to sea, heading east, in two long columns, six miles apart, our American battleship force being in the middle of the northern line. A light British cruiser was directed to meet the Germans who were heading west, and conduct them in between our two columns.

Here let me diverge for a moment and recall to the minds of any of you who have been in China or the Philippines the viciousness and antipathy which the domesticated carabao has for a white man. How ready they are to attack, while any native child can, with perfect safety and impunity, go up to the most

Painted by S. J. Woolf

Closely in the wake of the Allied armies as they advanced into Russia came the Red Cross with food and clothing, condensed milk for the babies, medical supplies, and all the things desperately needed by the Russian people.

On board the battleship *New York* at the time of the surrender of the German High Seas Fleet. King George does not seem depressed by the event. Left to right: Admiral Sir David Beatty, Admiral Rodman, King George, the Prince of Wales, and Admiral Sims

The German High Seas Fleet in the North Sea steaming to the rendezvous on the day of the great surrender. The picture was taken from the British destroyer *Seymour* while on her way to the historic scene at the rate of 30 knots an hour

The crews and officers of German submarines with their fangs pulled, on the day of the greatest naval surrender in history

German submarines, harmless at last, lying at anchor and out of commission in the harbor at Harwich, England

© Western Newspaper Union

The Kaiser reviewing his fleet at Kiel. This was when he still thought that "Germany's future lies upon the sea"

savage of them, take them by the nose and lead them where he pleases.

And so I was reminded of this when a little British cruiser rounded-to ahead of the much vaunted German High Seas Fleet and hoisted the signal, 'Follow me,' and led them down between our columns, where our battle flags were mastheaded, turrets trained toward the enemy, crews at battle stations, and all in readiness for any act of treachery that might be attempted.

At a prearranged signal our forces swung symmetrically through 180 degrees, and still paralleling the enveloped Germans, conducted them into a designated anchorage in the entrance of the Firth of Forth. Then came a signal from the Commander-in-Chief to the surrendered fleet: "At sundown lower your colors and do not hoist them again without permission." Surely no greater humiliation could have befallen them after their frequent and taunting boasts and threats.

There is little else to be told. After an inspection by British and American officers to gain assurance that the ships were disarmed, they were sent in groups, under guard, to Scapa Flow, in the cold, dreary, bleak, God-forsaken harbor in the Orkneys, where the Grand Fleet had spent many a dreary month and year, waiting like ferocious dogs in leash, watching and waiting, to pounce on the German Fleet should the opportunity ever occur.

Here the Germans now lie at anchor, in long lines, helpless, innocuous, harmless; their sting and bite removed, their national colors lowered for good and all as a token of submission to their masters. Corralled like wild and cruel beasts that have been hobbled and emasculated, guarded by a single division of battleships.

Our mission has been successfully accomplished; the German Fleet is a thing of the past; the seas are safe and free to our own and our Allies' ships. The value of sea power could have no better demonstration.

CHAPTER XII

IMMEDIATELY after the conclusion of the armistice began the work of carrying out its provisions. First of these was the evacuation by the enemy of those parts of France and Belgium in which his forces had been established. This was in fact the mere continuation of the general retreat which was in progress when the armistice silenced the thunders of our pursuing guns. But while the Huns would have been driven out, even had they not sued for peace, it is certain that their retirement in the face of a pursuing enemy would have been accompanied by those methods of devastation of territory, and barbarous oppression of the people which the Germans had shown themselves so well able to practice.

From this the armistice saved the portions of allied territory still in enemy hands. To many Americans, and to even more French and British, that capitulation seemed premature and its terms too mild to be applied to a piratical and savage foe. But as yet the world does not know to what extent it was hastened by apprehension lest the Germans, retreating under fire, should inflict upon the great Belgian cities held by them— Ghent, Bruges and Brussels—the same sort of devastation which had obliterated St.

Quentin and Ypres from the face of the earth, and reduced Rheims and other French towns to masses of ruins. As it was, while the terms of the armistice prohibited further destruction, the retreating Huns robbed without restraint the people of every community that had been cursed by their presence. Never in the history of warfare in the last three hundred years at least, has the spoliation of conquered peoples been so reduced to an exact science as by the German exponents of Kultur. We have to go back centuries for any adequate parallel.

When Alaric, first of the Huns whose deeds have been outdone by the Hohenzollerns, stood at the gates of Rome haughtily dictating to its terrified envoys the terms on which he would spare the Imperial City from complete destruction, they cried out in futile protest:

"If such, Oh King, are your demands what do you purpose to leave us?"

"Your lives," responded the Fifth Century prototype of Hindenburg.

Bismarck was a true descendant of the Huns and Vandals that almost destroyed European civilization fifteen centuries ago. Asked what he intended to concede to the French who were held at German mercy in 1871 he responded:

"We will leave the French people only their eyes to weep with."

Doubtless it was apprehension of the further barbarities that the Germans might perpetrate upon the people of the districts they still occupied that impelled the Allies to grant the enemy some respite from the annihilation which it was within their power to inflict. If a necessary concession it was still an unfortunate one. For it permitted the Germans to withdraw within their own territory armies aggregating at least 3,000,000 men which had not sustained any crushing defeat, and were not even effectively disarmed. The terms of the armistice, indeed, provided that there should be surrendered to the Allies 5,000 guns (2,500 heavy, and 2,500 field), 25,000 machine guns, 3,000 minenwerfer, and 1,700 airplanes. But while this would cripple the enemy it by no means wholly disarmed him. Possibly in the hope that the returning army would be a force for the maintenance of law and order against threatened revolutionary terror in Germany, the soldiers were not deprived of their personal arms—rifles, swords or pistols. The defeated armies were thus spared the igno-

The then Chancellor of State, Franz Ebert, addressing them, said in part:

Your deeds and sacrifices are unexampled. No enemy overcame you. Only when the preponderance of our opponents in men and material grew ever heavier did we abandon the struggle.

You endured indescribable sufferings, accomplished incomparable deeds, and gave, year after year, proofs of your unshakable courage. You protected the homeland from invasion, sheltered your wives, children, and parents from flames and slaughter and preserved the nation's workshops and fields from devastation.

With deepest emotion the homeland thanks you. You can return with heads erect. Never have men done or suffered more than you.

King Victor Immanuel of Italy and some of Italy's victorious soldiers celebrating victory around the statue of Dante

miny of returning home stripped of all insignia of the soldier, without arms and reduced to the quality of a mere mob.

The wisdom of this clemency is made doubtful by the deliberate misconstruction of the situation in Germany by the press and by official spokesmen of the government. The home coming soldiers entered Berlin like conquerors. Through the Brandenburg Gate and down Unter den Linden they marched, arms at shoulder and field guns in train, to the Palace whence the Kaiser had been ousted but from the galleries of which representatives of the government of the moment addressed to them words of compliment and praise.

The correspondent of a neutral paper commenting upon the scene wrote, "Berlin was once more a military town, full of enthusiasm for the soldiers and their deeds. There was nothing in the entry to call to mind the national defeat."

During the protracted sessions of the Peace Conference the attitude of the German government and press was sometimes defiant, more often suppliant, never apologetic. At times they declared that a Germany, ruined by harsh and oppressive terms might turn Bolshevist and menace all Europe. Again they threatened a new appeal to arms. But the note of contrition for the assault upon civilization was never sounded and not one voice in Germany—if

The spontaneous victory celebration after signing of the armistice on Fifth Avenue, New York—known as the Avenue of the Allies. Tons of paper were thrown from the windows by the excited celebrators

The victory celebration in Chicago where the crowds were even denser than in New York

American infantrymen, hot on the trail of the northward fleeing Germans, are here marching through the shell-swept streets of a village near Fresnes on the route from the Marne to the Vesle. They are in a formation that reduces to a minimum the danger of many men being killed by a single shell

we except that of a single rather sensational journalist—has been raised to express regret for even the most frightful atrocities committed by the German troops or in any plea for forgiveness for the perpetration of the greatest crime known to history. The attitude of the German nation toward those upon whom it so long worked its criminal will is haughty and unsubdued. It is only to be expected that some new Treitschke will presently arise to preach anew the gospel of war and devastation, and point out that by their excesses in France and Belgium the German armies instilled in the minds of their enemies such dread of what they might yet do as to snatch honorable terms of surrender from the jaws of ignoble defeat. Only by the exactions which the Peace Conference may lay upon the Teuton nations can they be made to feel their responsibility and to do penance for it.

Under the terms of the armistice the armies of the Allies followed the Germans as they retreated from France, and into the German territory that was set aside for Allied occupation. This territory included all of Germany west of the Rhine, and for a distance of ten kilometers east of it, together with the cities of Cologne, Mayence, and Coblenz, with a semi-circular expanse of territory, thirty kilometers wide, back of each. All of Belgium and France was of course to be evacuated, and the Belgian troops, long barred from their country, pressed close upon the heels of the retreating host so that on the 22nd of November King Albert rode in triumph into Brussels whence he had been driven into exile four years before.

Our American troops first entered Germany along the Sauer and Moselle rivers, occupying first the city of Treves. Coblenz, one of the chief bridgeheads along the line was occupied by them on the 9th of December. A corres-

pondent, Mr. Edwin L. James accompanied the army of occupation and from his account of the reception of our troops in these two German cities some quotations may well be made:

It was just five-thirty o'clock this morning, exactly one month after they broke through the German line,

Looking east on Locust Street from 8th Street, St Louis, Mo. A scene in the spontaneous victory celebration after the signing of the armistice. Not only in St. Louis but all over the country the people expressed their joy by throwing enormous quantities of paper out of the windows

north of Verdun and made the now famous dash toward Sedan, that the Americans quit hospitable Luxembourg for their trek into what the late and unlamented ex-Kaiser used to call the sacred soil of the Fatherland.

To one watching those business-like lads cross the international bridge of Wasserbillig in the sickly light of a cloudy dawn they seemed to march just as they did not so long ago, when the same lads were going into the hell which lasted five weeks over in the Meuse sector. Who could have told them a month ago that to-day they would be marching footfree into the land

The defeated German troops marching through Liege, Belgium, which they had entered four years before as the ruthless conquerors of a small county which they were pledged to protect

A night scene in the Far East in celebration of the signing of the armistice

of the enemy? But into Germany they marched, their eyes straight ahead, their rifles held tight, and their cartridge clips filled. There was nothing of the popular conception of a conquering army about them. They were solemn-faced lads, business-like and quiet, and, above all, ready for whatever was to come.

One was impressed by the general prosperous and sleek appearance of the whole city. The shop windows were well filled with all sorts of merchandise; the meat shops were far from empty. There was that air that one used to see about captured German officers—the same sullen apathy, the same insolent and disdainful manner. To one who smiled, many frowned; but most simply stood there and stared. We went out on the bridge over the beautiful Moselle to await the coming of the Americans.

It was just at 1 o'clock, German time, that Colonel Hunt appeared, leading the 6th Infantry of the 5th Division, which is to be the permanent garrison of the city during our occupation. Behind him came a brass band, formed by doughboys, who were a full regiment strong, and a company of machine guns. They were neat and nifty, these victorious young Americans, as they marched so solemnly into this Hun city.

It was so different from the entry into French and Belgian towns, where the smiles of little children and blessings and joyful tears of grown folks had greeted us. Here

was hostility lurking beneath the smirking surface hospitality of the Hun. I turned and marched with the head of the column into the ancient city, the German name of which is Trier.

No American was there but loved that bandmaster. He must have come from south of the Mason and Dixon Line, for as Colonel Hunt set foot into the city the strains of "Dixie" broke out. The tune quickened the heartbeats and footsteps of the Americans, but of all those thousands of Germans who lined our path none

© American Photo Service

An American shell stopped the flight of this German gun and crew, killing both the members of the crew and the horses

Germans retreating toward the Rhine drawn by oxen stolen from the peasants of the territories they are evacuating

German soldiers in the town of Hunigen during their evacuation of Alsace and retreat into Germany

showed the least feeling except the little children, who smiled at the soldiers, as all children will.

The crowd grew denser and denser as we reached the square. Here a band broke into "Suwanee River," and just then the standard bearer gave the Stars and Stripes an extra whirl, and the column passed on by the ancient Porta Nigra to their barracks.

After the triumphal and glorious march through France and Belgium and even Luxembourg the appalling silence almost frightened one. There was gloom everywhere. Even the German flags and arches which had welcomed the returning boche soldiers had been put away, and nothing remained undone to make the ceremony more sombre.

One was deeply impressed by the quiet dignity of the American soldiers to-day. These lads whistled and joked and played mouth-organs while going into battle, but marching through Germany to-day there wasn't a smile on their faces or a joke on their lips. They were dead serious.

At Coblenz the reception was very different, and the description given by Mr. James of the gayety and seeming prosperity of the city contrasts curiously with the pleas that even then were being made by German spokesmen that the Allies should feed their people lest they starve:

The reception of the Americans here was very different from that at Treves. There sullen silence greeted us everywhere. Here smiling delegations met us; pretty girls waved hands and handkerchiefs.

The river promenade was crowded with the curious, who were in remarkably good humor. Every one seems anxious to do what can be done for the Americans. One walks along the boardwalk here, which, if one did not look across the picturesque Rhine, one might imagine the Atlantic City promenade, and one rubs

The triumphal entrance of Marshal Pétain and his victorious troops into Metz on the Rhine from whose great fortress the Germans had threatened the French for forty-eight years

The 28th Infantry, 1st Division of the American Army of Occupation, marching down the valley of the Moselle to the Rhine. Whatever their motives, the people along the way are far from hostile

one's eyes to make one's self believe that this is a vanquished nation.

A German officer took me for a walk late in the afternoon. Thousands of well-dressed men and handsomely gowned women thronged the boulevard along the Rhine, the crowd in front of the magnificent Coblenzerhof reminding one of a Fifth Avenue holiday parade. The shop windows were filled with luxuries of every description. I bought excellent cigars and Waldorf-Astoria cigarettes.

My German guide took me into the city's finest tearoom. Here was matched the tearoom in Sherry's any December afternoon. Silks and satins and furs were on all sides. The tearoom itself was ornate and luxurious in its appointments.

Last night the cafés were filled with merrymakers up to 11 o'clock, and the theatres were running full blast. The gayety was as if Germany had won and not lost the war. The world knows Coblenz as one of the beautiful cities of Europe, and certainly the German defeat has dimmed none of its glory. Blooming prosperity is everywhere apparent, and if there is any scarcity of food I have not been able to find it. The famous old Monopol Hotel and the Coblenzerhof and numerous restaurants serve meals that would tickle the palate of an epicure.

At almost any other time one would have felt happy to be here; but now, seeing Coblenz, one at once remembers Rheims. Seeing Coblenz sleek and prosperous, one feels that Germany is not yet repentant.

Repentance, indeed, may come later. Germany suffered cruelly in men and loss of wealth in the war which she

Col. Milo C. Corey, the first member of the Second American Division to arrive in Luxembourg, inquiring his way to Mersch—one of the stopping points of the Division on its way to the Rhine

The 18th Infantry of the First Division American Army marching across the border line between France and Lorraine near Metz

so causelessly and wickedly provoked. The decision of the Peace Conference has indeed laid upon her a heavy burden of financial indebtedness, has stripped her of all of her colonies, some of her home territory, her most formidable forts, her entire navy. Her domestic indebtedness incurred by the war, combined with the heavy indemnities which she is condemned to pay to her victims, will lay upon her people a staggering load for generations yet to come. The Rhine is no longer a German river; the Kiel Canal is open to the world; Heligoland, its fortresses razed, may be left to the gradual disintegration before the assaults of the angry sea that threatened it when Germany began making it the most powerful stronghold in the world. The edifice of German military grandeur is shattered.

The former Kaiser, dethroned, a fugitive dependent upon the bounty and hospitality of a neighboring and friendly nation which for four years his armies had threatened with invasion, now faces trial in a world court on the charge of high crimes and offenses against international

morality. The nation which his inordinate ambition wrecked now faces ruin.

No nation of the world held a more enviable position than Germany in 1914. In philosophy and science her students ranked first in the world. German music stirred the hearts of all peoples, and musicians flocked to the Wagner theatre at Weimar, pilgrims to the Passion Play at Ober Ammergau and students to Heidelberg, Stuttgartt or Bonn.

An advance guard of the American Army of Occupation crossing the boundary between France and Germany

A party of German officers with a guard paying a visit to the headquarters of the American Army's First Division under a white flag to arrange for the transfer of German guns and ammunition to representatives of the American Army of Occupation

An American transport train in Germany, passing through Coblenz on the Rhine, on their way to take over the Fort of Coblenz

German inventions and manufactures flooded the world. In the chemical utilization of natural products she eclipsed all other nations, and in certain forms of chemical manufacture had established for her people a virtual monopoly. Her merchant marine under wise governmental encouragement had become second on the seas, and an army of state-aided and state-instructed salesmen invaded all markets with German made goods. The policy of peaceful penetration was winning everything for Germany and it was a sorry day for her people when their rulers thought they could hasten this method of assured conquest by adopting the course of international pirates. The world arose as a unit against this programme and beat Germany to the dust.

The Peace Conference at Paris, which began its sessions January 18, 1919, will rank as easily the most important and dignified international gathering ever held. Its task was to remake a shattered Europe, and to rearrange boundaries and powers in every quarter of the globe. The primary participants were the five chief belligerents on the Allied side—the United States, France, Great Britain, Italy and Japan. To these were added in a secondary capacity belligerent powers with secondary interests—namely Belgium, Brazil, the British Dominions and India, China, Cuba, Greece, Guatemala, Haiti, Hedjaz, Honduras, Liberia, Siam and the Czechoslovak Republic. From the opening session until the 7th of May when the completed treaty was published and offered for the acceptance of the German government the work of the delegates was continuous and engaged the attention of the whole civilized world. In that labor the chief share fell upon the delegates from the United States, England, France and Italy. President Wilson, casting precedent to the winds, established himself in Paris with a retinue as dignified and numerous as that of any monarch of the feudal days, and became easily the leading figure in the Conference. To him, perhaps more than to any other figure therein was due the incorporation in the treaty of the plan for a League of Nations by which it is hoped all danger of future wars may be averted.

The immediate fruit of the arduous and devoted work of the members of the Peace Conference has its expression in the official condensation of the treaty printed in the following pages. But to formulate a treaty is not necessarily to assure its ratification by all the parties in interest. No international document ever dealt with such varied and conflicting aspirations, pretensions and claims as this. None ever had a more world-wide scope, nor sought so much after the ideal in international relations. For this very reason the difficulties attaching to its general acceptance are vastly increased. The acquiescence of the defeated nations may be compelled, but the agreement of the victors is not so easily secured. Even in the

United States political criticism of the treaty ran high, and especially in relation to the League of Nations, threats of its repudiation were many and forceful.

What is to be the verdict of the future upon the outcome of the Great War and the work of the Peace Conference none can tell to-day. But of the war it may be said with all sincerity that never was there a world conflict in which idealism had a greater part. From Belgium's initial sacrifice to the belated but determinative entrance of the United States upon the conflict, the record is filled with instances of patriotic devotion without hope of reward. True the one great prize sought—the freedom of mankind from the dominion of the Hun—was won. With it came the emancipation of the world from autocracy. So far as may be the new map of Europe is made up of states composed of coherent, self-governing people of the same race. Russia still welters in the mire of anarchism, but even in that is more promise of human liberty than there was when the Czars were strong and their empire unshakable.

© International Film Service

The First Division of the American Expeditionary Forces crossing the famous old pontoon bridge leading into Coblenz, Germany

CHAPTER XIII

THE TREATY OF VERSAILLES—COVENANT OF THE LEAGUE OF NATIONS—FRONTIERS OF
GERMANY—MILITARY, NAVAL, AND AIR PROVISIONS—RESPONSIBILITY FOR THE WAR AND
TRIAL OF FORMER KAISER AND HIS CONFEDERATES—REPARATION AND RESTORATION—
FINANCIAL TERMS—INTERNATIONAL TRAFFIC REGULATION—INTERNATIONAL LABOR
ORGANIZATION—GUARANTEES DEMANDED—MISCELLANEOUS PROVISIONS

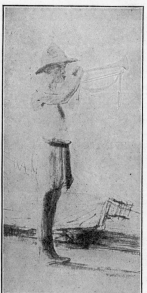

RESTORES Alsace-Lorraine to France.

Accepts the internationalization of the Saar basin temporarily and of Danzig permanently.

Agrees to territorial changes toward Belgium and Denmark and in East Prussia.

Cedes most of Upper Silesia to Poland and renounces all territorial and political rights outside Europe as to her own or her allies' territories and especially to Morocco, Egypt, Siam, Liberia and Shantung.

Recognizes the complete independence of German Austria, Czecho-Slovakia and Poland.

Reduces her army to 100,000 men, including officers.

Abolishes conscription within her territories.

Agrees to raze all forts within fifty kilometers east of the Rhine.

Must stop all importation, exportation, and nearly all production of war material.

Agrees to Allied occupation of parts of Germany till reparation is made, with the understanding that the army of occupation will be reduced at the end of each of the three five-year periods if Germany is fulfilling her obligations.

Agrees that any violation by her of the conditions as to the zone fifty kilometers east of the Rhine shall be regarded as an act of war.

Reduces her navy to six battleships, six light cruisers and twelve torpedo boats, without submarines, and a personnel of not over 15,000.

Must surrender or destroy all other vessels.

Is forbidden to build forts controlling the Baltic.

Must demolish the forts of Heligoland.

Must open the Kiel Canal to all nations and surrender her fourteen submarine cables.

May have no military or naval air forces except 100 unarmed seaplanes until October 1st to detect mines, and may manufacture aviation material for six months only.

Accepts full responsibility for all damages caused to the Allied and associated governments and nationals.

Agrees specifically to reimburse all civilian damages, beginning with an initial payment of 20,000,000,000 marks, subsequent payments to be secured by bonds to be issued at the discretion of the reparation commission.

Is to pay shipping damage on a ton-for-ton basis by the cession of a large part of her merchant, coasting, and river fleets and by new construction and is to devote her economic resources to the rebuilding of the devastated regions.

Agrees to return to the 1914 most-favored-nation tariffs without discrimination of any sort.

Is to allow Allied and associated nationals freedom of transit through her territories and to accept highly detailed provisions as to pre-war debts, unfair competition, internationalization of roads and rivers, and other economic and financial clauses.

Agrees to the trial of the ex-Kaiser by an international high court for a supreme offence against international morality, and of other nationals for violation of the laws and customs of war, Holland to be asked to extradite the former and Germany being responsible for delivering the latter.

The League of Nations is accepted by the Allied and associated powers as operative and by Germany in principle but without membership.

Index to the Treaty

Metz, the capital of Lorraine, protected by the mighty fortress of Ehrenbreitstein over which the Stars and Stripes float during the period of American occupation

PREAMBLE

The preamble names as parties of the first part these nations, described as the principal Allied and associated powers:

The United States,
The British Empire,
France,
Italy,
Japan;

And includes these twenty-two nations which, with the five named above, are described as the Allied and associated powers:

Belgium,   Liberia,
Bolivia,   Nicaragua,
Brazil,   Panama,
China,   Peru,
Cuba,   Poland,
Ecuador,   Portugal,
Greece,   Rumania,
Guatemala,   Serbia,
Haiti,   Siam,
The Hedjaz,   Czecho-Slovakia,
Honduras,   Uruguay.

Germany is described as the party of the second part.

The preamble states that, bearing in mind that on the request of the then Imperial German Government, an armistice was granted on November 11, 1918, by the principal Allied and associated powers in order that a treaty of peace might be concluded with her; and

Whereas, The Allied and associated powers being equally desirous that the war in which they were successively involved, directly or indirectly and which originated in the declaration of war by Austria-Hungary July 28, 1914, against Serbia, the declaration of war by Germany against Russia on August 1, 1914, and against France on August 3, 1914, and in the invasion of Belgium, should be replaced by a firm, just, and durable peace, the plenipotentiaries (having communicated their full powers found in good and due form), have agreed as follows:

From the coming into force of the present treaty the state of war will terminate.

From the moment, and subject to the provisions of this treaty, official relations with Germany and with each of the German states will be resumed by the Allied and associated Powers.

SECTION I

COVENANT OF THE LEAGUE OF NATIONS

The covenant of the League of Nations constitutes Section I of the Peace Treaty, which places upon the League many specific in addition to its general duties. It may question Germany at any time for a violation of the neutralized zone east of the Rhine as a threat against the world's peace. It will appoint three of the five members of the Saar commission, oversee its régime, and carry out the plebiscite. It will appoint the high commissioner of Danzig, guarantee the independence of the free city and arrange for treaties between Danzig and Germany and Poland. It will work out the mandatory system to be applied to the former German colonies, and act as a final court in part of the plebiscites of the Belgian-German frontier and in disputes as to the Kiel Canal, and decide certain of the economic and financial problems.

An international conference on labor is to be held in October under its direction, and another on the international control of ports, waterways, and railways is foreshadowed.

MEMBERSHIP

The members of the League will be the signatories of the covenant and other states invited to accede, who must lodge a declaration of accession without reservation within two months. A new state, dominion, or colony may be admitted, provided its admission is agreed to by two-thirds of the assembly. A state may withdraw upon giving two years' notice, if it has fulfilled all its international obligations.

SECRETARIAT

A permanent secretariat will be established at the seat of the League which will be at Geneva.

The assembly will consist of representatives of the members of the League, and will meet at stated intervals. Voting will be by states. Each member will have one vote and not more than three representatives.

COUNCIL

The council will consist of representatives of the five great Allied powers, together with representatives of four members selected by the assembly from time to time; it may admit additional states and will meet at least once a year. Members not represented will be invited to send a representative when questions affecting their interests are discussed. Voting will be by states. Each state will have one vote and not more than one representative. Decision taken by the assembly and council must be unanimous except in regard to procedure, and in certain cases specified in the covenant and in the treaty, where decisions will be by a majority.

ARMAMENTS

The council will formulate plans for a reduction of armaments for consideration and adoption. These plans will be revised every ten years. Once they are adopted, no member must exceed the armaments fixed without the concurrence of the council. All members will exchange full information as to armaments and programmes, and a permanent commission will advise the council on military and naval questions.

PREVENTION OF WAR

Upon any war, or threat of war, the council will meet to consider what common action shall be taken. Members are pledged to submit matters of dispute to arbitration or inquiry and not to resort to war until three months after the award. Members agree to carry out an arbitral award, and not to go to war with any party to the dispute which complies with it; if a member fails to carry out the award the council will propose the necessary measures. The council will formulate plans for the establishment of a permanent court of international justice to determine international disputes or to give advisory opinions. Members who do not submit their case to arbitration must accept the jurisdiction of the assembly. If the council, less the parties to the dispute, is unanimously agreed upon the rights of it, the members agree that they will not go to war with any party to the dispute which complies with its recommendations. In this case a recommendation by the assembly, concurred in by all members represented on the council and a simple majority

Premier Clemenceau of France, President of the Peace Conference: the "Tiger" whose righteous wrath the Germans have so feared

of the rest, less the parties to the dispute. This will have the force of a unanimous recommendation by the council. In either case, if the necessary agreement cannot be secured, the members reserve the right to take such action as may be necessary for the maintenance of right and justice. Members resorting to war in disregard of the covenant will immediately be debarred from all intercourse with other members. The council will in such cases consider what military or naval action can be taken by the League collectively for the protection of the covenants, and will afford facilities to members coöperating in this enterprise.

VALIDITY OF TREATIES

All treaties or international engagements concluded after the institution of the League will be registered with the secretariat and published. The assembly may from time to time advise members to reconsider treaties which have become inapplicable or involve danger to peace. The covenant abrogates all obligations between members inconsistent with its terms, but nothing in it shall affect the validity of international engagements, such as treaties of arbitration or regional understandings, like the Monroe Doctrine, for securing the maintenance of peace.

Prime Minister Orlando of Italy who temporarily left the Peace Conference rather than compromise regarding Fiume

THE MANDATARY SYSTEM

The tutelage of nations not yet able to stand by themselves will be intrusted to advanced nations who are best fitted to undertake it. The covenant recognizes three different stages of development requiring different kinds of mandataries. (A)—Communities like those belonging to the Turkish Empire, which can be provisionally recognized as independent, subject to advice and assistance from a mandatary, in whose selection they would be allowed a voice. (B)—Communities like those of Central Africa, to be administered by the mandatary under conditions generally approved by the members of the League where equal opportunities for trade will be allowed to all members; certain abuses, such as trade in slaves, arms, and liquor, will be prohibited, and the construction of military and naval bases and the introduction of compulsory military training will be disallowed. (C)—Other communities, such as Southwest Africa and the South Pacific Islands, to be administered under the laws of the mandatary as integral portions of its territory. In every case the mandatary will render an annual report, and the degree of its authority will be defined.

One of the latest and most characteristic pictures of David Lloyd George, Prime Minister of Great Britain and one of "The Big Four" at Paris

GENERAL PROVISIONS

Subject to and in accordance with the provisions of international convention existing or hereafter to be agreed upon, the members of the League will in general endeavor, through the international organization established by the labor convention, to secure and maintain fair conditions of labor for men, women, and children in their own countries and other countries, and undertake to secure just treatment of the native inhabitants of territories under their control; they will intrust the League with the general supervision over the execution of agreements for the suppression of traffic in women and children, etc., and the control of the trade in arms and ammunition with countries in which control is necessary; they will make provision for freedom of communications and transit and equitable treatment for commerce of all members of the League, with special reference to the necessities of regions devastated during the war; and they will endeavor to take steps for international prevention and control of disease. International bureaus and commissions already established will be placed under the League, as well as those to be established in the future.

Herr Gustav Noske, the German Minister of Defense, who so ruthlessly but successfully suppressed the risings of the "Reds" in Berlin

© Underwood & Underwood

Interior of the Chamber of Deputies in Paris

lesia, beyond and including Oppeln; most of Posen and West Prussia, 27,686 square miles; East Prussia being isolated from the main body by a part of Poland. She loses sovereignty over the northeasternmost part of East Prussia, 40 square miles north of the River Memel, and the internationalized areas about Danzig, 729 square miles, and the basin of the Saar, 738 square miles, between the western border of the Rhenish Palatinate of Bavaria and the southeast corner of Luxemburg. The Danzig area consists of the V between the Nogat and Vistula rivers, made a W by the addition of a similar V on the west, including the City of Danzig. The southeastern third of East Prussia and the area between East Prussia and the Vistula, north of latitude 53 degrees 3 minutes, is to have its nationality determined by popular vote, 5,785 square miles, as is to be the case in part of Schleswig, 2,787 square miles.

BELGIUM

Germany is to consent to the abrogation of the treaties of 1839, by which Belgium was established as a neutral state, and to agree in advance to any convention with which the Allied and associated powers may determine to replace them. She is to recognize the full sovereignty of Belgium over the contested territory of Morosnet and over part of Prussian Morosnet, and to renounce in favor of Belgium all rights over the circles of Eupen and Malmedy, the inhabitants of which are to be entitled within six months to protest against this change of sovereignty either in whole or in part, the final decision to be reserved to the League of Nations. A commission is to settle the details of the frontier, and various regulations for change of nationality are laid down.

LUXEMBURG

Germany renounces her various treaties and conventions with the Grand Duchy of Luxemburg, recognizes that it ceased to be part of

AMENDMENTS

Amendments to the covenant will take effect when ratified by the council and by a majority of the assembly.

SECTION II

WESTERN FRONTIERS OF GERMANY

ALSACE-LORRAINE

Germany cedes to France Alsace-Lorraine, 5,600 square miles in the southwest, and to Belgium, two small districts between Luxemburg and Holland, totalling 382 square miles. She also cedes to Poland the southeastern tip of Sithe German zollverein from January 1st last, renounces all right of exploitation of the railroads, adheres to the abrogation of its neutrality, and accepts in advance any international agreement as to it, reached by the Allied and associated powers.

LEFT BANK OF THE RHINE

As provided in the military clauses, Germany will not maintain any fortifications or armed forces less than fifty kilometres to the east of the Rhine, hold any manoeuvres, nor maintain any works to facilitate mobilization. In case of violation, "she shall be regarded as committing a hostile act against the powers who sign the present treaty and as intending to disturb the peace of the world." "By virtue of the present treaty Germany shall be bound to respond to any request for an explanation which the council of the League of Nations may think it necessary to address to her."

ALSACE-LORRAINE

After recognition of the moral obligation to repair the wrong done in 1871 by Germany to France and the people of Alsace-Lorraine, the territories ceded to Germany by the Treaty of Frankfort are restored to France with their frontiers as before 1871, to date from the signing of the armistice, and to be free of all public debts.

Citizenship is regulated by detailed provisions distinguishing those who are immediately restored to full French citizenship, those who have to make formal applications therefor, and those for whom naturalization is open after three years.

The last-named class includes German residents in Alsace-Lorraine, as distinguished from those who acquire the position of Alsace-Lorrainers as defined in the treaty. All public property and all private property of German ex-sovereigns passes to France without payment or credit. France is substituted for Germany as regards ownership of the railroads and rights over concessions of tramways. The Rhine bridges pass to France with the obligation of their upkeep.

For five years manufactured products of Alsace-Lorraine will be admitted to Germany free of duty to a total amount not exceeding in any year the average of the three years preceding the war, and textile materials may be imported from Germany to Alsace-Lorraine and re-exported free of duty. Contracts for electric power from the right bank must be continued for ten years.

For seven years, with possible extension to ten, the ports of Kehl and Strassburg shall be administered as a single unit by a French administrator appointed and supervised by the Central Rhine Commission. Property rights will be safeguarded in both ports and equality of treatment as respects traffic assured the national vessels and goods of every country.

Contracts between Alsace-Lorrainers and Germans are maintained save for France's right to annul on grounds of public interest judgments of courts held in certain classes of cases, while in others a judicial exequatur is first required. Political condemnations during the war are null and void, and the obligation to repay war fines is established as in other parts of Allied territory.

Various clauses adjust the general provisions of the treaty to the special conditions of Alsace-Lorraine, certain matters of execution being left to conventions to be made between France and Germany.

THE SAAR

In compensation for the destruction of coal mines in northern France, and as payment on account of reparation, Germany cedes to France full ownership of the coal mines of the Saar basin with their subsidiaries, accessories, and facilities. Their value will be estimated by the reparation commission and credited against that account. The French rights will be governed by German law in force at the armistice, excepting war legislation, France replacing the present owners, whom Germany undertakes to indemnify. France will continue to furnish the present proportion of coal for local needs and contribute in just proportion to local taxes. The basin extends from the frontier of Lorraine as reannexed to France north as far as Stendal, including on the west the valley of the Saar as far as Saarholzbach, and on the east the town of Homburg.

In order to secure the rights and welfare of the population and guarantee to France entire freedom in working the mines, the territory will be governed by a commission appointed by the League of Nations and consisting of five members—one French, one a native inhabitant of the Saar and three representing three different countries other than France and Germany.

The League will appoint a member of the commission as chairman, to act as executive of the commission. The commission will have all powers of government formerly belonging to Germany. Prussia and Bavaria will administer the railroads and other public services and have full power to interpret the treaty clauses. The local courts will continue, but subject to the commission.

Existing German legislation will remain the basis of the law, but the commission may make modification after consulting a local representative assembly, which it will organize. It will have the taxing power, but for local purposes only. New taxes must be approved by this assembly and in labor legislation it will consider the wishes of the local labor organizations and the labor programme of the League.

French and other labor may be freely utilized, the former being free to belong to French unions, all rights acquired as to pensions and social insurance will be maintained by Germany and the

Saar Commission. There will be no military service, but only a local gendarmerie, to preserve order. The people will preserve their local assemblies, religious liberties, schools, and language, but may vote only for local assemblies. They will keep their present nationality, except so far as individuals may change it. Those wishing to leave will have every facility with respect to their property.

The territory will form part of the French customs system, with no export tax on coal and metallurgical products going to Germany, nor on German products entering the Basin, and for five years no import duties on products of the Basin going to Germany or German products coming into the basin for local consumption. French money may circulate without restriction.

After fifteen years a plebiscite will be held by communes to ascertain the desires of the population as to continuance of the existing régime under the League of Nations, union with France or union with Germany. The right to vote will belong to all inhabitants over twenty, resident therein at the signature. Taking into account the opinions thus expressed, the League will decide the ultimate sovereignty. In any portion restored to Germany the German Government must buy out the French mines at an appraised valuation. If the price is not paid within six months thereafter, this portion passes finally to France. If Germany buys back the mines, the League will determine how much of the coal shall be annually sold to France.

SECTION III

OTHER FRONTIERS OF GERMANY

GERMAN AUSTRIA

"Germany recognizes the total independence of German Austria in the boundaries traced."

CZECHO-SLOVAKIA

Germany recognizes the entire independence of the Czecho-Slovak State, including the autonomous territory of the Ruthenians south of the Carpathians, and accepts the frontiers of this state as to be determined, which in the case of the German frontier shall follow the frontier of Bohemia in 1914. The usual stipulations as to acquisition and change of nationality follow.

POLAND

Germany cedes to Poland the greater part of Upper Silesia, Posen, and the Province of West Prussia on the left bank of the Vistula. A field boundary commission of seven, five representing the Allied and associated powers and one each representing Poland and Germany, shall be constituted within fifteen days of the peace to delimit this boundary. Such special provisions as are necessary to protect racial, linguistic, or religious minorities and to protect freedom of transit and equitable treatment of commerce of other nations shall be laid down in a subsequent treaty between the five Allied and associated powers and Poland.

EAST PRUSSIA

The southern and the eastern frontier of East Prussia as sucing [word obscure] Poland is to be fixed by plebiscites, the first in the regency of Allenstein, between the southern frontier of East Prussia and the northern frontier of Regierungsbezirk Allenstein, from where it meets the boundary between East and West Prussia to its junction with the boundary between the circles of Oletsko and Angerburg, thence the northern boundary of Oletsko to its junction with the present frontier, and the second in the area comprising the circles of Stuhm and Rosenburg and the parts of the circles of Marienburg and Marienwerder east of the Vistula.

In each case German troops and authorities will move out within fifteen days of the peace and the territories be placed under an international commission of five members appointed by the five Allied and associated powers, with the particular duty of arranging for a free, fair, and secret vote. The commission will report the results of the plebiscites to the five powers with a recommendation for the boundary, and will terminate its work as soon as the boundary has been laid down and the new authorities set up.

The five Allied and associated powers will draw up regulations assuring East Prussia full and equitable access to and use of the Vistula. A subsequent convention, of which the terms will be fixed by the five Allied and associated powers, will be entered into between Poland, Germany, and Danzig, to assure suitable railroad communication across German territory on the right bank of the Vistula between Poland and Danzig, while Poland shall grant free passage from East Prussia to Germany.

The northeastern corner of East Prussia about Memel is to be ceded by Germany to the Allied and associated powers, the former agreeing to accept the settlement made, especially as regards the nationality of the inhabitants.

DANZIG

Danzig including the district immediately about it is to be constituted into the "Free City of Danzig" under the guarantee of the League of Nations. A high commissioner appointed by the League and resident at Danzig shall draw up a constitution in agreement with the duly appointed representatives of the city and shall deal in the first instance with all differences arising between the city and Poland. The actual boundaries of the city shall be delimited by a commission appointed within six months from the peace and to include three representatives chosen by the Allied and associated powers, and one each by Germany and Poland.

A convention, the terms of which shall be fixed by the five Allied and associated powers, shall be concluded between Poland and Danzig which shall include Danzig within the Polish customs frontiers, though a free area in the port; insure to Poland the free use of all the city's waterways, docks and other port facilities; the control and administration of the Vistula and the whole through railway system within the city, and postal, telegraphic and telephonic communication between Poland and Danzig; provide against discrimination against Poles within the city, and place its foreign relations and the diplomatic protection of its citizens abroad in charge of Poland.

DENMARK

The frontier between Germany and Denmark will be fixed by the self-determination of the population. Ten days from the peace German troops and authorities shall evacuate the region north of the line running from the mouth of the Schlei, south of Kappel, Schleswig, and Friedrichstadt along the Eider to the North Sea south of Tönning; the Workmen's and Soldiers' Councils shall be dissolved; and the territory administered by an international commission of five, of which Norway and Sweden shall be invited to name two.

The commission shall insure a free and secret vote in three zones. That between the German-Danish frontier and a line running south of the Island of Alsen, north of Flensburg and south of Tondern to the North Sea north of the Island of Sylt, will vote as a unit within three weeks after the evacuation. Within five weeks after this vote the second zone, whose southern boundary runs from the North Sea south of the Island of Fehr to the Baltic south of Sygum, will vote by communes. Two weeks after that vote the third zone, running to the limit of evacuation, will also vote by communes. The international commission will then draw a new frontier on the basis of these plebiscites and with due regard for geographical and economic conditions. Germany will renounce all sovereignty over territories north of this line in favor of the associated governments, who will hand them over to Denmark.

HELIGOLAND

The fortifications, military establishments, and harbors of the islands of Heligoland and Dune are to be destroyed under the supervision of the Allies by German labor, and at Germany's expense. They may not be reconstructed or any similar fortifications built in the future.

RUSSIA

Germany agrees to respect as permanent and inalienable the independence of all territories which were part of the former Russian Empire, to accept the abrogation of the Brest-Litovsk and other treaties entered into with the Maxi-

Entrance to the Chamber of Deputies in Paris

© Press Illustrating Service

The beautiful main street of Strassburg which after almost half a century of German tyranny is now again a French city

malist government of Russia, to recognize the full force of all treaties entered into by the Allied and associated powers with states which were a part of the former Russian Empire, and to recognize the frontiers as determined thereon. The Allied and associated powers formally reserve the right of Russia to obtain restitution and reparation on the principles of the present treaty.

SECTION IV

GERMAN RIGHTS OUTSIDE EUROPE

Outside Europe Germany renounces all rights, titles and privileges as to her own or her allies' territories to all the allied and associated powers, and undertakes to accept whatever measures are taken by the five Allied powers in relation thereto.

OVERSEAS POSSESSIONS

Germany renounces in favor of the Allied and associated powers her overseas possessions with all rights and titles therein. All movable and immovable property belonging to the former German Empire or to any German state shall pass to the government exercising authority therein. These governments may make whatever provisions seem suitable for the repatriation of German nationals and as to the conditions on which German subjects of European origin shall reside, hold property, or carry on business. Germany

undertakes to pay reparation for damage suffered by French nationals in the Cameroons or frontier zone through the acts of German civil and military authorities and of individual Germans from January 1, 1900, to August 1, 1914. Germany renounces all rights under the conventions of November 4, 1911, and September 29, 1912, and undertakes to pay to France in accordance with an estimate presented and approved by the Repatriation Commission all deposits, credits, advances, etc., thereby secured. Germany undertakes to accept and observe any provisions by the Allied and associated powers as to the trade in arms and spirits in Africa as well as to the general act of Berlin of 1885, and the general act of Brussels of 1890. Diplomatic protection to inhabitants of former German colonies is to be given by the governments exercising authority.

CHINA

Germany renounces in favor of China all privileges and indemnities resulting from the Boxer protocol of 1901, and all buildings, wharves, barracks, forts, munitions of warships, wireless plants, and other public property except diplomatic or consular establishments in the German concessions of Tientsin and Hankow and in other Chinese territory except Kiauchau, and agrees to return to China at her own expense all the astronomical instruments seized in 1900 and 1901. China will, however, take no measures for disposal of German property in the legation quarter at

Peking without the consent of the powers signatory to the Boxer protocol.

Germany accepts the abrogation of the concessions at Hankow and Tientsin, China agreeing to open them to international use. Germany renounces all claims against China or any Allied and associated government for the internment or repatriation of her citizens in China and for the seizure or liquidation of German interests there since August 14, 1917. She renounces in favor of Great Britain her state property in the British concession at Canton and in favor of France and China jointly the property of the German school in the French concession at Shanghai.

SIAM

Germany recognizes that all agreements between herself and Siam, including the right of extraterritoriality, ceased July 22, 1917. All German public property except consular and diplomatic premises passes without compensation to Siam, German private property to be dealt with in accordance with the economic clauses. Germany waives all claims against Siam for the seizure and condemnation of her ships, liquidation of her property, or internment of her nationals.

LIBERIA

Germany renounces all rights under the international arrangements of 1911 and 1912 regarding Liberia, more particularly the right to nominate a receiver of the customs, and disinterests herself in any further negotiations for the rehabilitation of Liberia. She regards as abrogated all commercial treaties and agreements between herself and Liberia, and recognizes Liberia's right to determine the status and condition of the reestablishment of Germans in Liberia.

MOROCCO

Germany renounces all her rights, titles, and privileges under the act of Algeciras and the Franco-German agreements of 1909 and 1911 and under all treaties and arrangements with the Sherifian Empire. She undertakes not to intervene in any negotiations as to Morocco between France and other powers, accepts all the consequences of the French protectorate, and renounces the capitulations. The Sherifian Government shall have complete liberty of action in regard to German nationals, and all German protected persons shall be subject to the common law. All movable and immovable German property, including mining rights, may be sold at public auction, the proceeds to be paid to the Sherifian Government and deducted from the reparation account. Germany is also required to relinquish her interests in the state bank of Morocco. All Moroccan goods entering Germany shall have the same privilege as French goods.

EGYPT

Germany recognizes the British protectorate over Egypt declared on December 18, 1914, and renounces as from August 4, 1914, the capitulation and all the treaties, agreements, etc., concluded by her with Egypt. She undertakes not to intervene in any negotiations about Egypt between Great Britain and other powers. There are provisions for jurisdiction over German nationals and property, and for German consent to any changes which may be made in relation to the commission of public debt. Germany consents to the transfer to Great Britain of the powers given to the late Sultan of Turkey for securing the free navigation of the Suez Canal. Arrangements for property belonging to German nationals in Egypt are made similar to those in the case of Morocco and other countries. Anglo-Egyptian goods entering Germany shall enjoy the same treatment as British goods.

TURKEY AND BULGARIA

Germany accepts all arrangements which the Allied and associated powers make with Turkey and Bulgaria with reference to any rights, privileges, or interests claimed in those countries by Germany or her nationals and not dealt with elsewhere.

SHANTUNG

Germany cedes to Japan all rights, titles, and privileges, notably as to Kiauchau, and the railroads, mines and cables acquired by her treaty with China of March 6, 1897, and other agreements as to Shantung. All German rights to the railroad from Tsing-tao to Tsi-nan-fu, including all facilities and mining rights and rights of exploitation, pass equally to Japan, and the cables from Tsing-tao to Shanghai and Che-foo, the cables free of all charges. All German state property, movable and immovable, in Kiauchau is acquired by Japan free of all charges.

SECTION V

MILITARY, NAVAL, AND AIR FORCES

In order to render possible the initiation of a general limitation of the armaments of all nations, Germany undertakes directly to observe the military, naval, and air clauses which follow.

MILITARY FORCES

The demobilization of the German army must take place within two months of the peace. Its strength may not exceed 100,000, including 4,000 officers, with not more than seven divisions of infantry and three of cavalry, and to be devoted exclusively to maintenance of internal order and control of frontiers. The divisions may not be grouped under more than two army corps headquarters staff. The great German general staff

The city of Fiume on the Adriatic, which has been the chief bone of contention between the Italians and the Southern Slavs

is abolished. The army administrative service, consisting of civilian personnel not included in the number of effectives, is reduced to one-tenth the total in the 1913 budget. Employees of the German states, such as customs officers, first guards and coast guards, may not exceed the number in 1913. Gendarmes and local police may be increased only in accordance with the growth of population. None of these may be assembled for military training.

All establishments for the manufacturing, preparation, storage, or design of arms and munitions of war, except those specifically excepted, must be closed within three months of the peace and their personnel dismissed. The exact amount of armament and munitions allowed Germany is laid down in detailed tables, all in excess to be surrendered or rendered useless. The manufacture or importation of asphyxiating, poisonous, or other gases and all analagous liquids is forbidden, as well as the importation of arms, munitions, and war materials. Germany may not manufacture such materials for foreign governments.

CONSCRIPTION

Conscription is abolished in Germany. The enlisted personnel must be maintained by voluntary enlistments for terms of twelve consecutive years, the number of discharges before the expiration of that term not in any year to exceed 5 per cent. of the total effectives. Officers remaining in the service must agree to serve to the age of forty-five and newly appointed officers must agree to serve actively for twenty-five years.

No military schools except those absolutely indispensable for the units allowed shall exist in Germany two months after the peace. No associations such as societies of discharged soldiers, shooting or touring clubs, educational establishments or universities may occupy themselves with military matters. All measures of mobilization are forbidden.

FORTRESSES

All fortified works, fortresses and field works situated in German territory within a zone fifty kilometres east of the Rhine will be dismantled within three months. The construction of any new fortifications there is forbidden. The fortified works on the southern and eastern frontiers, however, may remain.

CONTROL

Interallied commissions of control will see to the execution of the provisions for which a time limit is set, the maximum named being three months. They may establish headquarters at the German seat of government and go to any part of Germany desired. Germany must give them complete facilities, pay their expenses, and also the expenses of execution of the treaty, including the labor and material necessary in demolition, destruction, or surrender of war equipment.

Heligoland, the impregnable German naval base, the fortifications of which are to be dismantled

William Howard Taft, ex-President of the United States and
now President of The League to Enforce Peace

NAVAL FORCES

The German navy must be demobilized within
a period of two months after the peace. She will
be allowed six small battleships, six light cruisers,
twelve destroyers, twelve torpedo boats and no
submarines, either military or commercial, with a
personnel of fifteen thousand men, including officers and no reserve force of any character. Conscription is abolished, only voluntary service being permitted, with a minimum period of twenty-
five years' service for officers and twelve for men.
No member of the German mercantile marine
will be permitted any naval training.

All German vessels of war in foreign ports, and
the German High Seas Fleet interned at Scapa
Flow will be surrendered, the final disposition
of these ships to be decided upon by the Allied
and associated powers. Germany must surrender
forty-two modern destroyers, fifty modern torpedo boats, and all submarines, with their salvage
vessels. All war vessels under construction,
including submarines, must be broken up. War
vessels not otherwise provided for are to be placed
in reserve or used for commercial purposes.
Replacement of ships, except those lost, can take
place only at the end of twenty years for battleships and fifteen years for destroyers. The largest armored ship Germany will be permitted will
be ten thousand tons.

Germany is required to sweep up the mines in
the North Sea and the Baltic Sea, as decided upon
by the Allies. All German fortifications in the
Baltic defending the passages through the belts
must be demolished. Other coast defences are
permitted, but the number and calibre of the guns
must not be increased.

During a period of three months after the peace,
the German high-power wireless stat ons at Nauen,
Hanover, and Berlin, will not be permitted to
send any messages except for commercial purposes
and under supervision of the Allied and associated governments, nor may any more be constructed.

Germany will be allowed to repair German submarine cables which have been cut but are not
being utilized by the Allied powers, and also
portions of cables which, after having been cut,
have been removed, or are at any rate not being
utilized by any one of the Allied and associated
powers. In such cases the cables, or portions
of cables, removed or utilized remain the property of the Allied and associated powers, and accordingly fourteen cables, or parts of cables, are
specified which will not be restored to Germany.

AIR FORCES

The armed forces of Germany must not include
any military or naval air forces, except for not
more than 100 unarmed seaplanes to be retained
till October 1st to search for submarine mines.
No dirigibles shall be kept. The entire air personnel is to be demobilized within two months,
except for 1,000 officers and men retained till
October. No aviation grounds or dirigible sheds
are to be allowed within 150 kilometres of the
Rhine or the eastern or southern frontiers, existing installations within these limits to be destroyed. The manufacture of aircraft and parts
of aircraft is forbidden for six months. All military and naval aëronautical material under a
most exhaustive definition must be surrendered
within three months, except for the 100 seaplanes
already specified.

SECTION VI

REPATRIATION OF PRISONERS OF WAR

The repatriation of German prisoners and
interned civilians, after the peace, is to be
carried out without delay and at Germany's
expense by a commission composed of representatives of the Allies and Germany. Those
under sentence for offences against discipline
are to be repatriated without regard to the
completion of their sentence. Until Germany
has surrendered persons guilty of offences against
the laws and customs of war, the Allies have
the right to retain selected German officers.
The Allies may deal at their own discretion with
German nationals who do not desire to be repatriated, all repatriation being conditional on

the immediate release of any Allied subjects still held in Germany. Germany is to accord facilities to commissions of inquiry in collecting information in regard to missing prisoners of war and of imposing penalties on German officials who have concealed Allied nationals. Germany is to restore all property belonging to Allied prisoners. There is to be a reciprocal exchange of information as to dead prisoners and their graves.

Both parties will respect and maintain the graves of soldiers and sailors buried on their territories, and agree to recognize and assist any commission charged by any Allied or associated government with identifying, registering, maintaining or erecting suitable monuments over the graves, and to afford to each other all facilities for the repatriation of the bodies of their soldiers.

SECTION VII

RESPONSIBILITY FOR STARTING WAR

"The Allied and associated powers publicly arraign William II of Hohenzollern, formerly German Emperor, not for an offence against criminal law, but for a supreme offence against international morality and the sanctity of treaties."

The ex-Emperor's surrender is to be requested of Holland and a special tribunal set up, composed of one judge from each of the five great powers, with full guarantees of the right of defence. It is to be guided "by the highest motives of international policy, with a view of vindicating the solemn obligations of international undertakings and the validity of international morality," and will fix the punishment it feels should be imposed.

Persons accused of having committed acts in violation of the laws and customs of war are to be tried and punished by military tribunals under military law. If the charges affect nationals of only one state they will be tried before a tribunal of that state; if they affect nationals of several states, they will be tried before joint tribunals of the states concerned. Germany shall hand over to the Allied and associated governments, either jointly or severally, all persons so accused and all documents and information necessary to insure full knowledge of the incriminating acts, the discovery of the offenders, and the just appreciation of the responsibility. The judge will be entitled to name counsel.

SECTION VIII

REPARATION FOR WAR DAMAGE

GERMANY'S RESPONSIBILITY

The Allied and associated governments affirm, and Germany accepts the responsibility of herself and her allies, for causing all the loss and damage to which the Allied and associated governments and their nationals have been subjected as a con-

The University Square of Strassburg, which next to Metz is the most important city of Alsace-Lorraine. This was the starting point for one of the German armies that were to capture Paris

sequence of the war imposed upon them by the aggression of Germany and her allies.

The total obligation of Germany to pay, as defined in the category of damages, is to be determined and certified to her after a fair hearing and not later than May 1, 1921, by an interallied reparation commission. At the same time a schedule of payments to discharge the obligation within thirty years shall be presented. These payments are subject to postponement in certain contingencies. Germany irrevocably recognizes the full authority of this commission, agrees to supply it with all the necessary information and to pass legislation to effectuate its findings. She further agrees to restore to the Allies cash and certain articles which can be identified.

As an immediate step toward restoration, Germany shall pay within two years 20,000,000,000 marks in either gold, goods, ships, or other specific forms of payment, with the understanding that certain expenses such as those of the armies of occupation and payments for food and raw materials may be deducted at the discretion of the Allies.

Germany further binds herself to repay all sums borrowed by Belgium from her allies as a result of Germany's violation of the Treaty of 1839, up to November 11, 1918, and for this purpose will issue at once and hand over to the reparation commission 5-per-cent. gold bonds falling due in 1926.

While the Allied and associated governments recognize that the resources of Germany are not adequate, after taking into account permanent diminution of such resources which will result from other treaty claims, to make complete reparation for all such loss and damage they nevertheless require her to make compensation for all damages assessed against her which may exceed her ability to pay. She undertakes to make compensation for all damages caused to civilians under seven main categories: (A) Damages by personal injury to civilians caused by acts of war, directly or indirectly. (B) Damage caused to civilians by acts of cruelty ordered by the enemy, and to civilians in the occupied territory. (C) Damages caused by maltreatment of prisoners. (D) Damages to the Allied peoples represented by pensions and separation allowances, capitalized at the signing of this treaty. (E) Damages to property other than naval or military materials. (F) Damage to civilians by being forced to labor. (G) Damages in the form of levies or fines imposed by the enemy.

In periodically estimating Germany's capacity to pay, the reparation commission shall examine the German system of taxation, first to the end that the sums for reparation which Germany is required to pay shall become a charge upon all her revenues, prior to that for the service or discharge of any domestic loan, and secondly so as to satisfy itself that, in general, the German scheme of

taxation is fully as heavy proportionately as that of any of the powers represented on the commission.

The measures which the Allied and associated powers shall have the right to take, in case of voluntary default by Germany, and which Germany agrees not to regard as acts of war, may include economic and financial prohibitions and reprisals and in general such other measures as the respective governments may determine to be necessary in the circumstances.

The commission shall consist of one representative each of the United States, Great Britain, France, Italy, and Belgium, and, in certain cases, of Japan and Serbia, with all other Allied powers entitled, when their claims are under consideration, to the right of representation without voting power. It shall permit Germany to give evidence regarding her capacity to pay and shall assure her a just opportunity to be heard. It shall make its headquarters at Paris; establish its own procedure and personnel; have general control of the whole reparation problem, and become the exclusive agency of the Allies for receiving, holding, selling and distributing reparation payments. Majority vote shall prevail except that unanimity is required on questions involving the sovereignty of any of the Allies, the cancellation of all or part of Germany's obligations, the time and manner of selling, distributing, and negotiating bonds issued by Germany, and postponement between 1921 and 1926 of annual payments beyond 1930 and any postponement after 1926 for a period of more than three years, the application of a different method of measuring damage than in a similar former case, and the interpretation of provisions. Withdrawal from representation is permitted on twelve months' notice.

The commission may require Germany to give from time to time, by way of guarantee, issues of bonds or other obligations to cover such claims as are not otherwise satisfied. In this connection and on account of the total amount of claims bond issues are presently to be required of Germany in acknowledgment of her debt as follows: 20,000,000,000 marks gold, payable not later than May 1, 1921, without interest; 40,000,000,000 marks gold bearing 2½ per cent. interest between 1921 and 1926 and thereafter 5 per cent., with a 1-per-cent. sinking fund, payment beginning in 1926 and an undertaking to deliver 40,000,000,000 marks gold bonds bearing interest at 5 per cent., under terms to be fixed by the commission.

Interest on Germany's debt will be 5 per cent. unless otherwise determined by the commission in the future, and payments that are not made in gold may "be accepted by the commission in the form of properties, commodities, businesses, rights, concessions, etc." Certificates of beneficial interest, representing either bonds or goods delivered by Germany, may be issued by the commission to the interested power, no power being entitled, however, to have its certificates divided into more than five pieces. As bonds are distributed and pass from the control of the commission, an amount of Germany's debt equivalent to their par value is to be considered as liquidated.

SHIPPING

The German Government recognizes the right of the Allies to the replacement, ton for ton and class for class, of all merchant ships and fishing boats lost or damaged owing to the war, and agrees to cede to the Allies all German merchant ships of 1,600 tons gross and upward; one-half of her ships between 1,600 and 1,000 tons gross and one-quarter of her steam trawlers and other fishing boats. These ships are to be delivered within two months to the reparation committee, together with documents of title evidencing the transfer of the ships free from encumbrance.

"As an additional part of reparation" the German Government further agrees to build merchant ships for the account of the Allies to the amount of not exceeding 200,000 tons gross annually during the next five years.

All ships used for inland navigation taken by Germany from the Allies are to be restored within two months, the amount of loss not covered by such restitution to be made up by the cession of the German river fleet up to 20 per cent. thereof.

In order to effect payment by deliveries in kind Germany is required, for a limited number of years, varying in the case of each, to deliver coal, coal-tar products, dyestuff and chemical drugs, in specific amounts to the reparation commission. The commission may so modify the conditions of delivery as not to interfere unduly with Germany's industrial requirements. The deliveries of coal are to be based largely upon the principle of making good diminutions in the production of the Allied countries resulting from the war.

Germany undertakes to devote her economic resources directly to the physical restoration of the invaded areas. The reparation commission is authorized to require Germany to replace the destroyed articles by the delivery of animals, machinery, etc., existing in Germany, and to manufacture materials required for reconstruction purposes: all with due consideration for Germany's essential domestic requirements.

COAL, ETC.

Germany is to deliver annually for ten years to France coal equivalent to the difference between annual pre-war output of the Nord and Pas-de-Calais mines and annual production during above ten-year period. Germany further gives options over ten years for delivery of 7,000,000 tons coal per year to France, in addition to the above, of 8,000,000 tons to Belgium, and of an amount rising from four and a half million tons from 1919

to 1920 to eight and a half million tons from 1923 to 1924 to Italy at prices to be filed, as prescribed in the treaty. Coke may be taken in place of coal in ratio of three tons to four. Provision is also made for delivery to France, over three years, of benzol, coal tar and of ammonia. The commission has powers to postpone or annul the above deliveries should they interfere unduly with the industrial requirements of Germany.

DYESTUFFS AND CHEMICAL DRUGS

Germany accords option to the commission on dyestuffs and chemical drugs, including quinine up to 50 per cent. of total stock in Germany at the time the treaty comes into force and similar option during each six months to end of 1924 up to 25 per cent. of previous six months' output.

CABLES

Germany renounces all title to specified cables, value of such as were privately owned being credited to her against reparation indebtedness.

DEVASTATED AREAS

As reparation for the destruction of the Library of Louvain, Germany is to hand over manuscripts, early printed books, prints, etc., to the equivalent of those destroyed.

In addition to the above, Germany is to hand over to Belgium wings now at Berlin belonging to the altar piece of the Adoration of the Lamb by Jan and Hubert van Eyck, the centre of which is now in the Cathedral of Saint Bavon at Ghent, and the wings, now at Berlin and Munich, of the altar piece of the Last Supper by Dieric Bouts, the centre of which belongs to the Church of St. Pierre, at Louvain.

Germany is to restore within six months the Koran of the Caliphs Othman, formerly at Medina, to the King of the Hedjaz, and the skull of the Sultan Okwawa, formerly in German East Africa, to his Britannic Majesty's Government.

The German Government is also to restore to the French Government certain papers taken by the German authorities in 1870, belonging then to M. Reuher, and to restore the French flags taken during the war of 1870 and 1871.

SECTION IX

PUBLIC DEBT AND OCCUPATION COST

The powers to which German territory is ceded will assume a certain portion of the German pre-war debt, the amount to be fixed by the reparations commission on the basis of the ratio between the revenue of the ceded territory and Germany's total revenues for the three years preceding the war. In view, however, of the special circumstances under which Alsace-Lorraine was separated from France in 1871, when Germany refused to accept any part of the French public

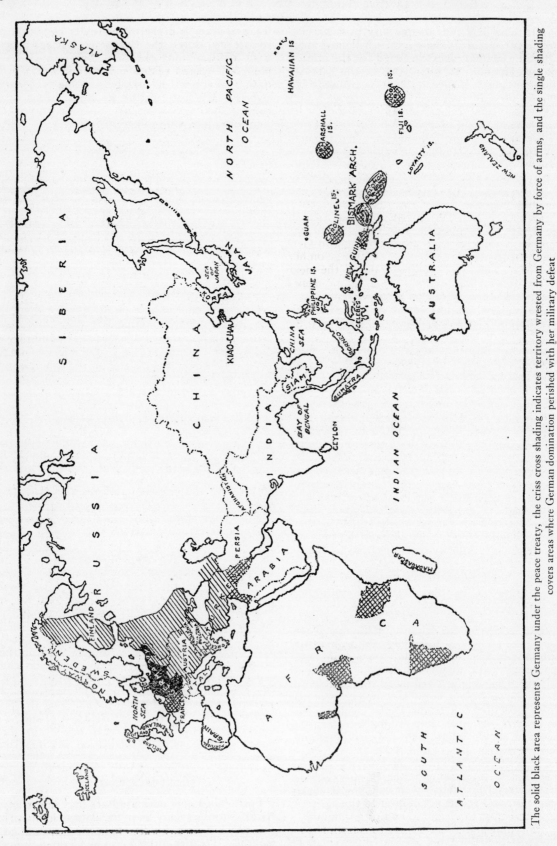

The solid black area represents Germany under the peace treaty, the criss cross shading indicates territory wrested from Germany by force of arms, and the single shading covers areas where German domination perished with her military defeat

debt, France will not assume any part of Germany's pre-war debt there, nor will Poland share in certain German debts incurred for the oppression of Poland. If the value of the German public property in ceded territory exceeds the amount of debt assumed, the states to which property is ceded will give credit on reparation for the excess, with the exception of Alsace-Lorraine. Mandatary powers will not assume any German debts or give any credit for German government property. Germany renounces all right of representation on, or control of, state banks, commissions, or other similar international financial and economic organizations.

Germany is required to pay the total cost of the armies of occupation from the date of the armistice as long as they are maintained in German territory, this cost to be a first charge on her resources. The cost of reparation is the next charge, after making such provisions for payments for imports as the Allies may deem necessary.

Germany is to deliver to the Allied and associated powers all sums deposited in Germany by Turkey and Austria-Hungary in connection with the financial support extended by her to them during the war, and to transfer to the Allies all claims against Austria-Hungary, Bulgaria, or Turkey in connection with agreements made during the war. Germany confirms the renunciation of the treaties of Bucharest and Brest-Litovsk.

On the request of the reparations commission, Germany will expropriate any rights or interests of her nationals in public utilities in ceded territories or those administered by mandataries, and in Turkey, China, Russia, Austria-Hungary and Bulgaria, and transfer them to the reparations commission, which will credit her with their value. Germany guarantees to repay to Brazil the fund arising from the sale of São Paulo coffee which she refused to allow Brazil to withdraw from Germany.

SECTION X

CUSTOMS, CONTRACTS, AND CONVENTIONS
TARIFF DUTIES

For a period of six months after the peace, Germany shall impose no tariff duties higher than the lowest in force in 1914, and for certain agricultural products, wines, vegetable oils, artificial silk, and washed or scoured wool, this restriction obtains for two and a half years more. For five years, unless further extended by the League of Nations, Germany must give most-favored-nation treatment to the Allied and associated powers. She shall impose no customs tariff for five years on goods originating in Alsace-Lorraine nor for three years on goods originating in former German territory ceded to Poland, with the right of observation of a similar exception for Luxemburg.

SHIPPING

Ships of the Allied and associated powers shall for five years and thereafter under condition of reciprocity, unless the League of Nations otherwise decides, enjoy the same rights in German ports as German vessels and have most-favored-nation treatment in fishing, coasting trade, and towage. Even in territorial waters ships of a country having no sea coast may be registered at some one place within its territory.

UNFAIR COMPETITION

Germany undertakes to give the trade of the Allied and associated powers adequate safeguards against unfair competition, and in particular to suppress the use of false wrappings and markings and on condition of reciprocity to respect the laws and judicial decisions of Allied and associated states in respect of regional appellations of wines and spirits.

TREATMENT OF NATIONALS

Germany shall impose no exceptional taxes or restrictions upon the nationals of Allied and associated states for a period of five years, and unless the League of Nations acts, for an additional five years, German nationality shall not continue to attach to a person who has become a national of an Allied or associated state.

MULTILATERAL CONVENTIONS

Some forty multilateral conventions are renewed between Germany and the Allied and associated powers, but special conditions are attached to Germany's readmission to several. As to postal and telegraphic conventions, Germany must not refuse to make reciprocal agreements with the new states. She must agree as respects the radiotelegraphic convention to provisional rules to be communicated to her, and adhere to the new convention when formulated. In the North Sea fisheries and North Sea liquor traffic convention rights of inspection and police over associated fishing boats shall be exercised for at least five years only by vessels of these powers. As to the international railway union she shall adhere to the new convention when formulated; as to the Chinese customs tariff arrangement, the arrangement of 1905; regarding Whangpoo and the Boxer indemnity of 1901; with France, Portugal and Rumania, as to the Hague Convention of 1903 relating to civil procedure, and Great Britain and the United States, as to Article 3 of the Samoan treaty of 1899 the other parties to the treaty are relieved of all obligation toward Germany.

BILATERAL TREATIES

Each Allied and associate state may renew any treaty with Germany in so far as consistent with the peace treaty by giving notice within six months. Treaties entered into by Germany since

Danzig, formerly the capital of West Prussia, which by the terms of the Treaty of Versailles, is to be a free city under the control of the League of Nations

August 1, 1914, with other enemy states and before or since that date with Rumania, Russia, and governments representing parts of Russia, are abrogated and all concessions granted under pressure by Russia to German subjects are annulled. The Allied and associated states are to enjoy most-favored-nation treatment under treaties entered into by Germany and other enemy states before August, 1914, and under treaties entered into by Germany and neutral states during the war.

PRE-WAR DEBTS

A system of clearing houses is to be created within three months, one in Germany and one in each Allied and associated state which adopts the plan for the payment of pre-war debts, including those arising from contracts suspended by the war, for the adjustment of the proceeds of the liquidation of enemy property and the settlement of other obligations. Each participating state assumes responsibility for the payment of all debts owing by its nationals to the enemy states except in cases of pre-war insolvency of the debtor, the proceeds of the sale of private enemy property in each participating state may be used to pay the debts owed to the nationals of that state. Direct payment from debtor to creditor and all communications relating thereto being prohibited, disputes may be settled by arbitration by the courts of the debtor country or by the mixed arbitral tribunal. Any Allied or associated power may, however, decline to participate in this system by giving Germany six months' notice.

ENEMY PROPERTY

Germany shall restore or pay for all private enemy property seized or damaged by her, the amount of damages to be fixed by the mixed arbitral tribunal. The Allied and associated states may liquidate German private property within their territories as compensation for property of their nationals not restored or paid for by Germany. For debts owed to Allied and associated nationals by German nationals, and for other claims against Germany, Germany is to compensate her nationals for such losses and to deliver within six months all documents relating to property held by her nationals in Allied and associated states. All war legislation as to enemy property rights and interests is confirmed and all claims by Germany against the Allied or associated governments for acts under reciprocal war measures are abandoned.

CONTRACTS

Pre-war contracts between allied and associated nationals, excepting the United States, Japan and Brazil, and German nationals are cancelled, except for debts for accounts already performed, agreements for the transfer of property where the property had already passed, leases of land and houses, contracts of mortgages, pledge or lien, mining concessions, contracts with governments, and insurance contracts. Mixed arbitral tribunals shall be established of three members, one chosen by Germany, one by the Allied and associated states and the third by agreement, or, failing which, by the President of Switzerland. They shall have jurisdiction over all disputes as to contracts concluded before the present peace treaty.

Fire-insurance contracts are not considered dissolved by the war, even if premiums have not been paid, but lapse at the date of the first annual premium falling due three months after the peace. Life-insurance contracts may be restored by payments of accumulated premiums with interest, sums falling due on such contracts during the war to be recoverable with interest. Marine-insurance contracts are dissolved by the outbreak of war except where the risk insured against had already been incurred. Where the risk had not attached premiums paid are recoverable, otherwise premiums due and sums due on losses are recoverable. Reinsurance treaties are abrogated unless invasion has made it impossible for the reinsured to find another reinsurer. Any Allied or associated power, however, may cancel all the contracts running between its nationals and a German life-insurance company, the latter being obligated to hand over the proportion of its assets attributable to such policies.

Industrial property rights as to industrial, literary, and artistic property are reëstablished; the special war measures of the Allied and associated powers are ratified and the right reserved to impose conditions on the use of German patents and copyrights when in the public interest. Except as between the United States and Germany pre-war licenses and rights to sue for infringements committed during the war are cancelled.

OPIUM

The contracting powers agree, whether or not they have signed and ratified the opium convention of January 23, 1912, or signed the special protocol opened at The Hague in accordance with resolutions adopted by the third opium conference in 1914, to bring the said convention into force by enacting, within twelve months of the peace, necessary legislation.

RELIGIOUS MISSIONS

The Allied and associated powers agree that the properties of religious missions in territories belonging or ceded to them shall continue in their work under the control of the powers, Germany renouncing all claims in their behalf.

SECTION XI

Aircraft of the Allied and associated powers shall have full liberty of passage and landing over

A typical mountain ravine near Fiume

and in German territory, equal treatment with German 'planes as to use of German airdromes, and with most-favored-nation 'planes as to internal commercial traffic in Germany. Germany agrees to accept Allied certificates of nationality, airworthiness, or competency, and licenses and to apply the convention relative to aërial navigation concluded between the Allied and associated powers to her own aircraft over her own territory. These rules apply until 1923, unless Germany will have previously been admitted to the League of Nations or to the above convention.

SECTION XII

FREEDOM OF TRANSPORT

GOODS IN TRANSIT

Germany must grant freedom of transit through her territories by mail or water to persons, goods, ships, carriages, and mails from or to any of the Allied or associated powers, without customs or transit duties, undue delays, restrictions or discriminations based on nationality, means of transport, or place of entry or departure. Goods in transit shall be assured all possible speed of journey, especially perishable goods. Germany may not divert traffic from its normal course in favor of her own transport routes or maintain "control stations" in connection with transmigration traffic. She may not establish any tax discrimination against the ports of Allied or associated powers; must grant the latter's seaports all factors and reduced tariffs granted her own or other nationals, and afford the Allied and associated powers equal rights with those of her own nationals in her ports and waterways, save that she is free to open or close her maritime coasting trade.

FREE ZONES IN PORTS

Free zones existing in German ports on August 1, 1914, must be maintained with due facilities as to warehouses, packing, and shipping, without discrimination, and without charges except for expenses of administration and use. Goods leaving the free zones for consumption in Germany and goods brought into the free zones from Germany shall be subject to the ordinary import and export taxes.

INTERNATIONAL RIVERS

The Elbe from the junction of the Moldau, the Moldau from Prague, the Oder from Oppa, the Niemen from Grodno, and the Danube from Ulm are declared international, together with their connections. The riparian states must insure good conditions of navigation within their territories unless a special organization exists therefor. Otherwise, appeal may be had to a special tribunal of the League of Nations, which also may arrange for a general international waterways convention.

The Elbe and the Oder are to be placed under international commissions, to meet within three months: that for the Elbe composed of four representatives of Germany, two from Czecho-Slovakia, and one each from Great Britain, France, Italy, and Belgium; and that for the Oder composed of one each from Poland, Russia, Czecho-Slovakia, Great Britain, France, Denmark, and Sweden. If any riparian state on the Memel should so request of the League of Nations, a similar commission shall be established there. These commissions shall, upon request of any riparian state, meet within three months to revise existing international agreement.

THE DANUBE

The European Danube Commission reassumes its pre-war powers, but for the time being with representatives of only Great Britain, France, Italy, and Rumania. The upper Danube is to be administered by a new international commission until a definitive statute be drawn up at a conference of the powers nominated by the Allied and associated governments within one year after the peace. The enemy governments shall make full reparations to the European Commission for all war damages; shall cede their river facilities in surrendered territory, and give Czecho-Slovakia, Serbia, and Rumania any rights necessary on their shores for carrying out improvements in navigation.

THE RHINE AND THE MOSELLE

The Rhine is placed under the central commission to meet at Strassburg within six months after the peace and to be composed of four representatives of France, which shall in addition select the president; four of Germany, and two each of Great Britain, Italy, Belgium, Switzerland, and the Netherlands. Germany must give France, on the course of the Rhine included between the two extreme points of her frontiers, all rights to take water to feed canals, while herself agreeing not to make canals on the right bank opposite France. She must also hand over to France all her drafts and designs for this part of the river.

Belgium is to be permitted to build a deep-draught Rhine-Meuse canal, if she so desires, within twenty-five years, in which case Germany must construct the part within her territory on plans drawn by Belgium; similarly, the interested Allied governments may construct a Rhine-Meuse canal, both, if constructed, to come under the competent international commission. Germany may not object if the Central Rhine commission desires to extend its jurisdiction over the lower Moselle, the upper Rhine, or lateral canals.

Germany must cede to the Allied and associated governments certain tugs, vessels, and facilities for navigation on all these rivers, the specific details to be established by an arbiter named by the United States. Decision will be based on the legitimate needs of the parties concerned and on the shipping traffic during the five years before the war. The value will be included in the regular reparation account. In the case of the Rhine, shares in the German navigation companies and property such as wharves and warehouses held by Germany in Rotterdam at the outbreak of the war must be handed over.

RAILWAYS

Germany, in addition to most-favored-nation treatment on her railways, agrees to coöperate in the establishment of through-ticket services for passengers and baggage; to insure communication by rail between the Allied, associated and other states; to allow the construction or improvement within twenty-five years of such lines as necessary; and to conform her rolling stock to enable its incorporation in trains of the Allied or associated powers. She also agrees to accept the denunciation of the St. Gothard convention if Switzerland and Italy so request, and temporarily to execute instructions as to the transport of troops and supplies and the establishment of postal and telegraphic service, as provided.

CZECHO-SLOVAKIA

To assure Czecho-Slovakia access to the sea, special rights are given her both north and south. Toward the Adriatic she is permitted to run her own through trains to Fiume and Trieste. To the north, Germany is to lease her for ninety-nine years spaces in Hamburg and Stettin, the details to be worked out by a commission of three representing Czecho-Slovakia, Germany, and Great Britain.

THE KIEL CANAL

The Kiel Canal is to remain free and open to war and merchant ships of all nations at peace with Germany; subjects, goods, and ships of all states are to be treated on terms of absolute equality, and no taxes to be imposed beyond those necessary for upkeep and improvement, for which Germany is to be responsible. In case of violation of, or disagreement as to, these provisions, any state may appeal to the League of Nations, and may demand the appointment of an international commission. For preliminary hearing of complaints, Germany shall establish a local authority at Kiel.

SECTION XIII

INTERNATIONAL LABOR ORGANIZATION

ANNUAL CONFERENCE

Members of the League of Nations agree to establish a permanent organization to promote international adjustment of labor conditions to consist of an annual international labor conference and an international labor office.

The former is to be composed of four representatives of each state, two from the government and one each from the employers and the employed; each of them may vote individually. It will be a deliberative legislative body, its measures taking the form of draft conventions or recommendations for legislation, which, if passed by two-thirds vote, must be submitted to the lawmaking authority in every state participating. Each government may either enact the terms into law; approve the principles, but modify them to local needs; leave the actual legislation in case of a Federal state to local Legislatures, or reject the convention altogether without further obligation.

The international labor office is established at the seat of the League of Nations as part of its organization. It is to collect and distribute information on labor throughout the world and prepare agenda for the conference. It will publish a periodical in French and English, and possibly other languages. Each state agrees to make to it, for presentation to the conference, an annual report of measures taken to execute accepted conventions. The governing body consists of twenty-four members, twelve representing the governments, six the employers and six the employees, to serve for three years. On complaint that any government has failed to carry out a convention to which it is a party, the governing body may make inquiries directly to that government, and in case the reply be unsatisfactory, may publish the complaint with comment. A complaint by one government against another may be referred by the governing body to a commission of inquiry nominated by the secretary general of the League. If the commission report fails to bring satisfactory action, the matter may be taken to a permanent court of international justice for final decision. The chief reliance for securing enforcement of the law will be publicity, with a possibility of economic action in the background.

The first meeting of the conference will take place in October, 1919, at Washington, to discuss the eight-hour day or forty-eight-hour week, prevention of unemployment, extension and application of the international conventions adopted at Berne in 1906, prohibiting night work for women; the use of white phosphorus in the manufacture of matches; the employment of women and children at night or in unhealthy work, of women before and after childbirth, including maternity benefit, and of children as regards minimum age.

LABOR CLAUSES

Nine principles of labor conditions are to be recognized, on the ground that "the wellbeing, physical and moral, of the industrial wage earners is of supreme international importance." With exceptions necessitated by differences of climate,

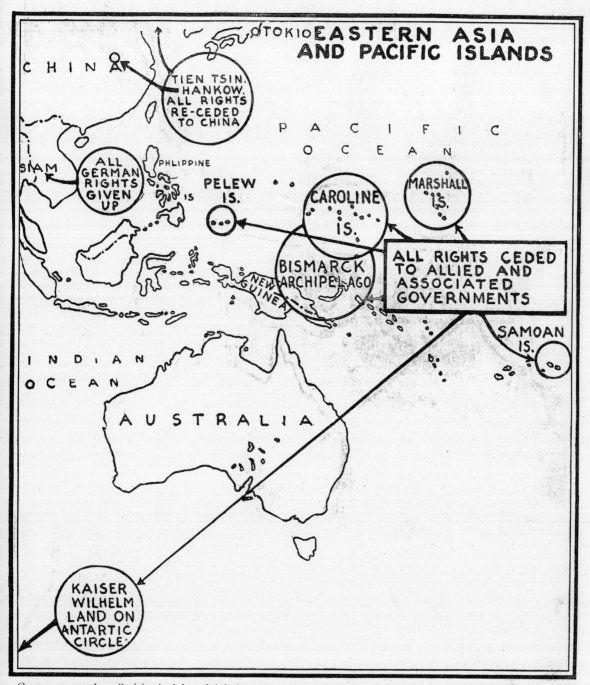

Germany surrenders all rights in Asia and Asiatic waters. The disposition of the Pacific Islands remains to be determined and sharp clashing of interests between the Allies may be feared. The mandatary principle of the League of Nations if it works out as planned should, however, avert serious trouble.

(X) Count Brockdorff-Rantzau, German Foreign Minister and head of the German peace delegation, and his staff of secretaries

One of the forts of Metz, the most heavily fortified city in the world, held by the American Army during the period of occupation

© Press Illustrating Service

habits and economic development, they include: The guiding principle that labor should not be regarded merely as a commodity or article of commerce; right of association of employers and employees; a wage adequate to maintain a reasonable standard of life; the eight-hour day or forty-eight hour week; a weekly rest of at least twenty-four hours, which should include Sunday wherever practicable; abolition of child labor and assurance of the continuation of the education and proper physical development of children; equal pay for equal work as between men and women; equitable treatment of all workers lawfully resident in any country, including foreigners; and a system of inspection in which women should take part.

SECTION XIV

GUARANTEES ASKED OF FOE

WESTERN EUROPE

As a guarantee for the execution of the treaty, German territory to the west of the Rhine, together with the bridgeheads, will be occupied by Allied and associated troops for fifteen years. If the conditions are faithfully carried out by Germany certain districts, including the bridgehead of Cologne, will be evacuated at the expiration of five years; certain other districts, including the bridgehead of Coblenz, and the territories nearest the Belgian frontier, will be evacuated

after ten years, and the remainder, including the bridgehead of Mainz, will be evacuated after fifteen years. In case the inter-allied Reparation Commission find that Germany has failed to observe the whole or part of her obligations either during the occupation or after the fifteen years have expired, the whole or part of the areas specified will be reoccupied immediately. If before the expiration of the fifteen years Germany complies with all the treaty undertakings, the occupying forces will be withdrawn immediately.

EASTERN EUROPE

All German troops at present in territories to the east of the new frontier shall return as soon as the Allied and associated governments deem wise. They are to abstain from all requisitions and are in no way to interfere with measures for national defense taken by the government concerned. All questions regarding occupation not provided for by the treaty will be regulated by a subsequent convention or conventions, which will have similar force and effect.

SECTION XV

FINAL CLAUSES OF THE TREATY

Germany agrees to recognize the full validity of the treaties of peace and additional conventions to be concluded by the Allied and associated powers with the powers allied with Germany, to

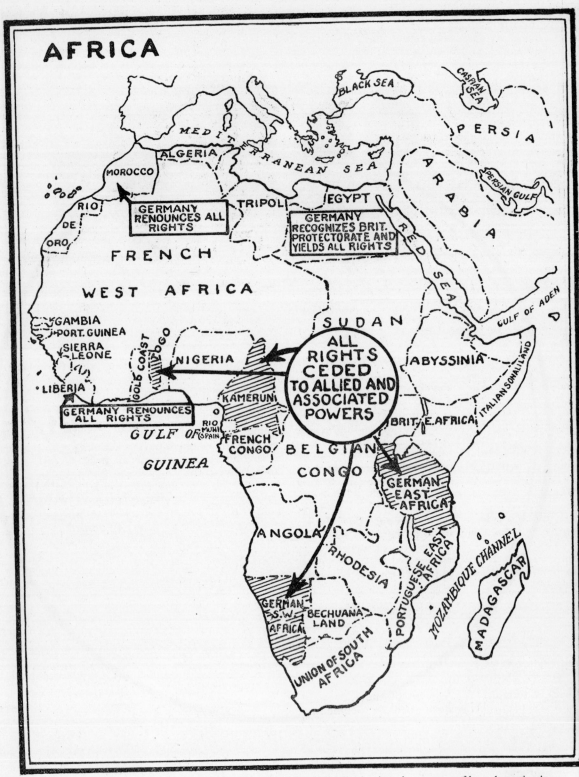

All German colonies in Africa are yielded to the Allies.   Their distribution is to be a matter of later determination

agree to the decisions to be taken as to the territories of Austria-Hungary, Bulgaria, and Turkey, and to recognize the new states in the frontiers to be fixed for them.

Germany agrees not to put forward any pecuniary claims against signing the present treaty based on events previous to the coming into force of the treaty.

Germany accepts all decrees as to German ships and goods made by any Allied or associated prize court. The Allies reserve the right to examine all decisions of German prize courts. The present treaty, of which the French and British texts are both authentic, shall be ratified and the depositions of ratifications made in Paris as soon as possible. The treaty is to become effective in all respects for each power on the date of deposition of its ratification.

THE SHANTUNG PENINSULA

The transfer of the Shantung Peninsula to Japan was opposed by the Chinese statesmen who claimed that Germany possessed no rights that should not properly revert to China

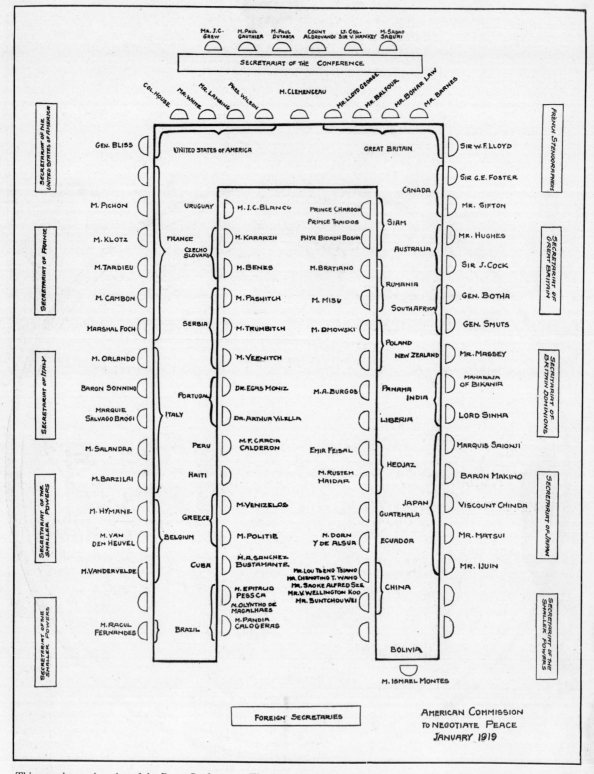

This was the seating plan of the Peace Conference. The five great powers occupied the outer seats at the head of the table and outward from it, while back of these seats sat the secretaries

Staff officers in Paris putting final touches on the redrawn map of Europe before its submission to the Peace Conference

French soldiers standing at attention on the arrival of President Poincairé to open the Peace Conference

AMERICA'S RECORD FOR TWO YEARS OF WAR

A FEW OF THE STATISTICS RELATING TO OUR ARMED FORCES, CASUALTIES, SHIPPING, AND ESTIMATED COST OF OPERATIONS, APRIL 6, 1917, TO APRIL 6, 1919

April 6, 1917—

Regular Army	127,588
National Guard in Federal service	80,466
Reserve corps in service	4,000
Total of soldiers	212,034
Personnel of Navy	65,777
Marine Corps	15,627
Total armed forces	293,438

November 11, 1918—

Army	3,764,000
Navy	497,030
Marine Corps	78,017
Total armed forces	4,339,047

Soldiers transported overseas	2,053,347
American troops in action, November 11, 1918	1,338,169
Soldiers in camps in the United States, November 11, 1918	1,700,000
Casualties, Army and Marine Corps, A. E. F.	282,311
Death rate per thousand, A. E. F.	.057
German prisoners taken	44,000
Americans decorated by French, British, Belgian, and Italian armies, about	10,000
Number of men registered and classified under Selective Service law	23,700,000
Cost of thirty-two National Army cantonments and National Guard camps	$179,629,497
Students enrolled in 500 S. A. T. C. camps	170,000
Officers commissioned from training camps (exclusive of universities, etc.)	80,000
Women engaged in Government war industries	2,000,000

BEHIND THE BATTLE LINES

Railway locomotives sent to France	967
Freight cars sent to France	13,174
Locomotives of foreign origin operated by A. E. F.	350
Cars of foreign origin operated by A. E. F.	973
Miles of standard gauge track laid in France	843
Warehouses, approximate area in square feet	23,000,000
Motor vehicles shipped to France	110,000

ARMS AND AMMUNITION

Persons employed in about 8,000 ordnance plants in United States at signing of armistice	4,000,000
Shoulder rifles made during war	2,500,000
Rounds of small-arms ammunition	2,879,148,000
Machine guns and automatic rifles	181,662
High-explosive shells	4,250,000
Gas shells	500,000
Shrapnel	7,250,000
Gas masks, extra canisters, and horse masks	8,500,000

NAVY AND MERCHANT SHIPPING

Warships at beginning of war	197
Warships at end of war	2,003
Small boats built	800
Submarine chasers built	355
Merchant ships armed	2,500
Naval bases in European waters and the Azores	54
Shipbuilding yards (merchant marine) increased from 61 to more than	200
Shipbuilding ways increased from 235 to more than	1,000
Ships delivered to Shipping Board by end of 1918	592
Deadweight tonnage of ships delivered	3,423,495

FINANCES OF THE WAR

Total cost, approximately	$24,620,000,000
Credits to eleven nations	8,841,657,000
Raised by taxation in 1918	3,694,000,000
Raised by Liberty Loans	14,000,000,000
War Savings Stamps to November, 1918	834,253,000
War relief gifts, estimated	4,000,000,000

THE COST OF THE WAR IN MEN AND MONEY

Up to and including February 14, 1919, General Pershing had reported the following casualties suffered by the United States Expeditionary Force:

Killed in action	30,868
Died of wounds	13,020
Died of disease	19,202
Died of other causes . . .	3,521
Dead from all causes . . .	66,611
Missing in action	11,200
Wounded	166,607

MARINE CORPS

Killed	1,562
Wounded	9,260
Missing	697

Very few details are available regarding the distribution of our casualties amongst the various branches of the service or regarding the proportions of officers and men. It is known, however, that the U. S. Air Service had total casualties of 442 members of its commissioned personnel of whom 109 were killed, 103 wounded, 200 missing, 27 prisoners, and 3 interned in neutral countries. To these must be added 159 who lost their lives while in training.

Included in the above grand total of losses suffered by the United States forces in Europe are also those of the various regiments of Marines. These amounted in all up to December 23, 1918, to 5,280, of which 192 were officers—90 killed, 101 wounded, 1 missing—and 5,088 non-commissioned officers and privates—1,908 killed, 2,792 wounded, 75 prisoners, and 313 missing.

BRITISH LOSSES TO NOVEMBER 19, 1918

	KILLED	WOUNDED	MISSING	TOTAL
France . . .	559,612	1,833,345	326,695	2,719,652
Dardanelles . .	33,522	78,518	7,689	119,729
Mesopotamia .	31,109	51,115	15,355	97,579
Egypt . . .	15,892	38,073	3,888	57,853
Saloniki . . .	7,615	16,876	2,827	27,318
East Africa . .	9,104	7,754	967	17,825
Italy	1,027	4,946	765	6,738
Other fronts .	823	1,515	959	3,297
Total . .	658,704	2,032,142	359,145	3,049,991

LOSSES OF THE BRITISH NAVY AND MERCANTILE MARINE

	KILLED	WOUNDED	MISSING	TOTAL
Navy: Officers .	2,466	805	237	3,508
Men . .	30,895	4,378	985	36,258
Mercantile Marine (all ranks)	14,661	?	3,295	17,956
Total . .	48,022	5,183	4,517	57,722

It will thus be seen that the total losses of all British forces on sea and land were:

Killed	706,726
Wounded	2,037,325
Missing	363,662
Total	3,107,713

These men, the M. P.'s of the 42nd or Rainbow Division, are lined up for guard duty along the Rhine near Coblenz. This is the new Wacht am Rhine

The former Kaiser and Count Bentinck walking in the garden of Castle Amerongen, where the former has been interned by the Government of Holland

In interpreting these figures it must be understood that the term "missing" includes men taken prisoners as well as those of whom no trace could be found. On the other hand "killed" does not include any except those actually fallen in action or who died from wounds. It will, therefore, be seen that the total of deaths will be considerably larger than 706,726 after those have been included who were listed as "missing," but are actually dead as well as those who died from sickness, and it has been stated on good authority that the total of British dead was very close to 1,000,000.

Regarding the losses suffered by our French allies, details are as yet more or less lacking. Official announcements give the total of dead up to November 1, 1918, as 1,071,300, of whom 31,300 were officers and 1,040,000 men. There were also 314,000 missing— 3,000 officers and 311,000 men—and 446,300 prisoners— 8,300 officers and 438,000 men. Those who died from wounds or disease numbered about 330,000, while some 800,000 more were wounded, but recovered. The grand total for France, therefore, may be reckoned at:

Killed	1,071,300
Died of wounds or disease . . .	330,000
Missing and prisoners	760,300
Wounded	800,000
Total	2,961,600

No figures, not even approximate estimates, are available covering the casualties suffered by the civil population in those parts of France in which the war was fought. The total, however, must have been very heavy, considering the brutality with which the Central Powers carried on warfare. The same lack of figures exists respecting the losses suffered by the civil populations of Belgium, Italy, Serbia, Rumania, Austria-Hungary, Russia, and of other parts of the world in which actual fighting occurred.

Casualty totals for the Italian forces vary—as estimated by various agencies—from 1,500,000 to 2,800,000. The latter figure is that of an estimate made by a Colonel of the Italian Army who distributes it as follows:

Killed in action	500,000
Died of wounds or disease . .	300,000
Wounded, missing and prisoners .	2,000,000
Total	2,800,000

Russian war casualties, too, have been estimated at widely differing numbers. The latest estimate amounted to 9,150,000, of which 1,700,000 were said to have been killed, 1,450,000 to have been totally disabled, 3,500,000 to have been wounded, and 2,500,000 to have been taken prisoners.

Other nations, fighting on the side of the Allies—Belgium, Serbia, Rumania, Greece, and Portugal—according to estimates lost by death altogether 530,000. While the grand total of their dead, wounded, and captured is placed at 1,310,000.

The German casualties up to October 25, 1918, are said to have been distributed as follows:

	DEAD	WOUNDED	MISSING	TOTAL
Prussia and small German states . . .	1,262,060	2,882,671	616,139	4,760,870
Bavaria. . .	150,658	363,823	72,115	586,596
Saxony . . .	108,017	252,027	51,787	411,831
Württemberg .	64,507	155,654	16,802	236,963
German Navy .	25,862	28,968	15,679	70,509
Total . .	1,611,104	3,683,143	772,522	6,066,769

Of the grand total of 6,066,769 of all casualties 140,760 were officers—44,700 dead, 82,460 wounded and 13,600 missing—and 5,926,009 non-commissioned officers and men.

Austria-Hungary's losses have been estimated at 4,000,000 of which 800,000—including 17,000 officers—are said to have been killed. Bulgaria and Turkey are believed to have suffered losses amounting to 1,000,000 each, of which the former lost some 250,000 and the latter about 300,000 in dead.

Summarizing all these figures we get the following stupendous totals for the cost of the war expressed in human lives, as shown in the table below:

The cost of the war expressed in dollars and cents, though, of course, not as tragic in its results as that in human lives, is hardly less staggering.

When the United States went to war in April, 1917,

	KILLED IN ACTION—DEAD FROM ALL OTHER CAUSES	TOTAL	TOTAL DEAD, WOUNDED, CAPTURED	GRAND TOTAL
Belgium	150,000		400,000	
France	1,330,000		2,961,600	
Great Britain	706,726		3,107,713	
Greece	25,000		100,000	
Italy	800,000		2,800,000	
Portugal	4,000		10,000	
Roumania	200,000		400,000	
Russia	1,700,000		9,150,000	
Serbia	150,000		400,000	
United States	58,478		264,856	
All Allies		5,124,204		19,594,169
Austria-Hungary	800,000		4,000,000	
Bulgaria	250,000		1,000,000	
Germany	1,611,104		6,066,769	
Turkey	300,000		1,000,000	
Central Powers		2,961,104		12,066,769
All Belligerents		8,085,308		31,660,938

The former Crown Prince of Germany in exile on the Island of Wieringen in the Zuyder Zee, Holland. These carriages are taking the former Prince and his party to the humble cottage in the village of Osterland where they are interned

President Wilson's Paris Guard of Honor standing at attention in front of the Prince Murat residence where President and Mrs. Wilson lived and which was known as the "White House" overseas. This guard was composed of two hundred and fifty picked men chosen for this duty by Major General Edwin F. Glenn

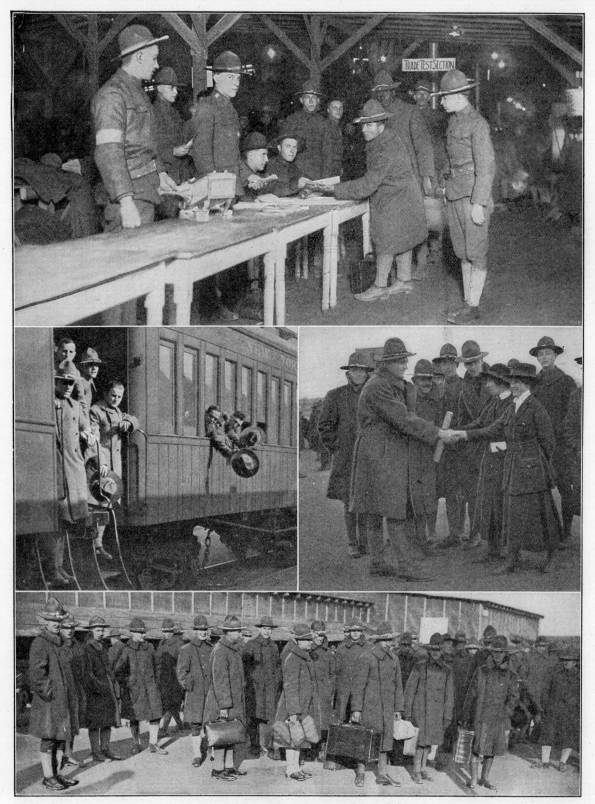

Being mustered out of the National Army after the signing of the armistice. Every man is tested as to his knowledge of a trade or vocation and his physical fitness before he is released

The President getting his first glimpse of France from the little despatch boat that took the Presidential party from the *George Washington* to Brest, France, on December 31, 1918

our public debt was somewhat under $2,500,000,000. By November, 1918, when definite figures for the subscriptions to the 4th Liberty Loan became available it had risen to over $20,000,000,000. This was accomplished by the flotation of four Liberty Loans and the sale of War Savings Stamps. The following figures give some idea of the gradual increase in our public debt:

	AMOUNT ASKED	SUBSCRIPTIONS RECEIVED	SUBSCRIPTIONS ACCEPTED	NUMBER OF SUBSCRIBERS
1st Liberty Loan	$2,000,000,000	$3,035,226,850	$2,000,000,000	4,500,000
2nd Liberty Loan	3,000,000,000	4,617,532,300	3,808,766,150	9,500,000
3rd Liberty Loan	3,000,000,000	4,176,516,850	4,176,516,850	18,300,000
4th Liberty Loan	6,000,000,000	6,989,047,300	6,989,047,000	21,800,000
War Savings Stamps			879,000,000	
Total	$14,000,000,000	$18,695,692,300	$17,730,699,300	54,100,000

President Wilson being welcomed in Paris which beautiful city has been called the capitol of the world

The returns from these loans, of course, only formed part of our war chest. To them were added part of our regular revenues from customs and taxes and other vast sums procured from special war taxes of many kinds. On the other hand not all of the moneys thus become available for war expenditures, can be considered pure expenditures. Much of it was invested rather than expended. Under this head come large amounts used in building ships, in building camps and barracks and guns, in advancing money to our Allies, railroads, and otherwise helping along temporarily certain undertakings of importance to our war activities.

Total appropriations and authorizations voted by Congress during the war amounted to $57,000,000,000. Of this vast sum $10,000,000,000 was set aside for war time loans to foreign governments. Up to the end of December, 1918, about 85 per cent. of this amount had been used, distributed as follows:

Great Britain	$4,195,000,000
France	2,445,000,000
Italy	1,210,000,000
Russia	325,000,000
Belgium	213,320,000
Greece	39,554,036
Cuba	15,000,000
Serbia	12,000,000
Rumania	6,666,666
Liberia	5,000,000
Czecho-Slovaks	7,000,000
Total	$8,473,540,702

Up to October 31, 1918, the army had been voted $24,281,000,000. Of this there had been disbursed about $10,327,000,000 and obligations had been incurred for the additional disbursement of $4,426,000,000. Out of this, it was expected that as a result of the cessation of hostilities $2,600,000,000 could be saved; to this sum must be added the unexpended and unobligated balance of $9,528,000,000, making the actual cost of the army during the war about $12,153,000,000.

Similar retrenchments in other departments, it was hoped, would amount to about $4,000,000,000. It may, therefore, be said that the total net war expenditure of the United States between April 6, 1917, and November 11, 1918, amounted to about $31,000,000,000.

The British Government between August 1, 1914, and November 16, 1918, spent $42,097,320,000. Of this $10,789,200,000 was provided by revenue and $31,308,120,000 from loans.

Again, as in the case of the United States, allowances must be made for sums loaned by Great Britain to its allies and dominions amounting for the same period to some $8,180,000,000. This would make the net war expenditure of Great Britain, not allowing for some $5,000,000,000 represented by "recoverable" expenditures, about $34,000,000,000.

The public debt of Great Britain on August 1, 1914, was $3,450,600,000. By November 16, 1918, it had reached $34,763,580,000. Included in this last figure, however, are some temporary engagements amounting to almost $10,000,000,000 so that for comparison with the pre-war public debt a present total of about $25,000,000,000 is more nearly correct.

Only estimates are available in regard to the war

© Committee on Public Information

President Wilson with President Poincaré leaving the railway station of Boulogne Woods, at the western portals of Paris, for a triumphal tour through the French capital to the home of Prince Murat, which is to be during the Peace Conference the "White House Overseas"

The American delegates to the Peace Conference. Left to right: Colonel House, Secretary of State Lansing, President Wilson, former Ambassador White, and General Bliss

America's fleet returning from the war and entering the mouth of the North River, followed by river craft and dirigibles overhead

costs incurred by the other belligerents. In the case of France these vary from $28,000,000,000 to $50,000,000,000. One put at $31,600,000,000 and announced late in Dec., 1918, by M. de Billy, Deputy High Commissioner of the French Republic to the United States, therefore, seems the most reliable. Of this sum almost $21,000,000,000 was raised by loans, over two thirds by internal loans, and the balance by loans from Allies and Neutrals.

Belgium's war expenditure is estimated at $4,000,000,000; Italy's (up to June, 1918,) at $11,500,000,000.

In the following compilation official or semi-official figures have been used, though in some cases these did not cover expenditures after August 1, 1918. However, the result, it is believed, will come very near to actual figures which will, of course, not become available until long after the end of the war.

These figures, include the expenditures for war purposes as well as the damages caused by hostile occupation, devastation, confiscation, air raids, submarine sinkings, etc. The latter, of course, are more or less hypothetical and in the case of Russia it is impossible under the conditions existing at the time general hostilities ceased to arrive even at an estimate of the damages caused by German-Austrian occupation, revolutions, etc.

WAR EXPENDITURES OF ALL BELLIGERENTS

	ACTUAL WAR COST	(FOR DEVASTATION, ETC.) SINKINGS DAMAGES CLAIMED	TOTAL
Belgium	$4,000,000,000	$1,400,000,000	$5,400,000,000
France	31,600,000,000	20,000,000,000	51,600,000,000
Great Britain	34,000,000,000	2,750,000,000	36,750,000,000
Italy	12,500,000,000	150,000,000	12,650,000,000
Japan	16,000,000		16,000,000
Portugal	280,000,000		280,000,000
Rumania	185,000,000	150,000,000	335,000,000
Russia	50,000,000,000	?	50,000,000,000
Serbia	55,000,000	50,000,000	105,000,000
U. S.	31,000,000,000		31,000,000,000
Misc.	100,000,000	500,000,000	600,000,000
All Allies	$163,736,000,000	$25,000,000,000	$188,736,000,000
Austria-Hungary	15,000,000,000	150,000,000	
Bulgaria	260,000,000	10,000,000	
Germany	33,000,000,000	50,000,000	
Turkey	170,000,000	50,000,000	
Central Powers	$48,430,000,000	$260,000,000	$48,690,000,000
All Belligerents	$212,166,000,000	$25,260,000,000	$237,426,000,000

The Lord Mayor presenting President Wilson with the freedom of the City of London. This is an honor seldom conferred upon the chief executives of other nations

CHRONOLOGY OF THE PART TAKEN BY THE UNITED STATES IN THE WAR

1917

February 3. Count von Bernstorff, German Ambassador to the United States, given his passports. United States Ambassador Gerard recalled from Berlin.

March 9. President calls extra session of Congress. Orders arming of American merchant ships.

March 24. Minister Whitlock ordered by President to leave Belgium.

April 2. President asks Congress to declare state of war existing between United States and Germany.

April 6. State of war declared.

May 16. Admiral Simms reports his torpedo squadron in European waters.

May 18. Selective draft law enacted.

June 5. Registration day under draft law; over 10,000,000 enrolled.

June 8. General Pershing reaches London.

June 15. First Liberty Loan subscription closed, subscriptions exceed $3,000,000,000.

June 19. Landing of first instalment of the American Expeditionary Force reported from France.

June 26. United States Marines landed at St. Nazaire.

July 18. Censorship of letters and telegrams established.

July 20. First drawing under the draft law.

July 24. Law enacted appropriating $640,000,000 for aviation.

July 27. Second contingent of American troops reaches France.

August 5. National Guard, approximately 300,000 men, drafted into service of the United States.

August 13. Mobilization of new National Army ordered.

August 28. President Wilson announces rejection of the Pope's peace plea.

October 6. War appropriation of $21,000,000,000 made by Congress.

October 17. Transport *Antilles* sunk; loss 67 lives.

October 28. Second Liberty Loan closed; subscriptions, $4,617,532,000.

November 3. First Americans killed in the trenches.

November 5. Patrol boat *Alcedo* sunk with loss of 21 men.

November 22. Third Liberty Loan completed; total $4,176,516,850. Number of subscribers 12,000,000.

December 6. Destroyer *Jacob Jones* sunk by torpedo; 65 lost.

December 7. Declaration of war upon Austria-Hungary.

December 28. United States Government takes over the railroads.

1918

January 8. President Wilson enumerates his famous "Fourteen Points."

January 26. Wheatless and meatless days prescribed by the President.

February 21. American forces penetrate German lines near the Chemin des Dames.

March 1. Americans repulse enemy near Toul. Hand to hand fighting with Germans near Chavigny.

March 10. Washington reports American troops on four sectors; Northwest of Toul; in Champagne; in Alsace near Luneville; on the Chemin des Dames in Aisne.

March 18. Germany announces seizure of all property owned by Americans within German boundaries.

March 22. American artillery in action east of Luneville.

April 5. Allies, including two regiments of American troops land at Vladivostok.

April 20. Americans in action at Seicheprey.

April 28. First division Americans take over sector near Breteuil.

May 1. Americans repulse attack at Villiers-Bretonneaux.

May 6. Americans sustain first gas attack in Picardy.

May 17. Presence of American troops in British war zone officially announced.

May 28. First division captures Cantigny.

May 31. Successful American raid near Woevre region.

June 3-6. Americans fighting hard in neighborhood of Château-Thierry, the Marne and Vieully-la-Potterie.

June 7. United States Marines drive two-and-one-half miles near Château-Thierry, storm Torcy and Bouresches, and with French take Vieully-la-Potterie.

June 10. Second Division attacked in Bois de Belleau, advancing the line 900 yards on a front of 1½ miles, capturing 300 prisoners, 30 machine guns, 4 trench mortars, and stores of small arms, ammunition, and equipment.

June 11. Second Division continued its advance in the Bois de Belleau, capturing more prisoners and machine guns and two 77 mm. fieldpieces.

Our aviators executed their first bombing raid, dropping numerous bombs on the railway station at Dommary-Baroncourt, northwest of Metz.

The artillery of the Second Division shelled the enemy in their areas. It discovered and dispersed a group of 210 machine guns in the wood south of Etrepilly. The Second Division captured the last of the German positions in the Bois de Belleau, taking 50 prisoners, machine guns, and trench mortars.

June 12-17. Americans hold their positions at Château-Thierry and Thiaucourt, repulsing persistent gas attacks.

June 20. Americans take German trenches in front of Cantigny and begin an advance on north side of Belleau Wood.

June 24. Belleau Wood reported clear of all Germans.

July 2. Americans capture village of Vaux and the Bois de la Roche.

One million Americans reported in France.

July 4. Australians and Americans capture Hamel.

July 6. Americans successful at Xivray and in the Vosges.

July 14. Lieutenant Quentin Roosevelt killed in aërial battle in the Château-Thierry sector.

July 15. Great German offensive launched. Americans repulse whole division on the Marne.

July 18. French and Americans in counter attack on the Marne.

July 19. U. S. armored cruiser *San Diego* sunk off Fire Island by a mine.

July 21. Germans driven from Château-Thierry. Allies steadily advancing.

July 28. Forty-second Division forces the crossing of the Ourcq.

August 4. Americans take Fismes by assault. The 32nd Division, after 8 days of fighting in which it decimated a crack division of the Bavarian Guard, entered the town in triumph.

August 10. British and Americans capture Morlancourt and Chipilly and drive forward on Bray.

August 12. Americans, coöperating with the British, reach the outskirts of Bray.

August 18. Americans gain more ground at Frapelle.

August 19. Americans and French push forward on the north bank of the Vesle.

August 23. Americans repulse violent attacks west of Fismes.

President and Mrs. Wilson visiting the Coliseum in Rome under the guidance of a famous archaeologist

August 24. Americans win a half-mile front on the Soissons-Rheims front west of Fismes.

August 25. Americans attack Bazoches and resist assault on Fismette.

August 28. Americans advance their lines at Chavigny and repulse German attacks at Bazoches.

August 30. French and American troops north of Soissons capture Chavigny and Cuffies and advance their line to the west of Crouy. Germans evacuate Bailleul; Americans take Juvigny.

August 31. Americans make gains eastward in the vicinity of Juvigny and the Bois de Beaumont.

September 1. Americans forge ahead two miles beyond Juvigny; Americans fight for the first time on Belgian soil and take Voormezeele and nearby strongholds.

September 2. Americans north of Soissons reach Terny-Sorny and the Soissons-St. Quentin highway.

September 3. Secretary Lansing announces the recognition of the Czecho-Slovaks as a belligerent nation.

September 5. French and American troops force a passage of the Vesle and occupy Chassemy, Bucy-le-Long, Branelle, Vauxcere, and Blanzy.

September 6. Germans retreat on a ninety-mile front from the posts of the Americans on the Aisne to the breaches in the Hindenburg line before Cambrai. Americans south of the Aisne make progress in the region of Villers-en-Prayeres and Revillon.

September 8. Americans advance northward on the Aisne in the vicinity of Vieil Arcy, Villers-en-Prayeres, and Revillon.

September 9. Germans throw in new divisions to check American advance on the St. Gobain massif.

September 12. First American Army attacks the St. Mihiel salient from all sides and advances on a thirty-mile front to a depth of five miles, aided by the French; St. Mihiel and several towns captured.

September 13. Americans wipe out St. Mihiel salient, re-ducing the front from forty to twenty miles, capturing 15,000 prisoners, and extending the battleline past Norroy, Jaulny, Xammes, St. Benoit, Hattonville, Hannonville, and Herbeuville.

September 14. Americans repulse counterattacks in the St. Mihiel sector and push on.

September 15. Americans in St. Mihiel sector advance from two to three miles on a thirty-three-mile front; guns from fortress of Metz in action against them; villages of Norroy and Vilcey captured.

September 17. Americans in Lorraine advance on extreme right of the line. Germans burn towns along the Moselle as American infantry advances.

September 18. Americans build strong front line in Lorraine, and threaten Metz and the Briey coal fields.

September 20. American guns fire on Metz.

September 26. American Army advances on 20-mile front between the Meuse and Aisne rivers; advances 7 miles first day, takes 12 towns and reaches the Kriemhilde line on the 28th—U. S. S. *Tampa* sunk by torpedo; loss 118 men.

September 29. Americans capture Breulles-sur-Meuse and Romagne.

September 30. Americans advance slightly in the Argonne; Bulgaria signs armistice amounting to unconditional surrender.

October 1. Americans push ahead in the Aisne-Meuse sector and repulse German counterattacks in the region of Cierges and at Apremont; Germans prepare to evacuate Belgium.

October 2. Germans begin evacuation of Lille and begin a retreat on a wide front on both sides of La Bassée Canal as Allies continue enveloping movement north and south of Lille, Roubaix, and Turcoing.

October 5. Americans break the Kriemhilde line and drive Germans back to a line two kilometers north of Binarville and Fleville; Americans join French in the Champagne and take part in operations north of Somme-Py.

Surgeon-General Gorgas and Col. Frank Billings, head of the Division of Physical Reconstruction, inspecting the Walter Reed General Hospital, Washington, D. C.

© Paul Thompson

The S. S. *Mauretania* in all the glory of her war paint

The first of the organized troops to return cheering from the deck of the *Mauretania* on first seeing the Statue of Liberty

The Palace of Versailles where the Supreme War Council met and where the armistice terms were agreed upon, Here is where King William of Prussia was crowned Emperor of Germany and where his grandson lost his heritage

Austria-Hungary appeals to President Wilson to effect an armistice.

October 6. German Chancellor proposes peace parley on "14 principles" laid down by Wilson.

October 7. Americans gain in the Argonne region, taking Châtel-Chehery and commanding positions on the Aire.

October 8. British, American, and French forces shatter twenty miles of Hindenburg defense system from Cambrai southward, advancing to an average depth of three miles.

October 9. American aviators active in the Argonne. One expedition of great number of planes bombarded many towns.

October 10. Americans clear the Argonne forest.

October 13. President Wilson notifies Germany that there will be no negotiations with an autocratic German government and no armistice while Germany continues its barbarous methods of warfare.

October 14. Americans advance west of the Meuse.

October 15. American troops land at Vladivostok.

October 16. Americans capture Grand Pre.

October 17. British and American attack on a 9-mile front northeast of Bohain and advance two miles.

October 18. Americans advance north of Romagne and take Bantheville.

October 19. President Wilson refuses Austria-Hungary's request for armistice on the ground that the Czecho-Slavs and Jugoslavs had been recognized as nations and must be consulted. Kriemhilde line pierced. Fourth Liberty Loan closed. Subscriptions, $6,989,047,000.

October 21. Germany renews suggestion of armistice. Declares her government has been popularized.

October 23. Americans on the Verdun front occupy Brieulles, the Bois de Forêt, and Banthéville.

October 24. Americans advance on both sides of the Meuse.

October 25. Americans clear Belleau Wood of Germans and hold Hill 360 in fierce fighting.

October 26. Turkey offers to surrender.

October 29. Americans shell Conflans region. Austria-Hungary again appeals for peace.

October 30. Turkey surrenders.

November 1. First American Army aided by the French attacks on a front of over fifteen miles north of Verdun, advancing nearly four miles at some points and freeing a dozen towns.

November 2. Americans break through Freya line on a wide front, taking Champigneulle, Buzancy, Fosse, Barricourt, Villers-devant-Dun, and Doolcon.

November 3. Americans continue advance north of Verdun, taking several towns, and joining with the French near Noirval. Austria-Hungary armistice signed.

November 5. Germans retreat on a 75-mile front from the Scheldt to the Aisne; Americans cross the Meuse at three points below Stenay. Lansing directs Germans to seek terms of armistice from Marshal Foch.

November 6. Germans order retreat across the Meuse on the front of the American Army; Mouzon in flames; Vervins, Rethel, and other towns won; Sedan fired upon.

November 7. Americans take Sedan.

November 8. French reach the outskirts of Mézières, advance beyond the La Capelle-Avesnes Road, and take Thon bridgeheads; Americans drive Germans out of last dominating position east of the Meuse.

November 10. Americans attack on extended front. Take Stenay.

November 11. Armistice signed by Foch and German delegates. Fighting ends at 11 A. M.

November 21. The German High Seas Fleet surrenders.

November 22. King Albert makes triumphal entry into Brussels.

November 26. French troops enter Strassburg, the capital of Alsace.

December 1. American troops of occupation enter German territory from Luxemburg and establish headquarters at Treves and the *Mauretania* reaches New York with the first American troops to return from Europe.

December 26. President and Mrs. Wilson cross the Channel and visit England and are entertained by the King and Queen at Buckingham Palace.

January 18. The Peace Conference meets at Paris in the Ministry of Foreign Affairs.

January 25. The Peace Conference declares for a League of Nations.

February 16. A renewal of the armistice is signed at Treves, the German Commission under protest accepting more severe conditions.

February 18. The Italian Delegation declines to accept the Jugoslav proposal for arbitrating rival claims to the Dalmatian coast.

May 7. Treaty of Peace is handed the German delegates at Versailles; fifteen days allowed for its consideration.

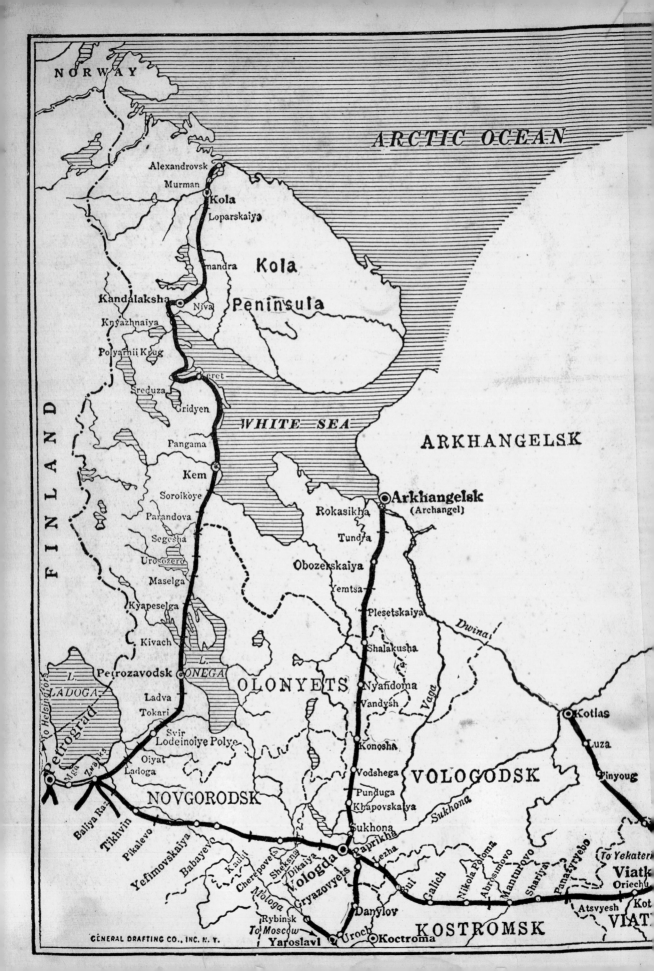